Faster, Louder, Riskier, Sexier

Faster, Louder, Riskier, Sexier

Learning to love ADHD

John Passmore

oldmansailing

oldmansailing

First published 2024

Copyright © 2024 by John Passmore

John Passmore has asserted his right under the Copyright, Designs and Patents Act of 1988 to be identified as the Author of this work.

All rights reserved. No part of this publication may be reproduced or transmitted in any form or by any means, electronic or mechanical, including photocopying, recording, or any information storage or retrieval system without prior permission from the Author.

No responsibility for loss caused to any individual or organisation acting on or refraining from action as a result of the material in this publication can be accepted by the Author.

ISBN: **9798308077749**

Book Cover Design: beyondbookcovers.com

Author's Note: I have now read through this book so many times that I truly believe I have weeded out all the spelling mistakes, typographical errors and grammatical howlers. However, if you spot an error – and you are the first to tell me about it – I will gladly refund you the cost of your book. Please send the mistake with the five words surrounding it exactly as it appears in the text (so that I can search for it) to john@oldmansailing.com. Thank you.

Photographs and a glossary of terms can be found on my blog at https://oldmansailing.com.

This is for Tamsin, who said: "The reason you can't write fiction is because you're not interested in other people. But you're good when you're writing about yourself."

*Life can only be understood backwards;
but it must be lived forwards.*

— SØREN KIERKEGAARD

Contents

Foreword xi
Chapter 1 Discovery 1
Chapter 2 Tradition 11
Chapter 3 Rebellion 31
Chapter 4 Work 39
Chapter 5 Boats 47
Chapter 6 Love 57
Chapter 7 Apprentice 71
Chapter 8 Craftsman 83
Chapter 9 Decision 97
Chapter 10 Escape 107
Chapter 11 Away 121
Chapter 12 Babies 137
Chapter 13 Home 151
Chapter 14 Departure 161
Chapter 15 Turmoil 173
Chapter 16 Return 185
Chapter 17 First 197
Chapter 18 Rescue 209
Chapter 19 Money 221
Chapter 20 Desperation 237
Chapter 21 Luck 251
Chapter 22 Excitement 261
Chapter 23 Health 279
Chapter 24 Rich 295
Chapter 25 Samsara 307
Chapter 26 Poor 317

Chapter 27 Fame 329
Chapter 28 ?@*&! 339
Chapter 29 Marriage 351
Chapter 30 Death 357
Afterword 369
Amazon Stars & Reviews 371
Books by the Same Author Also Available on Amazon 373

Foreword

This book has had a long period of gestation in the microchips. I wrote it during the year after I took the ADHD test in 2017. Apparently, not only did I have the condition, but I was in the 1% of the most severe cases.

At the age of 68, I had managed to excel at something!

That first year after the diagnosis was a confusing time. It is no small thing to have your entire life explained to you when you are nearly in your dotage. Now I had an answer to why I did so poorly at school, why I was so bad at relationships - why I had so few friends, could never remember people's names, constantly mislaid my glasses, my car keys, my children….

In the end, I dealt with the revelation the only way I knew how. I wrote it all down - a long and tortured explanation of how this peculiar mental kink accounted for a lifetime of never being entirely sure what was going to happen next.

Reading through it, I realised that what I had here was not so much an explanation as a long list of excuses. If this was an autobiography, I didn't much care for the central character. Apart from anything else, one of the characteristics of the condition is an unpleasant compulsion to **share inappropriate intimate details**.

So instead of showing the book to anyone, I wrote another - gutting the original for anything that might pass as entertaining and basing it around my passion for boats and sailing them long distances on my own. I had spent a lifetime writing for newspapers - something which is always done at breakneck speed. Writing two books back-to-back was no trouble. The version that emerged, I called Old Man Sailing.

It was a success. It topped the bestseller lists - well, it topped the bestseller lists in the Amazon sailing category.

That's one thing about writing for newspapers: You learn to make the dullest material sound interesting - even a troublesome life, dogged by poor decision-making and a good deal of inattention. I followed it up with four more sailing books.

Yet, all the while, the book of confessions stayed hidden away in a file that was moved from one computer to the next, to a Google docs folder, to a flash drive - still never seeing the light of day. It might have been in the restricted section of Hogwarts library.

Until now.

Now an undercover reporter for the BBC has exposed a number of online psychiatric clinics which hit on a clever wheeze for exploiting the interminable NHS waiting lists for ADHD consultations.

Since people who think they have the condition are notoriously impatient, there is a fortune to be made by charging them over the odds for a quick Zoom consultation, telling them they do have it - and then selling them the drugs to fix it.

Other interesting facts popped up in the report: It is estimated that 5% of the world's population have ADHD - that's 1.5 billion people. It's all over the Internet. One of the most popular UK podcasts is called "You're wrong about ADHD."

It's a hot topic.

So, maybe now is the time to put myself out there as a happy ADHDer. For yes, after seven years, I have come to terms with the man in the book.

Once I started to read it again - first at the age of 70 - and then another six times over the next four years as I got older and began to make sense of the whole absurd story, I learned to see the positive side. Certainly, I still have ADHD, but I don't see it as an affliction anymore - something to be "cured" with pills or years on a therapist's couch.

Instead, I embrace it.

After all, if I didn't have ADHD, would I be here now? Doing precisely what I always wanted to do? Would I have had half the life I've lived? Could it have been any Faster, Louder, Riskier, Sexier?

If you've got this thing. Take my advice and make the most of it.

Other people might not find it much fun - but you will have *the time of your life.*

Chapter 1

Discovery

Somebody walked in behind me. Everyone walked into my room behind me - that's what happens when your desk is under the window and your back to the door.

When people walk in like that, you have two options: Swivel round in your fake leather executive-style chair to see who it is - or keep looking out of the window and try to work it out from the footsteps. It helps if they speak - strange how often they don't.

So that left us with; who's in the house? What time is it? In this case, mid-morning on a Wednesday - I think it was a Wednesday. Who would be in the house on a Wednesday morning? Hugo was 14, so he would be at school. Lottie, at 16, was in her GCSE exam year, and so she might be home, supposedly revising. Theo? No, Theo had gone off to Liverpool University to study medicine. I'd been up there to see him on the way back from working on my new boat - well, she was hardly a new boat - 44 years old, to be exact. I had found her in Conwy in North Wales, and there was a lot of work to do before getting her into the water. Liverpool is right next door to North Wales, so it made sense to drop in.

Theo had shown me his room - very luxurious, like a budget hotel - not at all the way I imagined student living. We went to a couple of those huge Liverpudlian pubs with music blaring and bouncers on the door at six o'clock. A meal in Bella Italia (not what it was - Tamsin and I used to love Bella Italia and its two-for-one offer.) No, it couldn't be Theo.

Owen was home from University now, having graduated in English with Creative Writing from the University of East Anglia (I am still bursting with pride - and he does write well, even if I don't really appreciate the fantasy genre.) But whoever had walked in, it couldn't be Owen because - true to his creative nature - he writes all night (or video-calls his girlfriend). Anyway, Owen never rises before midday. So, it couldn't be Owen.

In that case, it must be Tamsin. That figured. The children always say what they have to say as soon as they walk in - often before they walk in - sometimes from a different room altogether. So, it had to be Tamsin. Tamsin and I had reached that stage in our marriage when we didn't say much to each other anymore. This was not because we were so in tune with each other that language was superfluous. Rather that we were so out of tune, it just caused trouble.

She tended to keep to the other end of the house. Over the past few years, we had become like those couples you read about who live separate lives under the same roof - cooking separate meals, devising an unspoken system to avoid finding themselves in the same room at the same time. We did meet for family dinner but for Tamsin to come down the passage to my end, this must be important.

She appeared at my shoulder. She was carrying a page from a newspaper. She put it down beside my laptop. She said: "Do you think you might have this?"

I kept quiet. Nothing annoyed Tamsin so much as people asking stupid questions - particularly me because I had a habit of doing it so frequently.

I looked at the page. It was the Family Section from the Saturday edition of The Guardian. Tamsin's parents took The

Guardian on Saturdays - their one paper of the week. Eddie removed the Family Section and handed it to Eira while he read the important parts. Eira considered the Family Section to be the important part. Then they swapped because Eddy and Eira had one of those marriages in which they did talk to each other. They discussed everything. By Wednesday, they would be finished with the Family Section and pass it on to Tamsin.

Tamsin always read the column by Tim Lott. This column was called Family Life. Tim Lott was a successful writer (he'd won awards for his novels). His Family Life column documented the slightly chaotic and often humorous goings-on in a typical North London literary household.

Except, from now on, it wouldn't. The Lotts were getting a divorce. Now, it's one thing to contrive interesting scenarios in the hope of avoiding the columnist's "nothing to write about" nightmare... but surely getting divorced would be classed as unseemly desperation?

Apparently, it all had to do with a column he had written about his "foregettery". I thought he had cleverly invented the word, but no - I find Google Docs' spellchecker accepts it (although, interestingly, it doesn't accept "spellchecker" - unless you put it in inverted commas, as it turns out…)

Anyway, "forgettery", according to Collins English Dictionary, means "A tendency to forget (humorous)" and, apparently, Tim Lott had this very tendency - in spades. It was something that provided him with endless copy - and which Mrs Lott found infuriating. He would go out to buy tomatoes and come back with potatoes - or forget why he had gone out at all. He was forever asking where he had put his car keys or his glasses. Whatever form his "forgettery" took, it was always a good source of column inches - although, invariably, Mrs Lott failed to see the funny side.

Then something unexpected happened. A reader wrote in alerting him to a much less humorous condition called Attention

Deficit Hyperactive Disorder (ADHD) - or, more appropriately, the adult version: Adult Attention Deficit Disorder (AADD).

Tim Lott took the letter seriously. As a writer preoccupied with his own small world, he found the possibility fascinating. He researched AADD online. He found the ADHD Foundation website. He checked the list of symptoms:

- Carelessness and lack of attention to detail.
- Continually starting new tasks before finishing old ones.
- Poor organisational skills.
- Inability to focus or prioritise.
- Continually losing or misplacing things.
- Forgetfulness.
- Restlessness and edginess.
- Difficulty in keeping quiet. Speaking out of turn.
- Blurting responses. Poor social timing when talking to others.
- Tendency to share inappropriate intimate details.
- Interrupting others.
- Mood swings.
- Increased desire for approval.
- Poor decision-making.
- Irritability and a quick temper.
- Inability to deal with stress.
- Extreme impatience.
- Taking risks in activities - little or no regard for personal safety or the safety of others…

Tim Lott sat down very hard. Later, after visiting the ADHD Foundation in Liverpool and taking their test - and finding that all sorts of well-known people had the condition (Justin Timberlake, Paris Hilton, Rory Bremner, Jim Carrey) – he was informed that he had it too. In my imagination, I pictured him trying to make light of it, but in the end, the prospect of no respite seemed like a life sentence - at least for Mrs Lott and her shopping list. The couple agreed to a divorce. Tim moved out. There would be no more Family Life to write about.

I did exactly what Tim Lott had done. I found the Foundation's website. I looked at the list of symptoms. I began to get a very bad feeling about this. There was an online questionnaire: Fifty questions along the lines of "Do you find that when you ask for directions, you can't remember what they were?" and "Do you forget people's names - even members of your own family?"

Yes, it sounds ridiculous, doesn't it? Am I really the sort of man who can't remember my own children's names? Well, yes, I do keep calling Hugo "Theo" and Lottie "Meg" (Meg is the dog).

Hold on a minute, it said ADHD was hereditary. Oh yes, very hereditary: Guess what is the world capital of ADHD - a country where the incidence is completely off the scale… to such an extent that it is accepted as part of the national character?

Australia.

Now, where did we send all the naughty people?

Come to that, if it's hereditary, look at my father, who had ten pairs of glasses so that he could always find one - who once rang my mother from a station platform demanding: "Why am I at Effingham Junction?" (He had got on the wrong train - but he kept insisting it was his usual platform).

What about *his* father, who went to Royal Ascot because of the social cachet - despite the fact that he hated crowds? Eventually, he panicked and started hitting out with his stick. The stewards had to restrain him.

I did the quiz and scored somewhere around 85% (Father would have managed 100%).

I took the Guardian page and went into the kitchen - something that, in the ordinary course of the day, I would think twice about. If Tamsin was in there, she might walk out - or ask: "Are you going to be long?"

I wondered if Tim Lott felt the same trepidation.

When you think about it, this was a ridiculous way to live, but it had crept up on us slowly. One thing we did know was that our relationship was in trouble.

Now we knew why.

I told Tamsin about the questionnaire.

"What are you going to do about it?" she asked.

Well, there were drugs, but I didn't want to take drugs. I had once taken a homoeopathic remedy that was supposed to help with memory and found myself consumed with the most violent urges. I remember it even now as one of the most terrifying episodes I have ever experienced. Certainly, it put me off psychotic remedies for life.

Meanwhile, I supposed the first thing to do was to get the ADHD confirmed. I made an appointment with the doctor. The doctor asked: "So you want a label, is that it?" She said she would refer me to a psychiatrist. It would take three months for an appointment.

Three months! What did the symptoms say? "**Extreme impatience.**"

I phoned the ADHD Foundation and asked if I could come and take their test that very week. The woman I spoke to knew all about Tim Lott. I had the impression I was not the first of his readers to call. Also, she was conditioned to understand the urgency. Within five minutes, I had an appointment for the following week. It would have to do.

The office was near Lime Street Station, on a corner in one of those enormous old buildings that make Liverpool seem such an important city. As I made my way up to the Foundation's floor, I felt that everyone was nodding to themselves, knowing where I was going. It was like asking the way to the Sexually Transmitted Diseases clinic.

A blonde woman in her 40s explained the test, but of course, I wasn't listening. Or at least I was, but I didn't take in anything she said. It doesn't matter. I can tell you what happened because it happened to me, and I remember what happens to me. Other people, not so much - as it says on the ADHD website: **The traits of talking over people in conversation, inattentiveness, and being easily bored can be draining on relationships. A person with ADHD can come across as insensitive, irresponsible, or uncaring**.

The blonde woman took me into a tiny room - a really tiny room. There was just enough space for a pale grey desk with a computer screen, a chair - and, on the wall behind the chair, looking down on the scene, a camera - although you didn't notice the camera when you walked in. I sat at the desk. I had to put a device on my head. It reminded me of those concave mirrors doctors used to wear in 1930s cartoons. This was so that my head movements could be tracked by a monitor on top of the computer screen. These movements were supposed to be minimal. I was supposed to be concentrating on the screen…

My task was to wait for little dots to appear. When they did, I was to click the mouse. That was all. Sounds simple, doesn't it? And it was only for 20 minutes…

Already, I had a sense of foreboding. I remembered the time I visited a hearing clinic: Tamsin had complained that I never listened, and I had said I hadn't heard her, so she insisted I was going deaf. I ended up at the clinic.

They put me in a soundproofed cubicle with a pair of headphones and a button. Then they played sounds of varying frequencies through the headphones. When I heard them, I was supposed to press the button.

I managed this for a couple of minutes. Then I got bored and fell asleep.

When I didn't press the button, the technician thought I was deaf - which meant I had the choice of being classified as deaf or difficult. I chose difficult. I was used to that.

I tried very hard with the foundation's dots, but it wasn't long before my feet started fidgeting. I moved them, but that didn't seem any better, so I moved them again - from in front of the chair to underneath it - to behind it, out to the sides. A little stamp with one ... and then the other...

The dots kept coming, and I kept on clicking the mouse, but I couldn't get comfortable on the chair. I shifted one way and then the other - all the time, still moving my feet around. Pretty soon, I was squirming about on the chair like a guilty suspect in a Columbo movie - all of which was recorded by the camera on the wall. I don't know what the device on the top of the screen made of my head movements. Meanwhile, the dots kept coming. Surely the 20 minutes must be up by now...

By the time they let me out, I had given up all pretence of clicking the dots. I couldn't sit still. I was looking all around the room. I knew this feeling. I knew it exactly. It was called *fidgeting*. I knew I shouldn't be doing this – I should be *concentrating* – but I couldn't help it. I started wondering when I had felt like this before. It was as if a door had opened, giving a glimpse into a long-forgotten room – and then closed just as soon as I recognised it.

The blonde woman came back. I felt there was a knowing look about her. She took me to another room, where I sat and waited on my own. This was almost as sparsely furnished as the first. Just another pale grey desk, a desk chair, one of those office cabinets with a box of tissues on it. Two small chairs with wooden arms facing each other across a coffee table. The blonde woman came back and took the other chair. She carried a sheaf of papers. She said: "I have the results of your test."

There are two other things I remember her saying:

"The tests indicate that you probably do suffer from AADD and that you are in the 1% of the most severe cases. However, a clinical diagnosis would require a psychiatrist."

Then she looked at me and added: "Yes, often it is an emotional moment. Rory Bremner was the same..."

She handed me the tissues. I took a handful and began to mop at the tears which had started streaming down my face. I do remember that I couldn't speak. The blonde woman sat and watched me weep, her face crumpled with concern - and also, I remember something else in her face. I supposed it was pity. I hated to see that. But it's a bit of a shock, at the age of 68, for the first time, to find that finally, your whole life makes sense.

Chapter 2
Tradition

It began when I was five years old.

I would be going to school soon. I was a big boy now. I didn't need a Nanny anymore.

My parents were what was then called "well-to-do". My father was a partner in his father's law firm in Piccadilly. We lived in a three-storey townhouse in Chelsea. I looked it up in Zoopla the other day, and you would need to be a hedge fund manager to live there now. But in 1955, my grandfather complained it wasn't at all suitable and asked why we didn't live in Belgravia. Possibly my parents considered it had potential because the whole of the opposite side of the street was a bomb site. We had a marmalade cat who would spend her whole day over there. I longed to go with her, but Nanny would not have approved.

Nanny had been with me my whole life, and on the day she was told that I was a big boy now and didn't need a Nanny anymore, she was so distraught that she packed her bags that very night and disappeared to her sister in Walton-on-the-Naze. She couldn't trust herself to say goodbye. It would be several years before relations were re-established - albeit tentatively. First, she began to reply to the card my mother had begun to send at Christmas. Later, we were duty-bound to visit her in the care home if ever we were in the area.

The odd thing is that I remember nothing about what should have been a traumatic parting. I wonder if my parents watched me carefully for signs of psychological damage - or at least, I wonder if my mother did. My father remembered he had three children when a family occasion arose - indeed, he would be delighted to enjoy the moment. It was just that he would just as quickly forget it had ever happened. No doubt my sisters will dispute this, but I know because I am just the same.

So, at five years old, I was fitted out with rust-coloured corduroy knickerbockers and a rust-coloured flat cap and, in the September, I started at Hill House School. This was the particularly unusual school hidden away behind Harrods. What made it especially interesting was that Prince Charles started at the same time. This meant that my mother quizzed me mercilessly every time I came home. What was he like? What did he say to me? What did I call him? I must have been a great disappointment. I had nothing to tell her. The Prince kept himself to himself - sensible chap.

He went on to Cheam - which he hated. I went to West Downs - which I hated.

West Downs prided itself on its "traditional values". In 1957 this meant sadistic prefects and paedophile teachers - not all of them, of course; but the music master liked to deal with errant flybuttons personally, and the maths teacher carried a whistle on a leather strap that would whip around a bare knee with the most satisfying slap.

Misdemeanours in the dormitory were punished by "running the gauntlet" - the victim was made to run from one end of the dorm to the other while all the other boys stood by their beds and beat the unfortunate miscreant with dressing gown cords as he passed. In 1957, these were proper, old-fashioned dressing gown cords with thick, knotted tassels at each end. If you held it in the middle, you could whack the wretched boy with both the hard, heavy knots at the same time. They left wonderful, red imprints on the skin.

From the victim's point of view, the trick was to leap out of bed the moment the bell rang and before anyone else remembered this was gauntlet day. The alternative was to hope they'd all forget, but there was always some sadist who had been looking forward to this moment all night - and he would make very sure everyone was armed and ready.

It hurt like hell, but you could show off the dressing-gown-cord-shaped welts with pride. The staff knew all about it. No doubt they considered it character-building - or at least, preparation for public school.

There was some doubt that I would ever get into public school. At the end of the first year, my form teacher - that is to say, the teacher in charge of the bottom form in the whole school - had to admit that I had failed to learn my multiplication tables. This was fundamental. I could not go up into the second year without knowing my times tables.

So, I was kept down. But what I had failed to learn in three terms, I certainly failed to learn in a fourth. I have no idea what consultations took place between the teachers of the first and second forms, but the headmaster thought it best not to inform my parents that their fees had not been transformed into nine eights are 72.

Of course, multiplication tables were not part of the second-year syllabus - or any syllabus beyond that all the way up to A-level. So, I never did learn my tables. I still don't know them. In fact, I had to use the calculator on my phone to write that line about 9x8=72. I thought it was 49 - but years of miscalculations have taught me always to check (unless I forget, of course).

I think it must have been at about this time that I acquired my nickname: "Thicky Passmore". I didn't mind. Indeed, I played up to it. Notoriety in a traditional prep school is a sure route to popularity. So, I made sure not to learn the dates of the Kings and Queens of England either. This made me even more popular. Think how great it would be if I failed to conjugate the Latin verb "amo".

Latin was taken very seriously at West Downs. It was taught by the headmaster himself, Jerry Cornes. Jerry had been a 1,500-meter Olympic silver medallist in the 1936 Berlin Games and bought the school with an inheritance in the early 50s. In those days, anyone could call themselves a teacher - especially if they owned the school.

Jerry was an enormously tall man with unruly grey hair and yellow index and second fingers on his right hand. You don't see yellow fingers today - nobody smokes enough. You had to be a really serious smoker to have yellow fingers - 60-a-day at the very least. I don't know how many Jerry got through, but on film show nights (the film projected onto a white sheet tied to a great wooden frame at one end of the hall, with a pause while they changed the reel), Jerry would arrive just before the opening titles carrying a huge ashtray, a silver Ronson table lighter and a box of 200 Players Navy Cut - unfiltered, of course. Nobody had heard of passive smoking.

Here was his technique for teaching me Latin: In silence (apart from the tapping and scraping of the chalk on the blackboard), he wrote "Puer amat mensam".

Then he asked me to translate.

I knew very well what "Puer amat mensam" meant. It was explained very clearly in *The Shorter Latin Primer,* a small red book, every single copy of which had been edited by previous generations of boys so that now it read *"The Shorter Eating Primer",*

"Puer amat mensam" meant "The boy loves the table". I knew that. You would have to be pretty dim not to know that, and I wasn't dim. I just didn't know my tables or my dates – or, to put it another way, numbers. I was OK with words, though. I really liked words.

Now that I had learned to read, I read voraciously. My mother used to send me the Boy's Own Paper every month - it came rolled into a cylinder and held together with a brown wrapper as "printed matter", which made it cheaper to send. To me, it just made it sound more exciting.

When you had twelve copies, you could send off for a hard-cover binder to keep them in. As the years went by at West Downs, I amassed five hard-cover binders, all full of adventurous boys who caught spies and rescued people from shipwrecks and climbed mountains and flew aeroplanes and generally enjoyed a life far removed from West Downs and Jerry Cornes and "Puer amat mensam".

Even more exciting than Boy's Own Paper was War Picture Library. These were 64-page pocket-sized comics, each one telling a full heroic tale of square-jawed Brits and dastardly Huns – also "Japs", "Eyties" and any other foreigners who happened to get in the way. The British said things like "Take that, Jerry!" and the Jerries said "Gott in Himmel!" and "Donner und Blitzen!" The Japs just said: "Banzai!" There were a lot of exclamation marks in War Picture Library.

There was only one problem: At West Downs, comics were not allowed. Or, to put it another way, since everyone collected and swapped them, they were classed as "Contraband". This meant they had to be read in secret - under the bedclothes by the light of a torch. I used to keep mine for a Saturday night. On a Saturday, the tuck shop opened, and for 6d (2½p) you could buy a Mars Bar. Under the bedclothes with a dim torch on a Saturday night, I could make a Mars Bar last a whole 64-page War Picture Library comic. I would be quite sticky by the end.

There was one thing that was better than the torch, the comic and Mars Bar: If you gave a second Mars Bar to a boy called

Boddington, he would lend out his uncle's flying helmet. This was a genuine World War II leather helmet complete with earphones and microphone/oxygen mask. Inside, in blue/black ink, was the name P/O Boddington. Once you had that on your head, breathing rubbery-smelling air mixed with the taste of Mars Bar while piloting a Spitfire through the flak of your imagination, you were invincible - even if you did have to run the gauntlet in the morning.

Of course, all this contraband had to be hidden somewhere. As far as we boys were concerned, the concealing of contraband was just a part of the never-ending battle with authority - rather like the PoW's in the comics putting one over on the "Goons". Every dorm had its secret hiding place - a loose floorboard under one of the beds. We would hide the comics down there in the certain knowledge that Matron would never find them.

I really believed this - until one day when I was confined to bed with something or other and lying there quietly at the far end of the dorm when Matron walked in. She was showing some prospective parents the traditional nature of the accommodation. She was particularly proud of the Victorian wash-stands, explaining that each morning these would be filled with hot water. In fact, what happened was that a pair of Portuguese domestics would get up at six o'clock in the morning and start ferrying enormous enamel jugs of boiling water up and down the stairs, and along the corridors in order to get round all the wash-stands before the bell went at seven o'clock. If your dormitory was the first on the round, the water would be stone cold.

Next, Matron pointed out the sturdy iron bedsteads - each one with its pronounced dip in the middle concealed by a tartan blanket stretched tightly across it like a drumskin. It would be some years before the "Continental Quilt" arrived in British prep schools.

Then Matron gave the parents a conspiratorial wink and - evidently forgetting that she had sent me to bed for the day -

casually lifted the loose floorboard to reveal our stash of contraband.

"It's important that the boys should feel they have some independence," she told the prospective parents. "Of course, we check regularly for anything unsuitable - which of course, there probably would be if we didn't turn a blind eye to the more innocent publications. It acts as a sort of safety-valve."

The parents nodded approvingly. I wonder how many of them sent their sons to West Downs based on Matron's seemingly progressive views. They should have seen her poking around in the lavatories with a disgusting stick to make sure our bowels moved every day.

Anyway, we're getting away from Jerry Cornes, who is still waiting for his translation of "Puer amat Mensam".

… by the way, if you are planning to continue with this narrative, you had better get used to this sort of digression. I have a habit of **continually starting new tasks before finishing old ones**.

Jerry took it one word at a time - as if addressing an imbecile. He pointed to the word "puer".

"What does 'puer' mean?"

"The boy."

"Excellent. And 'amat'?"

"Loves."

"Very good. And 'mensam'?"

"The table."

"Yes." Jerry produced one of his awful satanic smiles - all leer and yellow teeth. "So 'Puer amat mensam' translates as…"

There was a pause. It was a pause that lasted for more than half a century. Jerry Cornes waited for that pause to end right up to the day in 1988 when he retired and closed the school rather than let anyone else get their hands on it - and, presumably, it lasted beyond that until his death in 2001 at the age of 91, as a fine advertisement for the tobacco industry.

Actually, I did know what "puer amat mensam" meant. Good heavens, it had been explained to me word by word and, as I mentioned, I was not an imbecile. In fact, thanks to Boy's Own Paper - and, to some extent, War Picture Library, I had a certain appreciation for language. I knew beyond all doubt that "The boy loves the table" was possibly the most stupid sentence in any language - dead or alive.

Think about it: Did the boy love the table in some romantic sense? Hardly likely. Did he love it as an aesthetic object - a fine antique perhaps or as an attractive 1950s Formica laminate such as my mother might enthuse over in Peter Jones' furniture department? Boys, I knew, did not appreciate furniture in that way. No, the idea of any boy loving any table was so ridiculous as to be untranslatable.

So, I refused to translate it.

The rest of the class misunderstood my motives and presumed that Thicky Passmore was deliberately baiting the headmaster.

So did the headmaster.

He tried a few more times, going through the absurd sentence word by word and then attempting to get me to put it together. In the end, he snapped, just as the rest of the class knew he would. In two strides of his spidery legs, he reached my desk, grabbed me by the collar, hauled me to my feet and dragged me from the classroom shouting - and I remember this exactly - "Maybe the stick is the only thing that will teach you!"

As we made our way down the long, flagstoned green-and-cream corridor to his study, I could hear the gradually diminishing cries of my classmates as they banged their Shorter Eating Primers on their desks while conjugating that legendary Latin verb: "Bendo, Wackere, Ouchi, Sorebum…"

Being caned at West Downs always followed the same pattern.

It took place in the headmaster's study, an over-heated, dusty place with a cluttered desk, two leather armchairs either side of an ancient gas fire which popped and gurgled when Jerry lit it with a long wax taper - and then, so as not to waste the flame, applied the taper to a Players Navy Cut from the 200 box on the table beside his chair. There was a horrible purple hearthrug and, between it and the desk, a worn brown leather pouffe.

Since this was the very first time I had been caned, Jerry had to initiate me. He said: "Bend over that." Later he would just point with a long bony finger. Next, he walked around the back of the chair furthest from the window to a tall bookcase. It almost touched the ceiling, but he reached up with ease to the top shelf and took down the cane.

I had expected a thin, whippy thing with a curved handle like a walking stick. That was what Mr Quelch wielded in Billy Bunter. But no, this was a short, thick bamboo stick of the sort you find in a vegetable garden. It was well-used. Indeed, it seemed to be suffering from over-use since the splitting ends had been wrapped in tatty and greying Elastoplast.

Turning back to me and weighing the cane in his hands, Jerry saw me looking and pointed to the skirting board in front of me. I looked at the skirting board and, without more ado, he whacked me expertly four times on the bottom. It hurt like hell. Tears squeezed out of my eyes, but I refused to give him the satisfaction of hearing me cry out.

He replaced the cane on the bookshelf, turned back to find me still hunched over the pouffe and said: "Get up."

This was easier said than done. The pain gave no sign of abating. In fact, it seemed to be getting worse as more and more nerve-endings in other parts of my rear end woke up and protested. Movement of any sort was going to be difficult. I gritted my teeth and pushed myself up. Once again, Jerry grasped my collar and marched me back down the long corridor. As we approached the classroom, I was astonished to hear the sounds of "Bendo, Wackere…" My classmates must have kept it up the whole time. You would have thought one of the other teachers would have intervened (they had, but the class just started up again as soon as they left).

Once in the classroom, Jerry released his hold and pointed wordlessly to my desk. I sat down gingerly, taking as much weight as possible on my folded arms on the desktop. On the blackboard, the words "Puer amat mensam" glared at me accusingly. Well, I certainly wasn't going to translate them now. Jerry seemed to realise this. He took the board rubber and wiped them away in a cloud of chalk dust.

The incident was never mentioned again - unless you count the inclusion of the word "obstinate" in my end-of-term report.

As soon as the bell sounded, the rest of the class bore me gleefully *ad foricas*. If you don't know what that means, your Latin is even worse than mine. It means *To the Latrine* - where my shorts were lowered to reveal four identical and precisely parallel red stripes across both buttocks, rapidly turning purple. They hadn't broken the skin - which they would have done, undoubtedly, had all the strokes been in the same spot, but Jerry had placed them next to each other. How did he do that? He had placed them meticulously so that they took up every inch of available skin. Presumably, that was why I received only four of the best, not six. I would need a bigger bottom for six. Jerry might only have come second in the Olympics, but he was a champion with the cane.

I progressed through West Downs from the bottom of one form to the bottom of the next - always emerging at the end of the year, once again, at the bottom. Worst of all was Maths. Without the benefit of knowing my Times Tables, I had no idea where to start. The Maths master was a Mr Rawson, an ancient grey man in grey flannels and a rust-coloured sports jacket with leather elbows and cuffs. His only redeeming feature was that he could take a stack of foolscap paper and rotate his knuckle on the top sheet in small circles until the entire pile had fanned out like a cogwheel. His method of teaching was repetition, repetition - and endless repetition.

To this end, he set every class a test on a Friday and then, the following week, every wrong calculation had to be worked through again during a special session in his classroom after lunch. On the Monday almost the whole class would turn up - after all, there weren't many of us who didn't make a single mistake. On Tuesday, there were fewer - and the form room thinned out as the week went by. Until Friday: On Friday every week, I would be the only boy left - still with the whole list of wrong sums to wrestle over. Then, in the afternoon, there would be another test - and on the Monday the whole process would begin again.

However, despite Mr Rawson's sums and Jerry's wretched boy and his table, there was one subject at which I excelled. In English, invariably, I came top. The school could never understand why. After all, I was stupid, wasn't I?

The answer was simple: Mrs Cornes, a lady as fragrant and kind as her husband was smelly and irascible. She didn't seem to belong in a place like West Downs at all. Nevertheless, she was devoted to Jerry, and so there she was - and determined to make her mark. Every day after lunch, she would read to the new boys. We would go to her private sitting room - an oasis of light and calm and fresh flowers, absurdly just across the corridor from Jerry's dreadful study. She had a chintz three-piece suite and took the chair by the fireplace - a real coal fire in winter, a vase of flowers I summer. Around the edge of the floor was a strip of polished hardwood, where we left our shoes by the door. Covering the centre of the floor was the thickest, palest grey carpet I had ever seen. A few of the boys would tiptoe in their grey woolen socks to the sofa and the empty armchair. The rest of us spread out across the carpet in a semi-circle at Mrs Cornes' feet - the front row with their noses practically resting on her sensible shoes. Those further back lay on their stomachs, feet in the air to make room for the row behind and heads propped up on hands so they could look at the lady as she read.

It was important to be able to see her face because it was as much her expression as her knack for accents which brought to life the classics of children's literature: *The Borrowers, The Water Babies, The Railway Children...*

If my parents, shaking their heads over my dismal reports, ever wondered what they were getting for the fees they paid to Jerry Cornes three times a year, I would say they got their money's worth from Mrs Cornes.

On the first day of my second year, I presented myself as usual at her door after lunch. Of course, all the other boys were new - Story Time after lunch was for new boys. Mrs Cornes told me so in her kindly voice, suggesting I might like to run about with my friends in the second year. But I said they weren't my friends - that I had been kept down in the bottom class for an extra term. Whether that made a difference, or she recognised someone who loved stories as much as she did - or whether she was just being kind, I have no idea, but she let me stay. We started that second year with *Treasure Island*. For half an hour, I forgot all about Latin. My head was in the Spanish Main.

It was Mrs Cornes who edited the school magazine. This celebrated the victories of the cricket team, congratulated those boys who had gained scholarships to Eton and Winchester - and contained a collection of "Contributions from the Boys". These might be poems or essays - short pieces of a page or so.

I contributed an adventure story entitled "Green Flare". It was about the son of a lifeboat Coxswain. The lad had been helping his father by cleaning the engine when suddenly it burst into life, and the boat set off at high speed on a rescue mission - our hero still aboard.

You could tell he was going to be "our hero" because the style owed a good deal to Boy's Own Paper, and sure enough, when the entire crew of grown-up Lifeboatmen failed to rescue the shipwrecked fishermen - who weren't, of course, fishermen at all but dastardly foreign spies - it was the brave and resourceful youth who saved the day and saw that justice was done.

It was inevitable that I failed to cram all of that into a single page. In fact, I think it went on for some half-dozen pages. Mrs Cornes told me that she had overruled her husband and insisted on giving it space because it was so very good and exciting. I felt I had been awarded the Nobel Prize for Literature. From that moment, I determined to become a Writer with a capital "W". I would write adventure stories - thrillers. I graduated from Boys' Own Paper to John Buchan and Dennis Wheatley.

* * *

As West Downs grew, space in the dreadful dormitories came under pressure, and Jerry had to find somewhere else to sleep his surplus boys. When he bought the school in 1955, it came with an area of woodland called "Melbury" just across the road. This was where the school scout troop would light their campfires (using no more than three matches) and cook "damper" - a mixture of flour and water stirred with a stick and fried in lard. It was surprisingly delicious and tasted of woodsmoke. Anyway, down in Melbury was a lodge which had been converted to sleep a couple of dozen of these surplus boys. Every night they would troop down after prep, reappearing the next morning in time for breakfast.

The extraordinary thing was that I don't remember any member of staff sleeping on the premises. We were all in our last couple of years, and I suppose one of us must have been in charge, but - unbelievable as it sounds - I really think we were left to our own devices in groups of six in small dormitories.

Obviously, we got up to all sorts of mischief. I'm sure we went out into the woods, had midnight feasts and what-not. But whatever it was, all the japes pale into insignificance when compared to what became known in West Downs folklore as The Escapade.

I think we must have finished our midnight feast – eaten the last Smartie, the last crumb of rock cake snaffled from the tin in the sanitorium. After such a surfeit, the thing that 12-year-old boys crave in particular is a piece of chewing gum. Chewing gum was frowned on as much as War Picture Library. Certainly, it was not available in the Tuck Shop, and this made it all the more desirable.

However, you could buy chewing gum from the slot machine outside the newsagents on the way into town. We all knew this because we passed it when walking to and from the station for the school train at the beginning and end of term. The newsagent's shop was no more than a mile away down the hill. You could be there and back in half an hour. A penny would buy a packet of chewing gum. We pooled our pennies. In those days, pennies were real money - big, heavy chunks of brown metal that could weigh down a pair of shorts and make the wearer feel rich. By the time the whole dorm had pitched in their pennies, we had enough to empty the newsagent's machine - probably the bubblegum machine as well.

The next decision was who was going to go. I think we tried drawing lots, but that didn't work because the two boys who drew the short straws promptly backed out. After that, it became a dare, and as we know, ADHD means **taking risks in activities, often with little or no regard for personal safety or the safety of others.**

I volunteered, along with a boy called Dominic Wyhowski. We put on our clothes over our pyjamas. I still don't understand the logic of this since each leg now exhibited six inches of striped flannel between shorts and long woollen sock. Maybe somebody thought that since we were still technically dressed for bed, we could not really be considered to be out of it. Perhaps, if we were caught, we could pretend to be sleepwalking…

We loaded the coppers into our pockets and set off. I remember that it didn't seem to be nearly such a good idea once we got outside. There was a full moon, and the woods were lit up as if by floodlights. All the same, we walked in heavy silence, neither one of us wanting to admit that this was in fact, a terrible idea.

Once on the main road, it seemed even worse. By now it must have been one o'clock in the morning but regularly, cars swept up the road, their headlight playing across our pyjama-clad knees. All the same, we pressed on, still in terrified silence. We reached the newsagent a mile down the road. We pushed our pennies into the machines, exchanging the weight of copper for the bulk of sugar and gum.

On the return journey, we couldn't wait to get back fast enough. We didn't want to run - that would just draw attention. We would walk quickly, we decided. All the same, each time a car drove past, I'm sure we both held our breath. I know I was still holding mine when the police car stopped.

Police cars were black in those days; sinister things. The policeman on the passenger side cranked down his window. He looked at us. He said nothing. We said nothing. Somebody had to say something. Eventually, the policeman said: "Good evening."

"Good evening, Sir," we said in unison (we had been nicely brought up).

"So, where are you boys going at this time of night?"

"Um, we're going home, Sir."

The policeman was pleased to hear this. "Good," he said. "We'll give you a lift."

I don't know how it happened, but the next thing we knew,

we were in the back of the police car, looking at the backs of the policemen's heads and wondering how we were going to get out of this. The first thing to do was pretend we lived anywhere other than West Downs School.

"Sleeping Hill," I said when, inevitably, they asked us.

"Sleepers Hill."

"Yes, Sleepers Hill."

We drove to Sleepers Hill. We drove up and down Sleepers Hill because neither of us could remember the number. Nor, it transpired, could we recognise the house where - it was becoming increasingly obvious - we did not live.

Eventually, in the way of putting everyone out of their misery, the driver said: "Are you sure you're not from West Downs School?"

Silence from the back seat. The driver swung the car around, and two minutes later, we were crunching up the school drive.

Jerry Cornes answered the door in his dressing gown. I had never imagined him in a dressing gown. It was a mesmerizing sight. It seemed as faded and smokey as the rest of him.

I remember very little of what was said as the five of us stood in his study - apart from the repeated use of the word "Escapade".

Dominic and I stood there in our ridiculous attire, heads bowed, utterly terrified and dejected. The phrase "wishing the ground would open up and swallow me", which I had read so many times in Boy's Own Paper, suddenly had real meaning. However, I could see no escape - much less "with a single bound".

Then Jerry said: "These two, of course, will receive the *thrashing of their lives*", and that really terrified me. He thanked the policemen, insisted we thank them too, saw them out and then walked us round to his Morris 1000 shooting brake (pale blue with varnished woodwork) and drove us back down to Melbury where, amazingly, he deposited us once again - if I'm right - with no adult supervision.

Of course, the other boys in the dorm couldn't wait to hear about our "escapade" – and, amazingly, our pockets were still filled with chewing gum (nobody had thought to press us when we said we were out at one o'clock in the morning because we had decided we would like to "go for a walk".)

It was almost dawn by the time the debriefing was finished, and the last of the chewing gum had been stuck to the underside of the bedstead for tomorrow. But I didn't sleep. There was a phrase that was still going through my mind: "These two will receive the thrashing of their lives".

The thrashing was to be delivered after chapel - a magnificent memorial to all those former pupils who had died in two world wars. It was actually part of the structure of the building with a high vaulted ceiling and its own steeple and bell and the names of the glorious dead carved in gold into the wood panelling. Jerry ascended the steps to the pulpit, looking like a bird of prey in his old university gown. He chose as his theme *Retribution* with a good helping of *the wages of sin* and a side-order of *hellfire, brimstone and torment* and then a quick whip through the thesaurus under *pain and eternal suffering*.

Afterwards, Dominic and I waited outside his study, and I don't know how my accomplice in the Escapade felt, but I know that I was absolutely terrified. I knew that whatever happened in the next five minutes, I was going to remember all my life. It was, after all, going to be the *thrashing of my life*.

I think I was letting my imagination run away with me - wasn't the birch used for *thrashing*? Or perhaps it was the Cat o' Nine Tails – no, that was *flogging* (although *flogging* was school patois for masturbating).

In the event, Jerry stuck to his trusty cane. I noted that it had been awarded fresh Elastoplast since our last meeting. He tapped it against his palm as he explained that six strokes was the only possible punishment for an Escapade of this severity. Once again, it hurt like hell. Later, *ad foricas,* when Dominic and I gingerly lowered our shorts to show off our battle honours, I was pleased to hear that my bottom was now big enough to accommodate six parallel purple stripes.

***

I was never going to pass the Common Entrance examination. You needed 60% to get into any sort of decent public school, and I was destined for Charterhouse, my father's old school, which demanded 65% to be certain of a place. By pure chance, my aunt on my father's side had married a charming Scottish schoolmaster called Jock Reith, who was now a housemaster at Charterhouse. As such, he was allowed a good deal of autonomy about the boys he admitted to Gownboys house - but all the same, I would have to go through the motions.

My parents did more than go through the motions. In the holidays, I was sent to a "crammer". This was a dreadful Dickensian institution staffed by teachers who couldn't get jobs at proper schools and attended by pupils who were so stupid or - more usually, so stroppy - that they were incapable of learning anything at proper schools.

The best thing about the crammer was that you got to meet boys from other prep schools - and not the swots who were safe to go on tour with the First XI but the dregs of the system who were happy to swap scurrilous stories about how your new maths master had only got the job after he had been sacked from their school.

When it became clear that I was learning nothing at the crammer, my parents engaged Mr Fisher, a young and impoverished master from West Downs who spent the holidays staying with relations in Earls Court and came daily to sit at our dining room table and try to get some Latin into me. He was friendly - not at all like most of the staff - and seemed genuinely concerned that I should pass the Common Entrance. It would be a wonderful opportunity, he assured me. I started to do some work - not because I thought it would be a wonderful opportunity but because I really liked Mr Fisher and didn't want him to get the sack. I even translated the wretched boy and his blasted table.

As it happened, I didn't pass the Common Entrance exam. I only managed 57% - but Uncle Jock let me in. I don't think the family gave him much choice.

Chapter 3
Rebellion

At Charterhouse, I acquired a new nickname: "Rooty". It happened after the first three weeks when the class was called in front of the headmaster for a ceremony known as "Calling Over". The weather was still fine, so we were outside under a magnificent oak tree called, of course, The Charterhouse Oak.

The headmaster sat at a table which had been carried out especially. The form master, in his gown, hovered at the head's shoulder and muttered as they went through the class results. Boys who had achieved high marks were called up to be congratulated. Those who had returned low marks…

Well, let's just say my name was called. I was new, the headmaster was kind - somebody had to be bottom, after all. But, as he said: "Just make sure it isn't you again next time."

However, 13-year-old boys are not kind. I was, after all, bottom of the bottom class in the whole school - what was known as the "Root of the School": Hence, "Rooty".

Also, I was a fag - a servant to the older boys. This was 1962 - only a couple years after the trial of Lady Chatterley's Lover, during which Counsel for the prosecution asked the jury: "Is this a book you would wish your wife or your servants to read?"

The Public School system was still teaching young men to deal with the servants they would employ in later life. So, when a senior boy - a house monitor responsible for discipline in the house - instructed me to polish his brown brogues, I set to with a will. There was a room designated for the purpose of polishing not only shoes but also the many silver cups the house had won for everything from cricket to debating. The shoes came up beautifully, as you would expect from Lobb's of St James's - a deep, dark tan. Actually, a very dark tan. Indeed, the toe on which I was working so industriously was considerably darker than the heel.

It was at about this point I realised that, although I was using the dark tan polish, I was using the black brush - which obviously had a good deal of black polish still on it. I now put this down to a **lack of attention to detail**.

What to do about it? I couldn't see how I could get the black polish off now that it was on - and the monitor would see very quickly that the toes did not match the heels. The solution seemed to be to make the heels match the toes - by polishing them black as well. This made perfect sense. At no point did I suspect it might be an example of **poor decision-making**. I set to with renewed vigour - not only with the black brush but now also with the black polish.

A little late, admittedly, I replaced the gleaming black brogues just inside the door of the monitor's spacious and - thankfully empty - study.

And waited for the resulting explosion.

It was some hours in coming. But eventually, the monitor came to find me in the Junior Common Room. He was holding up the shoes like an exhibit.

"What are these?" he asked in the languorous tone he was practising, ready for the day he would be elected to White's Club.

"Your shoes, Farquarson Major." (Or whatever his name was.)

"These were brown."

"No, black. You can see they're black."

He looked puzzled. I looked innocent. Eventually, he gave a little shake of his head as if the world had somehow gone off on a tangent and left him behind. Then he wandered off back to the Senior Common Room.

I never heard any more about it. Maybe he just ordered another pair.

* * *

The incident of the monitor's shoes did wonders for my reputation. As time went by, I came by a new and rather better nickname than "Rooty". We had been sitting over lunch talking about names, and I happened to mention that my mother had wanted to call me "Ben", but my father hadn't cared for it.

"Ben": My friends loved it. Apparently, it suited me perfectly. They tried it out with a broad West Country accent: "Oo-aar, Ben" – a simple son of the soil. I remained "Ben" for the rest of my school days. Indeed, as time went by, there were people - including the staff - who were astonished to discover that it wasn't my name at all.

And, of course, I played up to it - remaining, resolutely, at the bottom of every class in every year - summoned to stand before the headmaster as regular as clockwork, every three weeks until he grew tired of calling me up - although I could hear the muttering with the form master:

"And Passmore, of course… "

"Yes, Sir, I'm afraid so…".

"Hmmm…"

And so, it continued along this path. When it came to 'O' Levels, I passed two: English, naturally, and something like biology. I was expected to pass at least five in order to enter the sixth form, so there was only one thing for it - I had to be kept down a year.

This, I resented hugely: Sixth-formers had all sorts of privileges. For one thing, they could drink beer in the Sixth Form Club. Suddenly all my friends had entered a different world denied to me - I was held down in the fifth form with a lot of boys with fluff on their chins who viewed me with pity. I determined to do something about it.

"Passmore!" said the form master at the first Calling Over of the Autumn Term (or, as it was called in the arcane manner beloved of public schools "Oration Quarter"). We were under the oak tree again, but this time the headmaster was smiling - a bemused sort of smile.

"Passmore," he said. "I see that your marks for the start of this term place you in the Number Three position of the form order. This is very good. This shows what you can do when you try. Well done. Keep it up!"

And I did. Retaking the 'O' Levels at the end of term, I passed another five - and with them, attained all the heady freedom that came with membership of the Sixth Form. I was given a study of my own - although, since I was the last to be allotted one, it was the smallest in the house. Really, there was hardly room to turn round - and certainly, none for swinging cats or, come to that, entertaining friends.

Entertaining in your study was a big thing at Charterhouse: We were allowed Primus stoves to make instant coffee and set fire to ourselves. We installed record players and huge, reel-to-reel tape recorders with miles of wire connected to a jumble of adapters plugged into the single light socket. This, in turn, necessitated stuffing a nail into the fuse box in place of the useless 30amp fuse wire which kept melting. How we didn't burn the place down, I have no idea.

And then there was the smoking.

No, of course, we weren't allowed to smoke – even in the sixth form. But this was the '60s. Smoking was big in the '60s. Smoking was cool. Smoking was sexy. I affected Gauloises Bleu, which smelled like French peasant's socks. We smoked in one of the attics accessed through a tiny trap door in the ceiling outside the top dormitory. If you could get up there, you could enjoy your post-prandial cigarette undisturbed by the roving housemaster (my Uncle Jock had retired by this time. Jock would never have interfered in our simple pleasures. Now we had the young and energetic Mr Green.)

Never mind; in those days, we learned our climbing skills by getting into the attic for a cigarette - none of your "climbing walls". You grabbed the lintel of the doorway, swung one foot up against the wall, transferred a hand to push open the trap door and, grabbing hold of the rafters, pushed up with the other foot against the opposite wall before wriggling your hips through the gap.

A boy called Tim Lee could never manage it. He wasn't unathletic, and he was a nice chap who would have been very welcome up there. But Tim had very wide hips - astonishingly wide hips. It wasn't just a matter of cutting down on the traditional 16-year-old's four slices of toast and jam at break: Tim's bones just stuck out too much - and there was nothing anyone could do about that…

Besides, we had other things to worry about: The young and earnest Mr Green had read all the theories about modern education and set out to be a friend to us. Unfortunately, he was also a passionate non-smoker and knew all about what was going on in the attic.

His problem was catching us at it. Obviously, he couldn't just come up with a step ladder because our lookout system would have been the envy of Stalag Luft III. So, what he did was get hold of some of that purple gunk used to identify burglars: You smear it on the window handles and then look round the tables in the dining room to see who has purple fingers from opening the windows to let the smoke out.

The only trouble was that, when he looked, every boy in the house had purple fingers – right down to the most junior fag.

As soon as we realised what was going on, we scraped off the gunk and smeared it all over the fifth formers - who promptly became the envy of the year below, so they volunteered to be smeared too… and so on down to the smallest new boy. After that, Mr Green left us alone.

Have you ever seen the film "If…?" It's based on real life - or, at least, what passed for real life in the '60s.

It was all about rebellion: Sending your trousers away to be tapered until you couldn't get your feet into them - sideburns below the top of the ear, hair below the collar. Loud music. Louder music.

I had a guitar (everybody had a guitar) and Burt Weedon's *Play in a Day* instruction book. Four of us took over an empty classroom one afternoon with three chords and a geometry box - if you bashed the geometry box with a couple of pencils, it sounded just like a snare drum. One of the guitarists was a boy with a long, permanently tanned face called Mike Rutherford. Mike was the only one of us who practised. In the end, he was spotted by a boy in the year above who practised even more and had a proper band with a real drum kit. That boy's name was Peter Gabriel…Yes, I played with that Mike Rutherford, and if only I hadn't been prone to **continually starting new tasks before finishing old ones** and practised my three chords, I might have been in Genesis too.

Just like West Downs, Charterhouse had a Memorial Chapel - just bigger and with more names of poor dead young men. You could sit where you wanted, provided you were in the right block and there were exactly ten boys in each row. Obviously, you would choose a row with your friends, so you had someone to whisper to during the sermon. At the end of each row was a small pad of paper. The idea was that the boy sitting on the end was supposed to check every day to see that everyone in his row had turned up. If there was someone missing, he was to write the name on the pad and hand the piece of paper to the master sitting at the back as they passed on their way out at the end of the service.

You might think there was a fatal flaw in all of this: If the boy on the end was possessed of a kind heart (or open to bribery), then the whole thing fell apart.

However, on the other side of the aisle was a similar block of pews - at the back of which sat another master tasked with counting the heads in the rows facing him to ensure that the boy in front of the pad didn't shirk his duty.

It was a very good system. It was simple. It had worked for decades. Miss chapel and you were in trouble.

However, any security system has a weak link (war picture library again) - and I found it at the end of my first year in the Sixth Form. It was simple - in fact, it was probably so simple, that everyone had overlooked it: If you never went to chapel at all, nobody would ever miss you. During the whole of my last year, I never went to chapel once. Of course, I couldn't be seen wandering around either. I had to stay in my study - but I was quite happy to do that. It was peaceful up there. The house was silent. I could read.

I should have been reading Vanity Fair, but I couldn't stick with it. Why on earth did these Victorian authors take so long to say everything? Dickens was just as bad - all that "And now, gentle reader, let us consider the predicament of our heroine…"

So, I studied Ian Fleming instead. I read all of James Bond - several times. I could quote complete passages. If 007 had been accorded the same status by the 'A 'Level examiners as David Copperfield, I would have ended up at Oxford. As things were, I'm afraid it all went downhill, rather. We had an enthusiastic and charismatic teacher called Mr Summerscale. The boy who won the Poetry Prize credits Mr Summerscale with setting him on the literary path - that boy was Peter James, who went on to write 68 books and has sold 20 million copies in his Roy Grace detective series alone.

I didn't go in for the poetry prize. I didn't go in for the Shakespeare prize either. It wasn't my fault. I seemed to have some sort of **inability to focus or prioritise**.

I didn't just fail to get an 'A' Level in English. They didn't even give me an 'O' Level. I got a complete 'Fail'. Here's how I managed it: I ignored the questions, whatever they were, and devoted the entire 90 minutes to writing an earnest and well-argued treatise on the theme that Shakespeare was a reasonably competent hack with a lot of money troubles who churned out plays as fast as he could to keep the creditors from the door. He would not have had time for sort of the convoluted thinking which had kept generations of academics in comfortable employment ever since.

In putting forward this theory, I somehow overlooked the fact that my paper was going to be marked by said comfortable academics…

Chapter 4
Work

My parents didn't know what to do with me. My preferred life choice - which we'll come to later - was a complete no-no. However, during a summer holiday when I was 16, I had been packed off to some family friends who had a farm. Still a year short of my driving test, I was thrilled to be allowed to drive tractors about the fields. Consequently, I agreed to be enrolled in the Royal Agricultural College at Cirencester - but first, I had to complete a year's practical experience on a farm.

Pond Park was in Essex - the sort of mixed farm which doesn't exist anymore - 350 acres of cereal, potatoes, sugar beet - we even tried asparagus. There was a small dairy herd and also a shed full of day-old chicks which became my first responsibility. The tractors had no cabs - just an old sack on the metal seat for comfort. We hoed the sugar beet by hand, walking sideways down the rows of seedlings. For the potato harvest, an extended family of gypsies arrived and built themselves little houses out of straw bales and tarpaulins to augment their caravans.

I had a caravan too. It was parked in what you might call a satellite farmyard a mile away – opposite the cowshed with the pond outside the door and the dung heap conveniently close (I had a chemical toilet). I loved that caravan. It was my first home of my own. In the evenings, with the stove lit and the curtains drawn, there was nobody to tell me what to do, nobody to tell me I had done it wrong or not at all. Revelling in the solitude, I cooked my dinner, listened to BBC radio comedy, and read the same books over and over again.

I earned £12 19s 6d a week - at a time when a gallon of petrol cost 2/6d and an evening's dinner and dancing at Francoise in Sloane Square would set you back £5. Of course, this being the '60s, the weekend didn't start until midday on Saturday. One Saturday, in particular, deserves to be remembered. I was anxious to get away (see Chapter 6 - Love) when the farmer informed me that I would spend the morning loading straw – the lorry would be arriving shortly. All I had to do was help the driver.

Pretty simple: I had loaded plenty of straw bales by this time - pitching them up onto the trailer with an old-fashioned pitch-fork: A bit of muscle but mostly technique and timing…

The lorry duly arrived at mid-morning, and I directed the driver as he backed up to the haystack. Then he climbed down and looked at me. I looked at him. There were just the two of us.

"OK," I said. "I'll pitch, and you stack."

He said: "What?"

I explained, but his expression still indicated that as far as he was concerned, I might as well have been speaking Serbo-Croat.

I might indeed have been speaking a foreign language because it turned out that:

A: The driver had never carried a load of straw before.

B: He had never collected any kind of load from a farm before – not straw bales, not sacks of grain – never delivered bags of fertilizer…

C: Actually, he had never driven a lorry before. He was a bus driver…

Also, there was some urgency because the reason he was driving a lorry today was in order to earn a bit of extra money because…

D: AT THREE O'CLOCK, HE WAS GETTING MARRIED.

What with all this discussion, it was now getting on for eleven.

He said: "Can't you load if I pitch?"

I had never done that before. Of course, I'd seen it done. The trick was to begin at the outside and prop the ends of the bales on the raised edges of the lorry bed. That made them lean inwards. The secret was to have all the outside bales leaning inwards right up to the top of the stack, and then the weight of the top layer would lock everything into place like the blocks in a game of Jenga… at least, I think that was the idea. They hadn't invented Jenga then. As I say, I'd never done it myself…

So, we started work. He pitched while I stacked – and, of course, we chatted as we worked. He told me all about his fiancée and the wedding. I think the honeymoon was going to be in Great Yarmouth or somewhere like that. In the light of what happened an hour later, it's hardly surprising that I don't remember the details.

I do remember him telling me that he had it all worked out: As long as he left by 12.30, he would just have time to dump the lorry at the haulage depot, rush home for a quick change and be at the church for three o'clock.

I stacked as fast as I could. I didn't want him to be late.

He pitched as fast as he could. He said it was hard work. He said he'd stick to driving a bus.

We got it all done in time. I laid the top layer to hold it all together. He threw up a rope. We lashed it down nice and tight with proper waggoner's hitches. We shook hands. I wished him luck for the future, and he climbed up into the cab, fired up the big diesel and lurched out of the farm gate.

I say "lurched" because years of heavy machinery driving in and out of the farm had opened up a large pothole on one side of the gateway. When it got too bad, we put a barrowload of hardcore into it and drove a tractor backwards and forwards to tamp it down. But it was a while since we'd done that, and as the lorry's nearside back wheels dropped into the hole, the entire chassis dipped to the left.

Now, you can tie a load of straw bales onto a flatbed lorry very securely – after all, you can get a good bit of purchase with a waggoner's hitch the way I'd learned as a competent farm worker (even if I was only worth £12 19s 6d a week).

However, the thing to remember about small bales is that not all of them will be secured by the rope. Some of them will be in the gaps between it - and if the weight of the top layer is not sufficient to lock them in place - especially if the ends of the bottom layer are not quite high enough because they're on a lorry and not a farm trailer... or maybe if the whole structure is fundamentally unstable because it has been stacked by somebody who is doing it for the first time and whose entire expertise is based on seeing someone else do it...

When that happens, the laws of physics come into play - in this case, the principles of kinetic energy as derived from the tilting motion of the lorry chassis when the nearside wheels dropped into the hole. The weight of the offside bales duly shifted onto those in the middle, and the resulting momentum was, in turn, transferred to those on the near side. Fortunately, some of these were secured by the stout rope and my masterful waggoner's hitches.

Unfortunately, others were not.

And, once some of the nearside bales fell out, those previously constrained by the rope were able to ooze into the gap left behind.

I say "ooze" which is an odd word to use when describing something as dry as straw, but it seemed to me that I was watching the unfolding disaster in slow motion. One after another, the bales found their way around the ropes and as they did so, began to bend – which is something you should never allow a small bale to do –

at least not until you want to break it open to spread the straw in your stable or strawberry field or wherever…

In this instance, it spread all over the road.

One by one, they toppled. Some bursting as they fell, others crashing onto the tarmac and going off like big golden bombs.

The lorry stopped with another lurch (which only helped to add impetus to the avalanche). The lorry driver/bus driver/bridegroom jumped down from the cab and took in the scene with an expression which I don't think I ought to attempt to describe because at my age, I should try and avoid undue excitement.

But it was while we were both standing there and watching the apparently never-ending cascade that the farmer arrived in his little grey Renault 4.

He stopped and got out. He nodded to the lorry driver/bus driver/bridegroom. He handed me my pay packet. He said: "Right. 12.30. You can go off for the weekend now."

"But… but…" I began. I gestured, mumbling, at the pile of loose straw which was now blocking the whole road.

"It's out of the farm gate," said the farmer. "It's not your problem. It's not mine, either. In you get."

And, with a further nod to my new friend, the driver, he drove me back to the home farm to pick up my bicycle, which – thanks to the Renault 4's legendary suspension – we were able to do without even noticing the pothole.

I collected the bike and returned to my caravan, where I was able to change back into my groovy 60's gear, jump into my Mini and head back to London, where I belonged.

But I have spent the rest of my life wondering what happened. How did the bus driver get all that loose straw cleared up? He couldn't get it back on the lorry. How long did it take? He was due at the church at three o'clock.

Did he miss his wedding altogether? Did the honeymoon in Great Yarmouth never happen? Have I ruined somebody's life just because I learned to tie a waggoner's hitch?

More to the point, was it something to do with ADHD? Was it **Carelessness and lack of attention to detail?** Was it **poor organisational skills?**

Actually, I don't think it was any of the above. It was something that could have happened to anyone. At least, I hope the bride saw it that way.

It is probably just as well that I never did become a farmer. Farmers are patient folk. They live by the seasons. In particular, they stay on the farm. Maybe it was just as well that I had stopped calling myself "Ben". After two terms at Cirencester, I disappeared in my Mini without telling anyone and went to Wales. Heaven knows what my parents must have thought, but I don't remember them ever mentioning it.

The problem was, I'd already told them what I wanted to do. It wasn't my fault they thought it was a stupid idea.

"Well, you'll have to do something," they said.

I went to work in Harrods. They started me off in Household and Garden Tools. I knew nothing about Household and Garden Tools and I wouldn't be allowed to handle money until I'd been there a month and been trained. But there was something I *could* do: I could direct people to other departments when they were lost - it takes customers years to learn their way around Harrods.

This meant I was lost too, but I compensated for this insignificant detail by putting on my most confident air and telling everyone: "Go down here through China and Glassware and you'll come to the lifts. Go up two floors to the fourth and head for Housewares. When you get to the washing machines turn left and you'll find it right in front of you (whatever it was).

I lasted a week - and I still have this recurring nightmare in which crowds of ancient shoppers mill aimlessly around washing machines.

Next came Futuristic Home Improvements. This sounded like the sort of forward-looking company in which I could prove myself. They needed "consultants". I could be a "consultant".

In fact, what they were looking for was door-to-door salespeople. Here was the deal: The professional salesman, a typical East London spiv, would load three of us young hopefuls into his Jag and drive us to Bedford where he would park outside a café and drink tea while we trudged up and down the neighbouring streets knocking on doors and offering affordable central heating.

Central heating was rare in those days and much sought after in Bedford because the town was full of immigrants who had come to work in the brick factory.

These were not the *Windrush* immigrants who had come from the Caribbean to be crammed into Rachman's Notting Hill slums. These immigrants came from India and bought their own houses. Admittedly the houses were small and cheap (and without central heating) and the immigrants were only able to afford them if the whole extended family lived together.

They had other ways of saving money, too: Readers of a certain age may remember "Tuf" shoes. These were cheap and durable – and guaranteed for life. This was ideal if you worked shifts in the brick factory in Bedford: There were three shifts so a father and his two sons could all work different shifts and share the same pair of shoes.

This is the sort of thinking Futuristic Home Improvements was banking on when it designed a system of linking cheap electric radiators to a time clock and calling it "central heating".

Since no one in India had any experience of central heating, the immigrants didn't know the difference. I would tell them the basic price on the doorstep and when they grabbed at the deal (who wouldn't?) I would go running down the street to the café to fetch the salesman who would drive me back in the Jag and together we would make the sale.

Then (and only then) would I get paid.

It worked brilliantly - until the second week when I was on my rounds and a customer came rushing up in a state of great distress and dragged me back to his house to beg to be allowed out of the contract. The radiators had still not been installed and now he could no longer afford the repayments. One of his children had been taken to hospital with some serious, possibly terminal, illness and his wife had given up her job to be with the child. The money from the brick factory (even with all the rest of the family chipping in) was not enough to pay the mortgage and…and…

I understood immediately. I ran to fetch the salesman. The salesman had not got to where he was by letting people wriggle out of contracts. He was backed up by the sales director, when I told him the sad story – and the Managing Director.

I resigned. On a point of principle.

It was the first time I had done anything on a point of principle. It felt wonderful.

Something else I learned was that, if you resign before they've paid you for all your other sales, they're probably never going to pay you.

Chapter 5
Boats

My first boat was a sleek racing yacht of the type that thundered up and down the Solent in the 1930s. Mine was smaller, of course – a model boat which had once belonged to the child of some family friends. Indeed, it may have been passed down through several generations of small boys.

Anyway, it had a long crack in the hull.

Nobody else noticed this, and I was so excited at the prospect of sailing it on the Round Pond in Kensington Gardens that I chose to overlook this one tiny defect.

My boat reached the middle of the pond and sank.

Even then, it appeared that I **didn't do detail.**

When I was five years old, we went on holiday to Cornwall, and my father hired a sailing dinghy on the Helford River. He gave me the tiller and said: "Steer for that yellow cornfield."

I did. Nobody told me to do anything else, and so I steered for the cornfield until we grounded on the other side of the river. I was amazed. I had brought us all this way. I distinctly remember being as thrilled as if I had crossed an ocean and discovered a New World.

Since nobody complained and neither my two sisters nor I had been sick or fallen in the water, when we got home, Father bought a 14ft dinghy called *Wilkie*. Every Sunday in the summer, the five of us would set out with the car full of sailbags and sandwiches, my mother waving to her friends as they queued to go into church. Mother would say: "I am sure the good Lord would rather we were out enjoying his nice fresh air than stuck in a stuffy old church." This was 1954, so she may have been risking arrest or at the very least, public outrage.

I think it all started with *Wilkie*. We sailed in the Walton Backwaters - that maze of saltings and creeks on the Essex coast where Arthur Ransome set *Secret Water* and Paul Gallico, *The Snow Goose*.

The important point was that, unlike the hired dinghy in Cornwall, *Wilkie* had a tiny foredeck and a little cuddy underneath where mother used to store the dry clothes. I was small enough to get in there too. I used to pretend it was my cabin. I would emerge in jerky little stages so that people on other boats would think I was coming up the companionway steps.

You can imagine my excitement when, three years later, Father had one too many gins in the Walton & Frinton Yacht Club and ordered a Folkboat. This was a 25ft Norwegian design. You could sleep on a Folkboat. We christened her Torgunn after the daughter of Thor, Thorgunna (Torgunn is the diminutive). The following year we found ourselves in Holland and learned what it means for five people to sleep on a 25ft boat.

Father was a yachtsman of the old school. He had owned a succession of boats before the war and got up to all kinds of japes (not being able to find his boat after a night in the pub at Bosham and sleeping on someone else's, rescuing a beautiful and naked girl off Bembridge, wiping his bowsprit down the side of a brand new millionaire's yacht in Cowes Roads (the paint came off like whipped cream). He liked to get up in the night to check the mooring warps. When he did this, he would step on my elder sister's face (Carol slept on the floor on a Li-Lo). Carol would scream. Everyone else would sit up and crack their skulls on the deckhead. Then they would scream too.

I still remember being rafted up in Haarlem and Father telling the man on the next boat that I was a "useful crew". Up until that moment, I don't think I had ever been happier - although that day was eclipsed when I heard my parents discussing how old I would need to be before I could be trusted to sail *Torgunn* on my own. The only cloud was that Mother insisted that 16 was too young and I should wait until I was 18. I was eight at the time. Eighteen was more than a lifetime away.

As things turned out, it was what happened three years later that tripped something in my head and sent life down a different track. In 1960, five singlehanded sailors raced across the Atlantic for the first time.

Singlehanded sailing was just beginning to claim the public's attention. It had been an established possibility for years: At the end of the 1800s, Joshua Slocum, a New England sea captain, became the first man to sail alone around the world. He had been left behind by the age of steam, and rather than retire, he rebuilt a derelict Boston oyster dredger called the *Spray* and defied all the gloomy predictions of the longshoremen by returning three years later to a hero's welcome and instant celebrity. His book is still in print today and regarded as one of the classics of the sea.

Among his many wonderful stories, he credited his success to the ghostly presence of the Pilot of the Pinta, one of Columbus's ships. Whenever conditions became particularly difficult, this spectre would appear at the wheel, and Slocum could sleep - or so he said.

And how about Vito Dumas? He was an Argentine who decided to give World War II a miss by taking his 32-foot *LEGH II* around the world via the four great capes - in other words, at the bottom of the world in the most ferocious weather it has to offer. He carried no radio in case one of the several warring nations should mistake him for a spy. At times he was so cold he stuffed his clothes with newspaper. Being a South American, he had named his boat after the initials of his four mistresses. Actually, that's not true. It was only one and she wasn't a mistress at all but a "benefactress".

But I prefer my version.

The British yachting establishment, however, remained resolutely unimpressed with singlehanded sailing. The editor of Yachting Monthly, the fiercely correct Maurice Griffiths, railed against the "physical impossibility" of a singlehander abiding by the COLREGS as they like to call the anti-collision regulations for ships. These demand that "Every vessel shall at all times maintain a proper look-out". How could such a thing be possible for one man alone? (It was always a man, of course).

But as so often happens, the rules were simply ignored. After all, if a singlehander not keeping a proper lookout was to collide with a ship, who would come off worse? Blondie Hasler, the inventor of the first efficient self-steering windvane, announced: "I shall drown like a gentleman."

It was this rather Edwardian philosophy which gave rise to the first Singlehanded Transatlantic Race: A handful of enthusiasts had been competing to become the first to make the crossing from east to west - so, why not make a race of it? The only trouble was that all the yacht clubs were run by The Establishment, and we know what they thought of the idea. In desperation, Hasler announced that if no club would adopt the race, then the competitors would organise it themselves, each putting in half a crown - winner takes all.

Ultimately, Francis Chichester solved the problem. He was a London map publisher who had made a name for himself before the war with a series of long-distance flights in small aircraft. Now he had taken up yachting and used his connections to persuade the Rear-Commodore of the Royal Western Yacht Club to organise the race.

Once The Establishment was on board, it was easy for Hasler to bring in The Observer newspaper as a sponsor - and so the Observer Singlehanded Transatlantic Race (The OSTAR) was born.

Of course, at eleven, I knew none of this. I was still at prep school. My idea of grown-up excitement was limited to Boy's Own and War Picture Library.

But then Francis Chichester won that first OSTAR - and it transpired that somebody at the Walton & Frinton Yacht Club knew the great man well enough to persuade him to come down from London one miserable winter's night and give an illustrated talk to the members.

My parents took me along. The slide projector broke down halfway through, and Chichester was as self-deprecating as only true heroes can be. But I could see through the casual asides about gales and gear failure. I could see the excitement in changing sail on a plunging foredeck, the thrill of being joined by a racing pigeon a thousand miles from land. One day, I said to myself, I would sail oceans too - singlehanded, of course. With a natural gift for exaggeration, even then, I took it a stage further: I would live on my boat all by myself. My adventures would be every bit as exciting as those of my youthful hero in *Green Flare*.

That was more than half a century ago, but I can still feel the thrill of anticipation - and remember the disappointment at my parents' reaction when I told them. I think the expression that comes to mind is: "That's nice, dear." Sometimes parents have no imagination.

But I didn't forget about it – and, inadvertently, they encouraged me: When I was 13, they sold Torgunn and commissioned a 28-footer called Bellrock. You could go anywhere in Bellrock. We explored Brittany in Bellrock. In my imagination, I was already in the Grenadines.

And I'm afraid the imagination wouldn't let go of me. Standing under the oak tree waiting to be called up by the headmaster, I imagined it. On the cricket pitch, letting the ball roll past me, I imagined it.

Eventually, the whole thing became too much, and I borrowed ten shillings from another boy, went down to the station and took the train home. Within ten minutes, my banker had sneaked, and the whole school knew that Passmore had Run Away.

It was the day my parents were due to join my grandfather on one of his disastrous outings to Royal Ascot. Once news of my absence reached them, my father went alone, leaving Mother to "deal with me". This meant that she sat and listened patiently while I explained I would like to leave school immediately, please, and go and live on a boat and sail the world, writing about it.

Patiently, she pointed out that I did not have a boat, and there was a world of difference between being good at English, getting your contributions into the school magazine and actually making a living from writing. With that, she drove me back to school. As I said before, sometimes parents have no imagination.

And so, for the next 13 years, the dream lay dormant - all through the short-lived marriage, the apprenticeship in journalism. It was not until I was 30 that I took out a bank loan and bought a boat of my own.

A very small boat – just 18ft 3in long, a Caprice; but I could sleep on *Amicus*. In fact, she had three berths so I could take my two small sons. Oliver was eight by this time, and George, six. We would have muddy adventures around Poole Harbour and splash about on the beach at Studland Bay.

Other times I would sail her by myself and, one day, missed the tide in the Solent and ended up sailing overnight from Portsmouth, round the back of the Isle of Wight and returned to Poole at breakfast time, eating boiled eggs in the cockpit and throwing the shells over my shoulder. I like to think the boats coming out for a day's sail imagined I must have come from

Cherbourg.

I did get to Cherbourg the following year – and all the way down the north coast of Brittany. In Treguier, a Frenchman on the next boat looked across and said: "Ah, so small but so beautiful."

And the crew, in a bikini, preened and smiled.

Of course, 18ft was all very well for a starter boat, but she wasn't what I imagined for crossing oceans – although a Caprice did hold the record for the smallest boat ever to sail around the world. But that one was sailed by an ex-Royal Marine who didn't mind roughing it. What I needed was something around 28ft – maybe 32ft. Best of all, I wanted a Rival.

These were the Land Rovers of the seas – tough ocean cruisers. Not particularly fast but able to cope with anything the elements could throw at them. Unfortunately, they came with a price tag to match.

But, in Warsash on the River Hamble, I found one I could just about afford. The reason for this was that *Margo* had been home-completed – by a man who was very much an amateur boatbuilder.

I didn't mind a bit of rough carpentry – not if the price was right. I did mind the name, though – *Margo?* Who was that, somebody's aunt?

Changing boats' names is notoriously bad luck, so I allowed myself just one letter. *Margo* became *Largo* – the musical notation for "broad and slow," it seemed appropriate.

Only after I took her in the 1987 Azores and Back Race did I discover the full price of a cheap boat. Hauling out at the end of the season, I noticed a crack running down the bow all the way to the waterline, where it disappeared under the anti-fouling paint.

I asked my friend Keith Dovkants at The Evening Standard to come and have a look. Keith had built his own boat – and renovated his flat. Keith was a perfectionist, and together we pulled all the clobber out of the fore-cabin. That was how we discovered that when the previous owner had come to build the front of his boat, evidently, he couldn't find a piece of wood big enough to reach all the way across. So, instead, he screwed three pieces together.

As *Largo* slammed again and again into those Atlantic rollers at the start of the race, the shock-like pressure had been transferred through the hull onto the three-piece bulkhead, which - not surprisingly - had given way; the three pieces sliding across each other, the screws chewing their way through the wood until the hull itself began to flex.

As Keith put it: "You're quite lucky the bow didn't fall off."

Over the next few weekends, we stripped out all the furniture and the remains of the bulkhead and glassed in a massive piece of marine ply bedded on foam and – for good measure – installed two "crash boxes" at the bow, filling them with foam which set hard as soon as it was exposed to the air. Keith said that now I had a bow like an egg-box. The way I liked to think of it, *Largo* was fit to shunt ice.

The following year, I entered her for the OSTAR - the singlehanded transatlantic race, just like my hero Francis Chichester.

Unlike Chichester, I did not win. I did not return to fame and glory. But it was enough that I was in the race. That's the thing about the OSTAR, it's like being allowed to enter your Morris Minor for the Formula One at Brands Hatch. In Plymouth, I was moored just behind Jean-Yves Terlain in his futuristic 60ft *UAP*. The public were allowed to wander up and down the pontoons looking at the boats. One man stood beside *Largo* and explained to his family: "This is one of the amateurs – probably take a year to get there."

If I hadn't been upside down in one of the cockpit lockers, I would have gone and remonstrated with him. But he was right in a way.

The "amateurs" had their own race and a very different one it was to the lonely battle with the elements at the front of the fleet. The Evening Standard had given me a long-range radio so I could send back reports for the paper, and this enabled me to join the "sked" – the radio schedule where a bunch of us would meet up three times a day to discuss progress.

At one of the sponsor's receptions before the start, I went to invite a Frenchmen to join us. He seemed good company, and he had a small boat. But he looked me in the eye and said: "With such a radio, you are not truly alone."

He was right, of course. But we did have fun. When James Hatfield was awarded the MBE in the Queen's birthday honours, we threw a party for him. I wore my white silk dinner jacket (really) and cooled a bottle of champagne in a bucket of Atlantic. I had to ask the guests not to park on the south lawn because the polo ponies were out.

Then one day, Robin Knox-Johnston failed to check in. When he had missed three schedules, we debated whether something had happened to him - whether we should raise the alarm...

Something certainly had happened. He had been moving his batteries for some reason or other and then connected them up again back to front. This most efficiently blew up his alternator. Isn't it nice to know that world-famous round-the-world yachtsmen, knighted for their services to sailing, can still do things like that?

Of course, we knew none of this at the time. However, the consensus was that Robin could look after himself and would be furious if we triggered a search and rescue operation. We were right – although he did arrive back in Falmouth, pumping almost constantly for the last thousand miles after *Suhaili* sprang a leak.

Then I fell across the cockpit and ended up with my teeth wrapped around the headsail sheet. I told the gang I was lucky it hadn't been the winch, or I wouldn't have any teeth left. Quick as a flash, one of the guys came back with: "I'm a maxillo-facial surgeon, and I have a full operating kit on board. If you had stopped so I could catch up, I could have wired your jaw back together." He was serious, too.

I got there in 32 days - 65th out of 96 starters. The Standard flew out a photographer who complained because I insisted on crossing the line in the dark. Just as well - I had tears streaming down my face.

Chapter 6

Love

Her name was Debbie. She was 14, and so was I - both of us on school ski holidays to Obergurgl in Austria. I went back the other year with my teenage children and tried to find the bar where we danced - all right, to find the dance floor where we had our first kiss.

It was true love all right: We exchanged 10 groschen pieces and wore them on chains around our necks. She lived in Surrey, a weekly boarder at a convent school. We wrote each other long letters and tried to read between the lines. If I cycled to Puttenham on a Sunday morning, we could talk on the phone until lunchtime for 2d (the phone box was broken). Debbie sat on the bottom of the stairs at home, blocking the way for anyone who wanted to get past. I could hear her father complaining.

What on earth did we find to say to each other for two hours? Later we graduated to meeting in Guildford and going to the pictures where we could sit in the back row – they had double seats in the back row. We didn't have to talk then.

Debbie and I went on for years – spooning and fumbling. Sometimes it was on, sometimes it was off. At one point, she found someone older and more sophisticated who had a sports car and took her to the West Indies. Another time I had to tell her she couldn't come to my 21st birthday party because I'd invited another girl as well and now had to choose between them, and I chose the other one (what an idiot!)

But then love and ADHD don't really go together. Tim Lott knew that, and it's something I have discovered, too – time and time again.

I got married when I was 23. Well, so did my parents - but, as they pointed out, that was in 1940. They thought they were going to be dead tomorrow. I got married, I realise now, because of a **desire for approval.**

If you have this condition, apparently it is quite likely you end up saying "yes" to everything just because you want people to like you. Normally this means nothing more complicated than having too many commitments. Other times it messes up everyone's life.

By this time I had embarked on a career in newspapers - on the Mitcham News and Mercury on the southern outskirts of London. They sent me away for two months to learn my trade at Harlow Technical College, along with 20 other baby journalists from all over the South East of England. One of them was a pretty girl called Marian from the Crawley Observer. She didn't have a car, so I volunteered to pick her up from her digs to join the gang in the pub.

I picked her up in my red Sunbeam Alpine. The Sunbeam Alpine was one of those sports cars which just looks right. Now you would call it a "Classic". The fact that it had twin Weber carburettors which were always out of tune so that it sounded like a tractor, and the back-end differential clonked every time you put your foot down didn't seem to trouble her - maybe because I kept a silver flask of 10-year-old Chivas Regal in the glove compartment. The car, the flask and the whisky had all been 21st birthday presents. I thought these were the sort of accessories James Bond would have.

When the two months came to an end, and we took our rudimentary shorthand and smattering of law back to our newspapers, Marian rang me and suggested a date. It was not something I had thought about, but there she was on the phone. I had to say something. I said," yes". Looking back over almost three-quarters of a century of bumbling through life, I can't remember when I've said "No" to anything.

Sure enough, we returned the following year to Harlow for the second "block" of our block release course, and this time, we applied for accommodation as a couple. Apparently, neither of us could bring ourselves to say "No".

It was a disaster. We were assigned a double room in a B&B which seemed to be a show house for Brentford Nylons: Nylon sheets, nylon curtains, nylon carpets... we nearly died from static electrocution. Worse still, the room and use of the pink plastic bathroom comprised the limit of our accommodation. Meals were served on a tray and eaten sitting side by side on the double bed - which seemed to dominate the room with its pink and slimy presence, crackling with static and sexual pressure – not a happy environment for an 18 year-old-girl and a 21-year-old boy completely out of their depth...

There is a moment in Four Weddings and a Funeral when Simon Callow's character, Gerald, announces that he has a new theory about marriage: "Two people are in love," he explains. "They live together – and one day, they run out of conversation. Totally. They can't think of a single thing to say to each other. That's it: Panic.

"Then suddenly, it occurs to the chap that there is a way out of the deadlock."

"Which is?" asks John Hannah's character, Matthew.

"He'll ask her to marry him. Brilliant: They've got something to talk about for the rest of their lives."

Charles, played by Hugh Grant - a man who has never got around to proposing to anyone, considers this: "So it's just a way out of an embarrassing pause in conversation?"

Gerald: "The definitive icebreaker!"

It is said that when it comes to Life, all the answers are in The Godfather: (What day is it? Monday, Tuesday, Thursday, Wednesday... What should I do? Leave the gun. Take the Cannoli...)

Similarly, when it comes to Love, all the answers are in Four Weddings and a Funeral: (Isn't she beautiful? She looks like a big meringue...What's bonking? It's like table tennis only with slightly smaller balls...)

And, of course: Nothing to say? Propose...

Come to think of it, you can find the same romantic wisdom in any Richard Curtis romcom. The man is the Marje Proops of film-making.

We were married in February 1972, and ten months later, our son Oliver was born. Marian was 19 and, as it says on the ADHD Foundation website: **"An adult with ADHD often has trouble in relationships, whether they are professional, romantic, or platonic. The traits of talking over people in conversation, inattentiveness, and being easily bored can be draining on relationships, as a person with the condition may appear insensitive, irresponsible, or uncaring."**

So, here's how this works in practice: The young mother is at home with a tiny baby. The baby is crying. There is no one else in the house - no one to hold the crying baby so she can lock herself in the bathroom for two minutes and scream at the mirror until she feels ready to return to doting mother mode. She wants to ring her husband at work and say: "The baby won't stop crying. I don't know what to do..."

She takes the broom and starts to sweep the kitchen floor. The head falls off the broom. This is the final straw. Now she is crying as loudly as the baby. The baby redoubles his efforts. Completely at the end of her tether, she succumbs and calls her husband at work.

The young husband answers the phone and hears his wife explaining between sobs that the head has fallen off the broom.

Her husband is a man. This is a bad start. What he hears is that the head has fallen off the broom. What he does not hear is: "The baby won't stop crying, and I don't know what to do, and I'm here all on my own, and I didn't know it would be like this, and now the head's fallen off the broom and I feel useless and helpless, and I just want someone to tell me it will be all right and that they love me and I'm not useless and - oh, I don't know… I just wanted to talk to you…"

However, being a sensitive man with some understanding of other people - possibly, even, some understanding of women - the husband looks behind the words, puts two and two together and says, wisely: "Oh, that's awful, poor you. Look, just leave the broom. Leave the floor. It doesn't matter. You're doing fine. I'll look at it when I get home. By the way, did I tell you I love you? Well, I do. Did you manage to get a sleep after lunch? Well done! Look, I'll see if I can get away early tonight…I love you, did I say that?"

If she's married to ADHD man, this is what she hears: "Put the head back on the broom and give it a bash on the floor."

This was never going to end well. In our case, it ended after five years, by which time we had another little boy, George.

I moved out and into a bedsit in Slough. The phrase "Bedsit in Slough" tells you all you need to know about that situation. It had that "old furniture" smell. Every night one of the other tenants would come home and use the communal kitchen to boil liver. The whole house smelled of boiled liver… and cabbage. He liked cabbage with his boiled liver.

Eventually, I bought a flat in Chiswick "in need of renovation". All the walls were covered in chocolate-coloured gloss paint. The little boys would come and stay with me and sleep on sunbeds. For cuddly toys, I rolled up towels and tied them with a piece of string. They loved these and called them Muppets – there's no accounting for children. On Monday morning, I would be late taking them to school.

In fact, I would be late taking them everywhere – or sometimes get the access arrangements mixed up completely. The saddest thing was to hear George, aged five or six, asking: "What's going to happen?" He asked that a lot. How could I tell him that I had no idea what was going to happen from one minute to the next? It wasn't his fault that I had **poor organisational skills**.

It wasn't helped by the fact that now I was working at the Daily Mail – the big league. I don't know if it's natural selection at work, but there is no doubt that a job on a big national newspaper works wonders for the love life. Suddenly, I found myself getting on for 30 years old, living the life I should have been living in my early 20s: London was full of attractive and accommodating young women – all very keen on meeting presentable and successful men.

I had the time of my life. That is not to say that I went home with a different girl every night – although many of my colleagues did exactly that (particularly after a night in La Valbonne). No, I was more pedestrian. My relationships ran for two or three years. In that time, you can really get to know someone – really get comfortable. At least, that's what I thought.

The difficulty was that, inevitably, one party in the relationship would decide that three years was probably the right time to move on to the next stage. They waited – with varying degrees of patience – and when it didn't move on, they did.

Time and time again, this happened - and then there would be a decent interval until the whole cycle began again.

And then something happened to break the cycle. It was 1987, the early autumn and getting on for the end of the sailing season when I would need to move the boat from her summer mooring in Portsmouth Harbour to the Elephant Boatyard on the River Hamble where she would spend the winter. On a whim, in the second week of October, I decided to move her that very Saturday, rather than wait for the end of the month. Looking back on it, I like to think this was a premonition (I had never had a premonition before. It sounds rather exciting). At the very least, it was a significant whim because, on the following Thursday, the Great Storm of 1987 wrecked virtually every boat on a mooring in Portsmouth Harbour.

More significantly, on the train back to London, a girl with long strawberry-blonde hair and laughing eyes sat across the aisle from me. We were at the end of the compartment, and so, when anyone came through the sliding door and left it open —which they invariably did - a howling gale would come whistling into the carriage. First, I got up to close it - and then she got up to close it. After the third or fourth time, when it was her turn, she got up to close it and smiled at me. Cécile possessed a smile that had melted hearts on three continents.

By the time I realised that mine was just another of them, it was too late. I was smitten like the 14-year-old boy in the 2p-for-two-hours phone box. The tough carapace that had kept emotion at a safe distance for more than a decade cracked open to expose the heaving mess within.

Heaven knows how, but I held it together for another three years. There was one more grown-up relationship – but only because she was older than me and truly sophisticated, not just playing at it.

Then one day, after I had moved to the Evening Standard, the paper's Medical Correspondent, Lois Rogers, came and stood beside my desk.

"John," she said. "I have a question for you."

"Yes?"

How's your love life?"

Well, it so happened that, a few days earlier, I had found an "x" at the top of my computer screen – sent by a colleague I didn't know. Since nothing in my romantic experience equipped me to deal with digital flirting, I had ignored it. Therefore, in answer to Lois's question, I said: "Um, quiet, I suppose."

"I thought so," she said. "I'm taking you out to lunch."

I should explain, at this point, that Lois was happily married to someone who had nothing to do with newspapers – and indeed, she had already rebuffed my drunken attentions during an incident which became embedded in Newsroom folklore as "Passmore's Lunge".

Anyway, we settled ourselves in a local restaurant, and Lois promptly instructed me to buy a copy of Time Out - in particular, the Lonely Hearts column.

No, I should not place an advert, she emphasised. Placing adverts was for the women. The men answered them - very bad form to get it the wrong way round.

So, I bought a copy of Time Out (you didn't argue with Lois) and sent three letters to promising-looking Box Numbers.

Box Number 316 was Tamsin Rawlins, the nurse at Highgate School in North London. She had been there for about a year, rather enjoying having a free flat in one of the most desirable parts of the capital but was also conscious that she wasn't meeting many people - or, to put it with brutal clarity: No one at all, who was not connected with the school.

Here is the advert Tamsin placed:

Woman 27, likes walking, skiing, crosswords, Scrabble and bookshops. Seeks man.

I responded with this:

Well, I can ski, but I'm hopeless with crosswords. Scrabble I can manage - it comes with being a newspaper reporter, but I've never got to grips with the cryptic bit.

So, I'm 42, 5 ft 11 and a non-smoker and wonder if I could interest you in sailing - it's what skiers should do in the summer. I have a 32-foot boat in Portsmouth.

Apart from that, I like small restaurants and sentimental films.

When the evening Standard doesn't send me to stupid places, I live in a big old mansion flat in Chiswick with the decorators and my 18-year-old son, who has come unexpectedly to live with me in his year before university. There's another of 16 away at school, and I'm divorced.

If you think it would be a good idea for us to meet, why not send me a letter with your photo, then we could progress to telephone calls and maybe even find a clock somewhere to stand under. Yours in anticipation…

She received more than 70 replies. She invited her old school friend Jan to come round, opened a bottle of wine, and together they began sorting the letters into three piles: Definitely not, Maybe and Possibly.

I'm pleased to say that I made it into the "Possibly" pile (unlike the man who sent a photo of himself bare-chested standing next to his sports car). Today there would have been dick pics.

We met on the corner of Bishopswood Road, just opposite Hampstead Heath. Tamsin appeared with her dog, Blue – a sort of Labrador but a lot thinner and with impossibly long legs – and a mission to chase anything with wings.

We walked all over Hampstead Heath that Sunday morning, told each other our life stories and, at one point, by way of conversation, Tamsin said carefully: "Have you ever thought you'd like more children?"

"More?" I said. "Good God, I'm not having any more!"

There was a pause as she filed this away - in a drawer labelled "Forward Planning."

Something else was quite significant during that first meeting: I lost my car keys. Well, I would, wouldn't I? If I was **constantly misplacing things?**

Actually, they weren't *my* car keys. I had crashed *my* car on the way to a court case in Lincoln. I was driving a replacement from the Evening Standard's car pool. So, what did I do? I did what any Chief Correspondent worth his salt would do, I rang the Newsdesk and asked the duty man to get another set of keys sent to the Cafe Rouge in Highgate.

Tamsin and I were sitting there over the first of many, many of the Cafe Rouge's excellent Marmite Dieppoises when a taxi driver walked in with a Jiffy bag asking for Mr Passmore. I went to meet him at the bar, tipped him generously and returned without a beat to Tamsin and the Marmite.

There are some moments when you can tell that a girl is impressed. If she had spent more time thinking about how I came to lose the keys in the first place rather than how very cool it was to get a spare set delivered to a restaurant, things might have turned out differently.

Five weeks later, we went skiing together. My boot bag was very nearly blown up as a "suspicious package" when I lost it at Gatwick. In the chalet, one of the other guests asked Tamsin: "You haven't known John very long, have you?"

"No, why?"

"He's very attentive…"

You bet. On the first day, there was a sudden and unseasonal thaw. A river of icy water gushed down the main street. Tamsin had only London street shoes. By the time we returned to the chalet, her feet were like blocks of ice. I put her to bed, peeled off her sodden socks and massaged her feet while feeding her cherry brandy.

I think that did it.

Actually, what did it was that Tamsin loved my boat as much as I did. We spent every weekend sailing along the South Coast to the West Country, across the Channel to France and the Channel Islands. She never complained, was never seasick and never tied a bad knot.

The emotional mess began to stir anew.

Pretty soon, we were talking about sailing the world together. I had told her on that first walk across Hampstead Heath that I planned to retire at 55 aboard my Ultimate Boat. However, that was still 13 years away. Would it be so awful to go at 50? After all, I had pots of money saved up – also, I had a regular column for Yachting World - I could probably pick up something else up if I was sailing full time.

Once that was settled, it was time to see what else was in the drawer labelled "Forward Planning".

We started buying books about children on boats. It didn't seem so bad - look at Rosie Swale and *Children of Cape Horn*. Children on the boat moved from "Forward Planning" to "That's settled, then".

We bought a new boat - not the "ultimate boat" - not the 43ft cutter for the Singlehanded circuit. Instead, we bought a 27ft catamaran – a floating caravan with central heating and a double bed. My sailing friends shook their heads over me. Clearly, John was a lost cause.

It didn't seem like that to me. I was in love. All that emotion that Cécile had unlocked was spewing out like a scene from Alien. This was new – and what do we know about anything new: **The ADHD brain constantly scans the environment for more stimulation – faster, louder, riskier, sexier…**

Sexier? We won't go there, it's not that kind of book. Just think: Traffic jam on the M3 sex. Nip-home-for-a-quickie-before-going-back-to-the-office sex. Stuck in a Russian hotel room telephone sex (I wonder if the Kremlin still has the tape?)

It was at this point that fate took a hand - alright fate took over: The Evening Standard management decided it was time to catch up with the rest of Fleet Street and bring an end to that wonderful old "Spanish Practice" of the Four Day Week.

There had been a time when it could have been argued that journalists worked a ten-hour day – for instance, from 7.00 a.m. to

5.00 p.m. But that was back in the days when the Standard printed six or eight editions every weekday. Saturday was a whole separate operation with the sports and racing editions. Now we barely managed more than three. Most days, it was all over by two o'clock: Time for a long lunch in Jimmy's Wine Bar and then look into the office to see what the subs had done to your copy before pushing off to the pub by half past four.

What was so great about this was that every three weeks, you got a five-day weekend - you could really sail somewhere in five days.

The problem for the management was that the four-day week was enshrined in our contracts. If we were going to be forced to return to a five-day week, we would have to be persuaded to sign new contracts. The stick and the carrot should do it.

The carrot was more money. The stick was: "If you don't sign the new contract, you will be unemployed when the old one runs out."

My contract was for a year. In a year, I would be 46. Already Tamsin and I had decided that 50 was too long to wait and had quietly settled on 48. This was only knocking off another two years…

Hardly able to suppress the giggles, I stood up in the staff meeting (union meetings were long gone) and announced that I would not sign.

In the same way that my singlehanded friends had shaken their heads over me for buying a cruising catamaran, so my newspaper colleagues began to stop me in the corridor with earnest entreaties: "Don't throw it all away…" and "There'll never be another job like yours."

Actually, they were right about that. What they were failing to consider was that I didn't want another job. A job stood for security – the daily grind…

No wonder they shook their heads: The Chief Correspondent

of the London Evening Standard, the highest-paid staff reporter in Fleet Street, the editor's personal Fireman, whose expenses no executive dared to question, who had it written into his contract that if any member of the Royal Family went skiing, he had to go too, considered his job to be "the daily grind".

Now, do you believe I was in love?

Chapter 7
Apprentice

"What experience do you have?" asked the *Herr Direktor* of the National Bellevue, the third-best hotel in Zermatt.

Zermatt is the third most fashionable ski resort in Switzerland (behind Gstaad and St Moritz). What it can boast – which the others cannot – is the perfect view of the Matterhorn. The 14,692-ft peak is so instantly recognizable that, in 1971, when the Weetabix Corporation named their new breakfast cereal "Alpen", it was the Matterhorn they put on the front of the packet.

I had stayed in Zermatt for a skiing holiday when I was 13 and been captivated by the place: You arrived by mountain railway and were taken to your hotel in a horse-drawn sleigh – the luggage following behind on a little electric cart. Cars were banned, but goats were positively encouraged: Twice a day, the town's herd would be driven along the main street – each one with a bell around its neck. The noise was deafening – the sight unforgettable.

Yes, Zermatt was the place I wanted to see again. It was 1967. I was 18. I had left school and joined my parents for a sailing holiday to Brittany. We made it halfway down the west coast, and then it was time for them to turn around and go home.

Not for me, though. I was not due for my year's practical on the farm until the autumn. The whole summer stretched before me: Four months of exciting possibilities with The Continent at my feet.

"I'll go hitch-hiking," I explained when the parents asked what on earth I was going to do if I jumped ship.

"Where will you go?" My mother wanted to know.

"I won't know until I get there" (even more **exciting** - where did this need for constant excitement come from?)

My parents discussed this in private - although, of course, there isn't much privacy in a 36-foot boat.

Mother: "He can't just go off…"

Father: "He'll be fine. He's grown up. It won't do any good trying to tell him he can't - he'd probably just go anyway…"

So, I packed my belongings into a sausage-shaped blue kitbag, hoisted it onto my shoulder and started off up the hill from the harbour. It never occurred to me that I was depriving them of their crew. Later, my mother was to tell me that she thought I looked just like the sailor on the Seagull Outboard advert – and she was thinking that it might be the last sight she had of me.

In fact, when she got home, she found a letter on the mat asking her to pack a suitcase and send it care of the Hotel National Bellevue. I was going to be there for the summer, and I attached a list of requirements.

I had told the *Herr Direktor* I was 22 years old, not 18, and had two years' experience as a waiter on cruise ships (a friend had joined P&O as an assistant purser and was full of stories of rich American divorcees).

The *Herr Direktor* looked doubtful. However, he was a man faced with a problem: Every summer, he recruited half his seasonal staff from British catering colleges, and one of his waiters had failed to turn up. He summoned his secretary and dictated rapidly in German. She went into the next room and clattered away on her typewriter while he continued to look at me as if I was a fraud (very astute, the *Herr* Direktor). All the same, he signed the letter and told me to take it to the outfitters in the square.

There I exchanged my letter for two white shirts, two pairs of black trousers, a white clip-on bow tie and a pair of black shoes. Then the housekeeper showed me to the House of the Devil.

It really was called that – in Italian, "La Casa del Diavolo" – named by the older female staff because that was where the hotel lodged its younger male staff.

However, I wasn't interested in sin. I was above all that. I was a Writer: The main reason I needed that suitcase from home was because, at the top of the list, was my grandfather's Remington portable typewriter. Now I remember it, how I wish I'd never got rid of that typewriter: In a wooden case and weighing a ton, it had a retractable lever on the right-hand side which raised the typebars in a cone so they could strike down on the roller (or the platen before we lose the historic terminology completely). The keys, of course, were round and white with black letters, and you could stick a biro down between them to wiggle the metal connectors when they got stuck. It made a most satisfying "clack-clack-clack," did Grandfather's Remington Portable.

Every morning, after we had cleared away breakfast in the dining room, we had an hour and a half of free time before lunch. I would climb the stairs to the very top of the House of the Devil, throw open my windows to the most perfect view of the Matterhorn (wearing her little white cloud which always seemed to stick to the summit) and begin the serious business of the day, I would remove the wooden lid of the Remington, raise the typebars - and Write.

Of course, before I could write anything, I had to learn to touch type. After all, surely all Writers could touch-type. Years later, when I took my 40 words-a-minute to Fleet Street, I found that the greatest of them stuck religiously to two fingers (albeit at the speed of light).

Never mind, at the back of the wardrobe, I found a couple of wire coat hangers which - together with a piece of cardboard - I fashioned into a shield over the keys. Unable to see my fingers, I was forced to learn where to put them by touch: If I hit the wrong key, the wrong letter appeared on the paper. It was just as well I hadn't thought about what I was going to write…

Meanwhile, in the dining room, it took Tony, the head waiter, no more than five minutes to realise that I knew nothing about waiting tables. He took me to one side: "Now tell me. John - and tell me true: You no waiter, eh?"

"No."

"Never, no experience - niente?"

"No."

"OK. Andrea!" Here, he called over one of the Italian waiters, an impossibly handsome young man with liquid eyes and the reputation for justifying the *Casa del Diavolo's* name all by himself. "Andrea teach you. Andrea, you teach him."

And Andrea did. Andrea taught me to carry four plates of Osso Buco alla Milanese all at once - or a dozen empty wine glasses in one hand. More importantly, he taught me that the biggest tips would be left under the plate, not on top of it (and if I didn't check immediately after the guest left the dining room, one of my colleagues would snaffle it).

As the summer progressed, I liked to think I became rather a good waiter. But it was Tony who taught me the most important lesson - and the one which makes me such an impossible restaurant customer today: "What is your first job?" He wanted to know. "What is it you must do every moment you are in the dining room - from the moment you come in until the moment you leave - your most important job in a first-class restaurant?

"*You look!*

"You look all around. You look at your customers all the time. All the time, you look! You know how I tell a bad restaurant? If I see a customer raise their hand. They should not raise their eyebrow! If they need you, you will know it - but only if you look. Capisci?"

Once the season was properly underway, the silver service and the five-franc tips gave way to mass catering for tour groups, and it was all a bit more like school dinners. Most interestingly, once the American school vacation began, we started getting large parties of teenage girls - 30 or 40 at a time. Andrea thought he had died and gone to heaven. His room was directly below mine, and the Casa del Diavolo had been built before anyone thought of soundproofing. I retaliated by typing long into the night. Clack-clack-clack went the keys of Grandfather's ancient Remington. Bang-bang-bang went Andrea's bed against the wall…

Whatever it was that I wrote that summer in Zermatt, it has long since disappeared. I hope it was thrown out in disgust. It probably had something to do with spies (James Bond again) and would have been set in the mountains (no imagination).

But the ambition to be a writer endured all through agricultural college - I spent more time on a correspondence course in short story writing than I did reading through lecture notes about crop rotation.

Finally, in exasperation, Father advised: "Well, if you really insist on being a writer, I suppose you'd better learn to do it. You should go and work on a newspaper."

"I'll call Arthur Christiansen," said Mother. She was forever helpful and had once partnered the legendary editor of the Sunday Express in a mixed Stableford four at Frinton Golf Club.

But no, I was going to do this myself. I took a train to Southampton. Right on the Solent, Southampton was full of boats. I could write for the newspaper about boats…

Half an hour after a brief interview with the editor of the Southern Evening Echo, I was back on the train to Winchester to try the Hampshire Chronicle. It's amazing to think of it now, but you could do that in those days - just walk in and ask for a job.

Now you need a degree and a personal recommendation.

The editor of the Hampshire Chronicle was a man who respected tradition (his paper carried advertisements on the front page - putting news on the front would have been terribly vulgar.) He sent me round the corner to the Southern Sentinel.

This was not a traditional paper. In fact, it was an upstart. Printed by the new web-offset process, not only did it have pictures on the front page - but colour pictures! The editor obviously thought this was enough to sell the paper all by itself, and it was sufficient to employ an editorial staff of a news editor and one reporter (and me, if he gave me a job).

Here was the deal: If I could bring him a story that made the paper, I could have a job.

I rushed out to find a story - and was very nearly run over by a police car, an ambulance and a fire engine, in that order.

I followed them.

On foot.

The story - when it appeared all over the front page - described in the most lurid detail HORROR ON DEATH BEND!

What had happened was that as dusk fell on that autumn evening in 1968, there had been a perfectly straightforward collision at the bottom of a particularly steep hill out of the town. The emergency services had been summoned, and the district nurse, who lived in an adjacent cottage, supervised her neighbours in removing the casualties to the grass verge, where she was busy ministering to their minor injuries.

At this point, an 18-year-old driving a souped-up Ford Prefect came thundering down the hill, saw the two crashed cars in his headlights and took evasive action by steering onto the grass verge...

...where he ran over the casualties and bundled the district nurse into the hedge.

As if this wasn't enough, an enormous Alsatian was trapped in the back of one of the cars, trying to bite the firemen. They had to send for the vet to sedate it.

The front-page story which appeared that Friday was undoubtedly libellous and should have got me and the Southern Sentinel into the most dreadful trouble. The reason it didn't was because nobody read the Southern Sentinel. People in Winchester read the Hampshire Chronicle. They had never heard of the Southern Sentinel.

The editor – who was also the owner – attempted to solve this problem by maintaining the 3d issue price on the front page but, at the same time, giving several bundles free to every newsagent in town. The newsagents (not wanting to clutter up their shops with a lot of newspapers nobody was going to buy) gave the bundles to the delivery boys.

And the delivery boys (who were not being paid any extra to distribute them) left a whole bundle on each doorstep until they were shot of them.

So, the circulation of the Southern Sentinel was probably never more than a few dozen. This had some unexpected consequences: Every week, the crossword competition was won by the same reader - maybe she was the only reader. Since we had to publish the name of the winner, this soon became embarrassing. Then somebody came up with the clever wheeze of making up a fictitious name and address and taking the £1 prize money down the pub.

This was fine until the real winner turned up, protesting: "I've checked, and there ain't no Number 15, Acacia Avenue, and there ain't no Maurice Spiggings neither - and I want my £1."

We had to have a whip-round to get rid of her.

I didn't stay long on the Southern Sentinel. It had been a mistake to make me the sports reporter: Newcastle United came to play Southampton, and my interview with the manager came to an end when he said: "You don't know much about football, do you, lad?"

I awarded myself the following Saturday off and went for an interview with the South London News Group - proper papers with a proper training scheme under the auspices of the National Council for the Training of Journalists. They gave me a job on their Mitcham News and Mercury - just as well because the dreadful editor of the Southern Sentinel promptly sacked me for taking an unauthorised day off.

Never mind, I was on my way. As with all local papers, the job was to fill the space between the adverts. What went into that space didn't much matter - wedding reports, lists of flower show results - and if a church fete could be stretched out to half a column, the editor felt he had discovered a rare talent.

I could make a church fete last for half a page. Let's face it, you're still reading this and nothing much has happened (no, it hasn't. It's just the way I tell it…)

Sure enough, when the Mitcham office closed, and we were all shipped over to Wimbledon, they gave me my own office, two pages to fill every week and left me to my own devices. These were broadsheet pages, remember - positively acres to fill. Never mind, I devised "Looking in at your local", which entitled me to spend a day in a pub on expenses and "Profile", which was an interview with a local personality - any personality, from the Town Clerk to the cricket club groundsman (who was much more interesting). Even the taciturn president of the National Association of Fish Fryers warranted his space (he had a wonderfully ancient gas fire that made burbling and popping noises during the interminable silences - so I wrote about that instead.)

By this time, I was 23. I was married with a baby. It was time I made my mark on the literary world. I had thrown out the old Remington (terrible shame) and bought a flashy Brother portable for £12 19s 6d from WH Smith in Sloane Square. That little typewriter was with me all the way up to the advent of computers.

Heaven knows how many hundreds of thousands of words it must have clattered out from the battlefields of Iran to the Australian outback. Towards the end, the carriage return only worked thanks to a strategically placed paper clip, and the crack in the lid from the Belfast funeral of the Gibraltar bombers ended up being patched with epoxy paste from the *Largo's* bosun's locker.

But I christened it by writing a novel called The Season's The Reason. I had to write it on the tiny slips of the Wimbledon News's yellow copy paper so that nobody would know that I had dashed off my "Profile" by elevenses and proposed to spend the rest of the day writing comic scenes about spies and debutantes (the fact that I knew nothing about either spies or debutantes might have had something to do with the fact that it was never published.)

However, I did know a lot about The Wombles - those furry creations of children's author Elisabeth Beresford. Remember them? They cleaned up Wimbledon Common and ended up on television. For years, I wrote a weekly "Great Uncle Bulgaria's Diary" for the children's page - it carried on long after I left the paper and moved up to the Evening Mail at Slough.

This was a much bigger paper, covering a vast area of the Thames Valley and heaven knows how many local authorities. This caused a problem for a reporter with ADHD - particularly if he didn't know he had it: Several times a week, I would find myself in council chambers or committee rooms reporting on the interminable machinations of local government - which meant I had to attribute the right quotes to the right councillors (can you imagine the fuss if I got it wrong?)

As the local reporter, I was supposed to know all the names – or at least ask and remember them for next time. In years to come, this wouldn't be a problem - reporters will always help each other. However, the Spelthorne & District Council Planning Committee did not warrant a press bench filled to capacity. I was on my own, facing a room of what seemed to me to be total strangers.

In the end, I devised a code based on where they were sitting and in my notebook, instead of a name next to the quote, there would be a little symbol representing, for instance, the end of the table and the third chair along…

It was a system that served me well for the next 20 years. It never occurred to me that other journalists just remembered the names. What with that and stretching the copy by applying the "Mitcham Flower Show Technique" of filling all the gaps with extravagant adjectives, I graduated to Feature Writer (where it's more important that you know your adjectives rather than a lot of boring old names).

This was the way it worked for young journalists: If you kept moving up to bigger and better papers, then it was inevitable that one day you would end up in Fleet Street. Not with a single bound, of course. First, you had to do night shifts which meant leaving the evening paper at the end of their working day - probably around four o'clock and driving up to town to start at six. If you were lucky, you would finish at two in the morning, ready to hit the sack at three - and be up again for a seven o'clock start at the day job. Not always, of course. Sometimes two o'clock would find you in Hastings or Ross-on-Wye…

Junior hospital doctors are expected to consider that sleep is for sissies, and obviously, the same went for young journalists in the 70s. If you didn't quit and you didn't screw up, eventually, they gave you a "Summer Relief", which meant you had regular employment for six months through the holiday season. Obviously, you had to give up the evening paper … with no guarantee that the six-month contract would turn into something more permanent come September.

The trick was to get yourself noticed – to write something that came to the notice of the editor - and David English was a writer's editor. If he found someone like Vincent Mulchrone or John

Edwards - Peter Lewis, come to that or Lynda Lee-Potter - he promoted them and paid them handsomely and gave them champagne. He made them stars.

I wanted to be a star. Of course, writing something that gets you noticed is a bit of a risk. If it doesn't work, it will be just as noticeable as a pretentious failure. For a young journalist just getting started on his summer relief contract, it might be better to keep your head below the parapet.

But we know what I thought about **taking risks**. Also, I had been throwing adjectives onto the page ever since the Mitcham News and Mercury and all those church fetes. The Mail sent me down to the Isle of Sheppey to see if I could find a strike-breaking steelworker (the Mail loved making heroes of strike-breakers). I found one. He was sitting at home among his astonishing collection of china shire horses, his wife beside him looking equally glum, and holding a letter from the Iron and Steel Trades Confederation stating that, after 30 years, his membership was cancelled with immediate effect.

Unfortunately, he was so shocked he appeared to have been stuck dumb. After half an hour of questioning, my notebook contained one page of monosyllabic answers. I wrote about the shire horses instead.

When I got back to the office, Ina, the exotically red-headed editor's secretary, came out with two bottles of Piper Heidsick and a note which, I still remember, contained the phrase "high-quality journalism".

How did David know that the shire horses - like the president of the fish fryers' burbling gas fire - were nothing more than a device to keep myself from getting bored while I was writing it? I just presumed everybody else was like me when it came to anything **boring**. Better to ramble on about anything than write something **boring**. As long as it's entertaining, people will keep reading (admit it, you've made it this far).

But then, The Mail had always been a writer's paper: In his history of the paper *Mail Men,* Adrian Addison goes back to the early part of the 19th Century, when a man named George Warrington Stevens would be given licence to eulogise the ordinary (he once wrote about an empty London street on a bank holiday Sunday). As the paper's co-founder Alfred "Sunny" Harmsworth put it: "He showed genius in his extraordinary power of observation and his entirely new way of recording what he had seen."

If I had any sense of modesty, I would not place myself in the same company. But it appears that I don't do modesty any more than I do boring.

I got the job.

Chapter 8
Craftsman

After seeing what I could do with proper stories, The Daily Mail started sending me to cover events that weren't strictly stories at all just to see what I would make of them:

Oh, the fun we had: In fact, I think this is the time to tell you about Wally the Walrus.

Wally the Walrus washed up on a beach in Skegness one August morning in about 1980.

This posed a question: What do you do with a lost Walrus? Well, you send him back to Greenland, of course.

How do you do that?

This is where the fun begins - and it lasted for the best part of a week: First, the local council has to knock up a crate for him. Who does this? The council's works department... no, no, no, you're losing the thread: The council carpenter is who - as in *The Walrus and the Carpenter*. This means that one of the sub-editors with a poetic bent gets to write a pastiche of Lewis Carroll.

Next, you persuade Iceland Air to air freight the Walrus for nothing more than the publicity it will generate (or rather, with the threat of the bad publicity that will be heaped on the company if they refuse).

The World Wildlife Fund and the RSPCA both sent their experts (including a very young Mark Carwardine) to see to Wally's welfare, and of course, there was Mail's wildlife photographer Mike Hollist - a man with enough patience for all of us. We even had a fishing boat organised at the other end to convey the party across the Denmark Strait to Greenland. What could possibly go wrong?

Well, I hoped something. There is nothing so dull as a newspaper stunt that goes according to plan - and this had the makings of a story I would tell my grandchildren, not to mention the readers…

It started looking promising as soon as we arrived at Keflavik International Airport in Iceland - and the man who owned the fishing boat backed up his lorry to load Wally's crate. It turned out that not only did he own the fishing boat but also, he owned Reykjavik Zoo - where, he announced, Wally would be spending the night… and as many days and nights thereafter until enough visitors had paid to come and look at him.

Mention of the word "Zoo" did not go down well with the RSPCA and the WWF. A quick inspection of a muddy park and a few bedraggled animals confirmed that Wally might have been better off staying in Skegness. As it was, he was stuck on the tarmac with the wind whistling straight off the icecap. The RSPCA's young woman vet, who had spent much of the journey so far with her nose pressed up against the bars of the crate, communing with Wally, announced that the present situation could well be classified as cruelty – and blamed me.

Right next to Wally's crate was an enormous hanger, wide open and inviting.

"Would he be all right in there?" I suggested.

"He'd be out of the wind."

We pushed him in.

"Shouldn't we ask someone?"

"Take too long…"

This was absolutely true. One thing I had learned about big

organisations was that nobody ever wants to take responsibility for anything - and this was a very big organisation indeed. This was the United States Air Force. Pretty soon, I found myself being wheeled in to see the commanding officer – a man with very short hair and more medal ribbons than you could easily count. He sat behind an enormous desk under an enormous flag and, according to the block of hardwood in front of him, was called something like Hiram B. Sidewinder III.

He was also bored to tears. Everyone at USAF Keflavik was bored to tears. The only reason they were there was to provide a Search and Rescue facility should a B52 come down in the North Atlantic. No B52 had ever come down in the North Atlantic. Colonel Sidewinder was "Go" for excitement.

"Here's what we're gonna do," he said with the certainty of JFK announcing the Moon Landing Program. "We're gonna take the refuel tank out of a C130 - should make enough room for your Wally's crate. Now you guys get some shuteye, and we'll have Go for 0600."

So, we closed the big roller doors on Wally and booked into the surprisingly luxurious hotel where we didn't so much get some shuteye as have a celebratory dinner and go for a dip in one of the natural volcanic hot spas that litter Iceland like puddles in Manchester.

The following morning, we were back at the airport, all ready for "Go" at 0600. However, now the Colonel had morphed from JFK into Jim Lovell with "Houston, we have a problem."

We certainly did. Someone had told the Pentagon.

It was like this: If the C130 was going to be out of commission, another one would have to be flown up from mainland USA to cover for it - after all, the C130 was there to refuel the Air Sea Rescue helicopter that would go to the aid of the crew of the downed B52 - if one should happen to come down for the first time ever during the precise 12 hours it would take to fly Wally to Greenland, fly back and replace the refuel tank.

So, what we had was a "No-Go".

I began to shake my head. This was not good. So far, Skegness Council had helped save Wally by building him a crate, a North of England haulage company had helped save him by driving him to Heathrow, and Iceland Air had helped save him by flying him free and gratis to Keflavik, and now... and now...

I placed my cup of disgusting, weak American coffee with obligatory cream on the edge of the desk and began to excuse myself: My deadline was approaching. The Daily Mail and its six million readers would be waiting for news of Wally... however disappointing and, possibly, tragic that news might prove to be.

With a heavy heart and heavy tread, I rose to leave and impart to a waiting world... etc...etc...

"Wait!" The Colonel held up his hand - not an easy thing to do, given the weight of gold braid on his sleeve.

What happened over the next few hours, I can only surmise. I never saw the colonel again - but I did see a lot of a harassed young Captain who had been tasked with rescuing the international reputation of USAF Keflavik, the United States Air Force in general and God's Own Country as an animal-loving nation.

One day that young Captain would be a Colonel - even a General. Here's what he did from his little office in Iceland: He got the Pentagon to call the State Department - and the State Department to call the US embassy in Reykjavik... and the ambassador to call the Icelandic Foreign Minister - who called the Fisheries Minister - who handed the mission to the commander of their Fishery Protection Fleet.

For 72 hours, the Icelandic Fishing fleet in the Denmark Strait would be left unprotected while a little grey ship – a sort of cross between a destroyer and a lifeboat - would take Wally home. The vet rushed off to tell him the news.

Sure enough, the whole circus moved to the harbour, where Wally was winched aboard and lashed to the deck (the vet giving him a running commentary through the bars).

The captain was a bemused man with a bushy beard and piercing blue eyes revelling in a name that sounded something like Gunnarssonnjohanssensen. The weather forecast was excellent - we should have a smooth crossing (which might well have had something to do with the Icelandic authorities agreeing to desert all those fishermen).

And so, we ate our way to Greenland. Ask Mark Carwardine about it if you don't believe me - he spends a lot of his time living on freeze-dried rations in desolate parts of the world while he makes his documentaries. But on this trip, we had six meals a day.

We started with breakfast - very Scandinavian, lots of raw and smoked fish, hearty breads to exercise the beard muscles. Then, for a mid-morning snack, we were offered a selection of cakes and flatbreads with more smoked fish and coffee. On to lunch which was a full meal of four courses with a choice of two or three dishes for each one. Tea followed at four o'clock with more cakes and then dinner at 6.30 – the sort of meal that would not have disgraced a Mayfair restaurant. It took a couple of hours, but then we didn't have much else to do – at least not until the table was filled once more with cakes and breads at 11.00 p.m. to fend off night starvation.

It was all very relaxing - except for the vet, who kept up her vigil, nose to nose with Wally's bristling moustache.

Then, finally, in brilliant sunshine, we arrived off the sparkling shores of Greenland - about a couple of miles off them.

"This is as close as we can go," said the captain.

"As close as we can go!" I think I may have exploded slightly.

We had come all this way, from Skegness beach (with the carpenter) down to London thanks to the friendly haulier - Iceland Air's free freight - Colonel Sidewinder and Captain PR… not to mention the Pentagon, the State Department, the Icelandic Foreign Minister and his Fisheries counterpart…. and after all that, the unpronounceable captain proposed to stop a couple of miles short of the destination…

"Some things you cannot do," he said in the sort of measured tones you would expect from serving up ancient Norse wisdom.

Actually, he had a point. The final mile was blocked with pack ice.

"Wally will be fine," said the Captain. We move the crate to the edge of the deck, we open the door, he dives in. All good!"

Mike Hollist, the Mail's patient wildlife photographer, had been listening patiently to all this and spotted a fatal flaw. It would take Wally about a second to dive from crate to water. The motor drive on Mike's Nikon F4 might be able to crank out five frames in a second. In other words, the best part of a week of everybody's time and thousands of pounds of other people's money was all going to be zeroed into five frames - all of them pretty much identical.

We went back to the drawing board. We considered dragging the crate across the ice. We considered calling in a helicopter - the Americans could refuel it on the way…

"We could put him on the ice," said Mike - which showed why he kept winning awards for his animal pictures. "Put him on the ice; he crawls around for a bit, then he dives in. How's that?"

Mike looked at me. I looked at the Captain. The Captain looked at the ice.

"Maybe," he said. "Not the pack ice. But maybe we can get close to a big floe. Lower the crate onto the floe…"

"Open the crate," said Mike.

"With you on the floe…" I suggested (this was looking promising).

But the Captain had seen that go wrong before: "Loose ice like this - very unstable. Can break up - *crack* - no warning. No people on the ice floe. Just Wally. He swims good."

And so, it was arranged: Two little rubber boats were launched to go and fetch an ice flow and drive it towards the ship. Mike stayed aboard because, as he rightly pointed out, if he was in one of the boats, he would have the ship in the background, not Greenland. If we didn't have Greenland in the background, who was to say we weren't dropping Wally into the Serpentine?

The ship's derrick hoisted the crate high into the air and over the rail. The two rubber boats revved up and pressed the ice floe more firmly against the side of the ship.

And it was here that the Laws of Physics came into play. Oh, how I hate the Laws of Physics! Remember the trouble they caused with the Load of Straw? If the number of times the Laws of Physics were divided into the sum of human endeavour, you would get a very frustrating number indeed.

On this occasion, the Force generated by the two outboard motors was applied to the Object (the ice floe) and from that to the ship (the outboards were still revving). This meant we had Leverage – and with Leverage, you get a Fulcrum (In this case, the centre-point of the ship). This caused the whole vessel to turn (the ice floe, Wally and the two little rubber boats with their revving engines, turning with it.)

"Wait, wait, stop!" I cried (I was on the bridge with the mistaken idea that I was directing operations).

The Captain raised a bushy eyebrow. Evidently, he was not used to people countermanding his orders.

"I'm losing Greenland!" came the faint voice of Mike from his vantage point on the rail.

"We're losing Greenland!" I relayed to the captain in the manner of John Mills addressing Noel Coward.

"...and the sun," Mike added for good measure.

But the Captain had had enough: "Mister," he said. "This is a ship. It is floating in water. *You cannot park it like a car!"*

The pictures weren't great when I saw them in the paper several days later. Wally emerged as a shapely black blob – backlit against the ice.

But Greenland was there – as large as life – in all its desolate glory with mountains and ice in all directions.

"Hammersmith," said Mike, coming up behind me.

Hammersmith means taking two photographs, cutting them up, pushing them together and photographing them again. It got its name from the fiasco surrounding the newly-constructed Hammersmith Flyover in the early '60s. It was so huge that even the widest wide-angle lens could not encompass all the diverging and converging lanes and bridges. So, the photographer who was sent to cover the opening took several photographs, intending that they should be fitted together later.

They were - just in the wrong order, that was all. So, what you ended up with was roads disappearing into the sides of buildings, bridges which ended in mid-air…

Now, they would mess it up with Photoshop.

I got another two bottles of the Editor's Piper Heidsieck for that. It even meant I could get away with failing to recognise him when the IRA blew up Airey Neave in the House of Commons car park. I was standing at the police tape waiting for something to happen, and David turned up in pressed jeans and a designer sweater with one very expensive camera round his neck (he lived just around the corner). I asked him which paper he was from.

I remember he gave me that sort of look you give someone who you never knew was an imbecile but has now provided irrefutable proof, and you can't quite believe it.

When I still didn't say: "Oh, my God, I'm sorry, David! I didn't recognise you out of a suit…" (or come to that, out of the office), he leaned over conspiratorially and said: "I'm your editor."

(ADHD notes: Forgetfulness can be damaging to careers

and relationships because it can be confused with carelessness or lack of intelligence.)

Of course, I didn't know this at the time. I just thought I was an imbecile and wished I had gone into accountancy.

Whatever the editor thought, he must have put it down to eccentricity, which in those days was seen almost as a pre-requisite for fine writing.

Like alcoholism.

And so I embarked on years of lost parrots, cats with two homes (and two owners who ended up fighting it out in court), daft old men in leaky old boats being rescued by one Lifeboat after another as they navigated down the coast in the vague direction of palm trees with the aid of the AA road map...I covered them all.

In fact, Captain Calamity – as the daft old man with the road map became known when he appeared every summer in one guise or another – became a major contributor to Passmore's Dictionary of All-Purpose Intros.

The Intro - the first dozen words - count double in newspapers. The great Peter Lewis, writing about the even greater (his view) Vincent Mulchrone, said that the intro should give off a fizz like a wave running up dry sand.

I was just coming along on the coat-tails of people like this. Mulchrone used to arrive at the office at mid-morning but turn right into the back bar of The Harrow, where he would hold up two fingers to Len, the landlord – two fingers signified a Fernet-Branca and a quarter bottle of champagne, if Len would be so kind. After that, the larger-than-life Irishman would be ready to make history out of another day. When he died, they turned the back bar into a shrine – which is still there today with some of his greatest intros immortalised on the walls.

I was going to give you just the first line of this one from his coverage of Churchill's funeral - but, hey, why stop at the first line? Have the whole intro: *Two rivers run silently through London tonight, and one is made of people. Dark and quiet as the night-time Thames itself, it flows through Westminster Hall, eddying about the foot of the rock called Churchill.*

If I were you, I would stop and think about that. That is great literature. The fact that it wrapped fish and chips the next day does not detract from its genius one iota.

As Mulchrone wrote, equally famously: "The news story must be the only human activity which demands that the orgasm comes at the beginning."

I grew up reading him. All through my school days and into my years on local papers, Mulchrone was a fixture in the Daily Mail, and I modelled my style on his just as faithfully as a generation of young actors studied Laurence Olivier and pop stars copied Elvis.

I went back and looked at "The Mulchrone Bar" a while ago. It was empty. Upstairs, in the "Top Bar" where we used to be "locked in" if Len got fed up with trying to throw us out, a roomful of twenty and thirty-somethings - all far better dressed than we had been - turned to stare at the old man who appeared at the top of the stairs. A young woman, much more composed than any of the young women I remember there, came and informed me that this was a "private party". I asked quietly whether she would indulge a sentimental old hack for a few minutes while he had one drink at the bar for old times' sake.

She looked at me as if I was mad.

You should never go back. It's a mistake.

The other important piece of advice is to recognise important turning points for what they are: If I had been more on the ball, these would have been obvious. After all, how often did the Deputy Editor come and invite me for lunch? He was a man named Stewart Steven, best known for (not) finding the Nazi, Martin Bormann, in the jungles of South America for the Express.

He suggested lunch the following day. I said tomorrow was my day off (rather than an important turning point in my career). Stuart said: "I am sure you can bring yourself to come in on your day off to have lunch with the deputy editor".

We went to The Boulestin - that incredibly expensive establishment in St James's where businessmen, bankers and politicians lunch each other with the obvious intention of being seen doing so by other businessmen, bankers and politicians. We travelled by chauffeur-driven car and were shown to "Mr Steven's usual table" - positioned on some sort of dais so as to see and be seen even more ostentatiously.

Almost immediately, a waiter appeared bearing a huge salver of langoustines. They were arranged so artistically that it would have been rude not to have exclaimed in admiration.

The trouble was that having been so enthusiastic, I could hardly avoid ordering the wretched things **(desire for approval).** And, as every sophisticate knows (not me, though), langoustines are impossible to eat with any delicacy. Order them on a romantic weekend in Paris, certainly. Do not order them for a business lunch.

Of course, now you can look up on Google "Tips for attending a business lunch" (I just did). One of the tips says: "The table is a test: Will this person be able to handle themselves at all levels of society."

So, I suppose dropping a langoustine on the floor, reaching down and putting it back on your plate would mean failing the test…

For that is what I did - after all, I couldn't very well leave it on the floor, could I? (Actually, I just looked that up, and the answer is: "It's better to leave it there and mention the mishap to your server. Fumbling around the floor is not in keeping with a fine – and hygienic – dining experience.")

I can't remember what we discussed during the remainder of the lunch. Certainly, it was of no consequence, and whatever highly-paid position on the paper I was being considered for, it never materialised.

Just imagine how differently life would have turned out if I had ordered smoked salmon. I would never have left the Mail in 1987 to go to Robert Maxwell's short-lived London Daily News - nor ended up on the Evening Standard when the Mail refused to take me back because I insisted on six weeks off for the Singlehanded Transatlantic Race.

If I had not been at the Evening Standard, Lois would never have invited me for lunch - never suggested I should buy a copy of Time Out. Tamsin and I would never have met on Hampstead Heath, run away to sea together. Owen, Theo, Lottie and Hugo would never have been born...

Turning points...

But thinking about it now, maybe a dramatic change of some kind was inevitable: I had been working for newspapers for nearly 20 years, and in ADHD terms, that is an interminably long time to be doing the same thing. Compared to a career in accountancy or food processing, my life was filled with variety. Indeed, as Mikhael Gorbachev introduced *Glasnost* and communism began to falter, it could be argued that I was witnessing at first hand one of the most exciting periods in history.

In 1989 I was in Tiananmen Square when the People's Army started shooting; I was in Prague to see Vaclav Havel appear on the balcony to tell 200,000 people in Wenceslas Square that communism was finished. I joined the East Germans as they streamed through Czechoslovakia, Hungary and Austria, turned right into West Germany and pulled down the Wall from the other side.

And finally, sitting at a table for ten in a Moscow hotel with a bunch of American correspondents who were positively fizzing with excitement, I announced heavily: "If I have to stand in one more public square watching one more crowd make a mess of pulling down yet another statue while singing patriotic songs out of tune, I really think I may scream."

The Americans were aghast. They were all Moscow correspondents. They had been cooped up there watching democracy blossom all over Eastern Europe while saying: "Ah yes, but It could never happen here…"

And suddenly, out in the streets, a public demonstration was winding its way through the city demanding the overthrow of the government (we saw it from a window while eating Baskin Robbins ice cream and watching the coverage on Russian state TV).

When I left the Evening Standard, the head librarian came down to the newsroom and dumped a pile of brown envelopes on the empty desk next to me – my "Corres file". Everything I had ever written for the Mail and now, the Standard, had been filed – not just under the subject and name of everyone mentioned in the story – but also under my name as the correspondent who had written it. It was astonishing to see it all heaped up in wire trays: A mountain of words. Of course, at the time, I was finished with the Evening Standard – and certainly finished with the Daily Mail. Without a second's thought, I swept them into the wastepaper basket. They filled it and spilled out all over the floor – political scandals, celebrity gossip, the inevitable animal stories, all the April Fool spoofs which seemed to be my speciality - all scattering together under the desks and the wheels of the office chairs.

The news editor was aghast: Philip Evans had rescued me when the Mail wouldn't take me back with all my prima-donna demands.

"You can't do that!" said Philip. "That's a life's work!"

Yes, so it was – but a different life. A life that I was shedding as surely as a snake must shed its skin in order to grow.

Chapter 9

Decision

Tamsin's Lonely Hearts advert had mentioned sailing – she had been on a dinghy sailing holiday in Greece - they sailed over to a little island and had a barbecue. It had been an adventure. Clearly, Tamsin liked adventures.

If she thought whistling up a spare set of keys in a taxi was impressive, what do you think happened when she heard about sailing to France, The Azores, America? That lunch in Cafe Rouge went very, very well.

And don't forget that we met in November. By the time the sailing season started, we had been skiing together, spent hedonistic weekends in country house hotels and talked over our plans and excitements across more restaurant tables than seems entirely possible. By the time Largo went in the water, I was smitten. Now: if only she really did like sailing…

Tamsin liked sailing all right. She liked everything about it. She liked the "Where shall we go aspect of it. She liked the getting there - she could steer a course better than I could (there's nothing more boring than steering a course – or maybe it has something to do with spending hours staring at a compass when you have an **inability to focus***)*.

But there were other dimensions Tamsin brought to sailing – dimensions, I had never appreciated. She made every meal an occasion: Suddenly, Largo's galley blossomed with little jars of herbs. The mugs lost their coffee stains. We had fresh ingredients trying to keep cool in the bilges.

I had never seen the need for a fridge - after all, fridges on boats are nothing but trouble and turn the skipper into a slave to electricity generation. Instead, we would wrap a bottle of white wine in a tea towel and stand it in a bucket of seawater, reasoning that the process of evaporation might lower the temperature by a degree or two...

Best of all, Tamsin turned every destination into an adventure. Until now, I had viewed harbours as a place to tie up and replenish the water tank (Largo only carried 12 gallons). Suddenly they were filled with tiny backstreets and antiquarian bookshops, undiscovered restaurants and pub gardens – and long, long beach walks.

Because, of course, along with Tamsin, came Blue - the dog with the impossibly long legs and the compulsion to chase anything with wings. We bought him a lifejacket and he became a proper boat dog (being able to hold onto his bladder for what seemed an extraordinarily long time).

Of course, this did mean that as soon as he leapt ashore (usually while the dinghy was rather further from the beach than he imagined) he would make for the first lamp post and - without any thought for the audience which inevitably gathered - stand on three legs for what seemed a very long time indeed while the puddle grew into a lake...

While we're on this distasteful subject, perhaps it is the time to explain that Largo's mooring was in the middle of Portsmouth Harbour, and the boatyard operated a ferry service to get people on and off their boats. It worked rather well, you never had to wait long...or, at least, it didn't seem long if you weren't crossing your back legs after being on the boat for more than 12 hours...

For Blue and his amazing elastic bladder, this would have been manageable if only we had devised a way of getting him off the boat and into the launch which did not involve lifting him by the convenient handle on the top of his lifejacket ... which was attached to him by means of straps round his chest and ... er ... abdomen.

Poor animal, he was so embarrassed. Tamsin and I smiled and nodded at all the attention he was getting from the other passengers - until we realised that this was because he was looking appalled at his own lack of self-control as he drained into the bilges. The ferry coxswain was very calm about it: "Happens all the time...just pumps out...

We explored the Solent and the West Country. We went to Brittany and Normandy and the Channel Islands. Tamsin stood a night watch by herself - and experienced that wondrous feeling of being alone with the universe - and also the rude awakening when a ship creeps up behind you when you're not looking.

And she never complained, and she never tied a bad knot.

Here I was in unfamiliar territory: After more than a decade of managing relationships to suit myself, I found I was succumbing to the first signs of domesticity: If a girl wanted to buy new plates or started lingering outside estate agents' windows, I knew it was time to move on - and did.

This was different: It wasn't estate agents' adverts we trawled through together, it was the "Boats for Sale" columns of Yachting Monthly – and this was worrying.

I had never met anyone as enthusiastic as I was - at least not as enthusiastic about the same things as I was. You can love someone because they make you feel happy or they make you feel sexy or secure or special - you can love someone for any number of reasons. But if you have never loved someone because they want to do what you want to do - but with even more enthusiasm than you have ever felt for it; then you have never been helplessly, hopelessly, completely in love.

For years my "giving up everything and going sailing" date had been set for April 4th 2004 - my 55th birthday. This was the earliest date I could draw my pension - and it would be plenty. I had been pouring money into Additional Voluntary Contributions. I had watched my salary - on which the final figure depended - climb inexorably up and up. All I had to do was keep my head down, my nose clean and be moderately patient - after all, it was only another 13 years.

It's just that when you've been waiting your whole life to do something, 13 more years sounds like an eternity. I was resigned to waiting, I told myself - it wouldn't be so bad: I had Largo. I had long holidays to do long trips - the Standard even bought me a long-range radio, sent me off across the Atlantic and published my despatches.

But in those days, I didn't know that waiting for anything at all was entirely against my nature. I didn't have the list of ADHD symptoms back then. I thought everyone wanted things and had to force themselves to be patient.

And then there was Tamsin. She wasn't patient. Why couldn't we go now? She wanted to know.

"Well I don't get my pension for another 13 years…"

As I said it, I could hear how it sounded. The very words seemed swollen with images of pipe and slippers, begonias and privet hedges - I could see myself in a knitted cardigan, a member of the bowls club. Was that really me?

That's what happens when you have a good job – when you start accepting employment as the norm and looking to the company to keep you safe from all the surprises life has to offer - things like not enough money and failing health. I didn't even have to worry about the gearbox falling out of the car (or, come to that, losing the keys). I realised I was in a bubble.

Tamsin painted a picture of another life: With Anne Hammick's *Ocean Cruising on a Budget*, propped up against her knees, she opened my eyes to waving palms and blinding white sand, the warm trade wind bowling us along mile after unravelling mile…

Gradually, I started thinking of waiting only until I was 54 - after all, I had enough saved up to bridge the gap for a year - and think how much more material there would be for the yachting magazines…

But then the doubts would come muscling in: To jump free - with no safety net. What if…

What if the boat needed some hugely expensive repair? What if one of us became ill or suffered some sort of serious accident and had to be repatriated? What if it all went wrong, and we had to come back with our tails between our legs … and I had to beg for my old job back?

In other words, what if it didn't work? What if we were poor? Now I looked at the plan in terms of reality rather than possibility, I was startled to discover that what I was really frightened of was being poor - and, of course, the more frightened I became, the more I kept thinking about it. When you are saddled with a natural predilection for thinking about yourself, ideas like these can go round and round - privately, of course. ***The desire for approval*** did not allow for flies in the ointment. We were set on a course and my doubts had to be kept to myself.

And then, as it always will if you look for it, the answer appeared. It was handed to me in a press release: A run-of-the-mill story that was picked out for me, as usual, from the bottom third of the news schedule, as in: "Looks a bit dull but let's see what Passmore can make of it..."

I looked at the brief: American self-help guru Tony Robbins launches new book.

In those days, "Self Help" was one of those joke fads that made their way across the Atlantic on wings of hype - only to fall flat on the prickly shores of British scepticism. It sounded right up my alley.

The launch was held - as all the best book launches are - in one of those big London hotels where publishers convert money directly into publicity without troubling the critics. It was probably the Dorchester or the Savoy or somewhere like that. Tony Robbins turned out to be an impossibly tall American with a chin the size of Mount Rushmore – which he could carry off because of his impossibly large and gleaming white teeth. Honestly, you needed sunglasses just to look at him.

We were each given a copy of his book - a doorstop of a thing, called *Ultimate Power!* I remember writing that if he had been a British self-help guru, it would have been called *My mother thinks I have potential!* (but, without the exclamation mark). The accompanying press notes explained, with suitable hyperbole, just how big this guy was in American life-coaching circles.

Life coaching? Personal development? These concepts were new to the British press corps. Call it by its name. This was Self-Help, wasn't it - all rather pathetic…

Tony Robbins talked earnestly. He had taken charge of his own life (apparently, he had started out as an overweight nobody). He had helped millions of people take charge of their lives - reach their potential - achieve their goals…

You can do anything you want to do. You can be anything you want to be… Just buy the book…

True to form, the British Press corps put up their hands, asked how this was possible - and Tony Robbins flashed his enormous teeth and had an answer for every question (most of which mentioned chapter and verse as if he was some southern preacher quoting The Bible).

And while all this was going on, the reporter from The Sun sat at the back in an attitude of terminal boredom, the fresh page of his notebook completely unmarked. The Sun delighted in demolishing pretension wherever it could be rooted out. After quarter of an hour of earnest questions and Tony Robbins' practised answers (buy the book), the man from the Sun raised his hand and asked his question.

The question had been crafted to be as offensive as possible and was delivered with a sceptical sniff more appropriate to the public bar of an East London pub than the Savoy's River Room. This was it: "What makes you think that your pseudo-psychological American claptrap is going to cut it with the British public, eh?"

What happened over the next two minutes was quite extraordinary. Without breaking stride - without so much as blinking or allowing his luminous smile to flicker, Tony Robbins totally demolished the man from The Super Soaraway Sun and gathered the rest of the room into the palm of his hand. It was like a magic trick. I wouldn't have believed it if I hadn't seen it done. I once saw Muhammad Ali demonstrate levitation, but then he rather spoiled the effect by showing how it was done. (The Magic Circle were furious.)

But on this occasion, there appeared to be no sleight of hand - no secret compartment or trapdoor in the stage. All the same, I remember not quite believing what I had just witnessed.

And so, I did not use Tony Robbins' book as a doorstop. I read it. It was the first book on personal development I had ever read - and it was a revelation: If this man was right, then if you didn't like the way your life was turning out, you could change it. You could change it just by changing your thinking.

True, we all know the poem about the two men looking out from prison bars: One sees mud. The other sees stars...

But was it really true that you could change your reality by the power of your thinking? He said it was - and he had a very persuasive way of arguing his case. Of course, first you had to decide what you wanted.

What did I want?

Did I want to be safe? Did I want to be sure that I was going to be paid a large amount of money at the end of every month... and continue doing as I was told every day? Did I want to have to pack up the boat on Sunday night and clamber back onto the M3 to London - and sit in the traffic jam on the Winchester bypass?

Or did I want to sail off with Tamsin? Wake up in the morning and stick my head out of the hatch and only then decide what to do with the day - pile into the dinghy with the dog and go exploring - or haul up the anchor and set sail for somewhere new... every day an adventure.

What did I really want? There was a whole chapter on working out what you really wanted. I didn't need it. I knew what I wanted. I had wanted it since I was 11 years old. I'd just never met someone who wanted the same thing - who egged me on to "seize the day"... who said things like: "Don't worry, we'll manage..." Also, I had never read a book that said: Just go and do it...

But I did worry. I worried all the time. If there was half an hour when Tamsin was not there to make me feel that everything would be all right, I worried.

I didn't worry about sinking or being shipwrecked. I didn't even worry about having babies on the boat (the books said there was nothing to it). What worried me was being poor. What if nobody wanted to buy my writing? That was all I had to sell - and just at that moment, I was selling it for a very high price indeed. Did I mention that Philip Evans told me I was the highest-paid staff reporter in the country? And he should know because he was the one who agreed my salary.

I liked being able to go out for lunch just because it seemed like a nice thing to do. I liked not having to worry about the car because it didn't belong to me. I liked keeping Largo properly maintained - no matter what it cost. I liked an awful lot of what I was considering giving up.

And then I started reading the book again. If I had ever read the books I was given for 'A' Level English, I would have known how to study a book: First, you read it through to find out what it's about – and then you begin studying it until the margins are filled with notes. This is how I read *Ultimate Power!* and it might very well have been my first experience of the ADHD symptom **Hyperfocus.**

A person with ADHD can become so engrossed that they become unaware of anything else around them. This kind of focus makes it easy to lose track of time and ignore those around you, which can lead to relationship misunderstandings.

First came the chapter on working out what you really want (make lists). Then there was the - much more difficult - matter of making the decision. In order to do this, I had to overcome that massive obstruction The Fear of Being Poor. We had plenty of books about families who had cruised the world on not much more than sunshine and coconuts. Look at the title of Anne Hammick's book: That was called *Ocean Cruising on a Budget*. At one point, I had met Nick Skeates aboard Wylo II (and bought a pair of oil lamps at what must have been a 1,000% mark-up on what he had paid for them in South Africa). But all the time, in quiet and weak moments (when Tamsin wasn't around to bolster my confidence) the nagging fear would return…

Of course, Tony Robbins knew this would happen. I was beginning to see why he had such a following (and why The Sun was so wrong). He told me to construct two technicolour images in my head: One depicting everything I wanted, just as I wanted it to happen - and the other showing my greatest fear in all its bewildering panic. That second image was to be fixed on a page - one of those pages in a ring-bound notebook that could be ripped off with the satisfying sound of tearing paper.

Then I was to imagine it being ripped away and flying off in the wind - to leave the permanent image of everything going *right*.

And I was to do this several times a day - and certainly every time I felt that doubts were beginning to creep in.

And it worked. Within the space of a couple of weeks, I had stopped worrying. We would be all right. Something would turn up. We had our health, we had each other - what more could we ask for? Life didn't offer guarantees. Besides, it was exciting.

And we know how compelling an idea can be if it is **exciting**...

And so, it was decided. We would leave our safe, secure, well-paid jobs. We would take a leap into the unknown - a leap of faith.

We would Go.

Chapter 10
Escape

Falstaffian - a great word. It was the word people used to describe Geoff Pack. He was enormous - in physical presence as much as in personality. Geoff didn't just live life. He devoured life with a chip shop scoop.

And he was the sort of man who should not have been allowed to die from Hodgkins Lymphoma, a particularly virulent form of cancer, at the age of 39, leaving his wife Lou-Lou and four young children devastated.

Geoff had been a presence at Yachting Monthly for as long as I had been reading the magazine - and certainly for as long as I had been writing for it. Mind you, his was an intermittent presence since he kept finding reasons to resign and go off sailing with Lou-Lou - first in an impossibly small home-built Wharram catamaran which started to disintegrate in mid-Atlantic (they rebuilt it and carried on).

Returning to the magazine in his mid 20's, he immediately set about fitting out a more suitable boat for world cruising - the Rival 34 *Euge* - and it was his experience with this boat that became the basis of his book Ocean Cruising Countdown (later entitled Blue Water Countdown).

Tamsin and I made our plans with that in one hand and Anne Hammick in the other.

Geoff was probably the only one of my sailing friends who did not think I was mad. After all, he had done just the same (three times, in fact) and warned us off the 40ft steel cutter in favour of a tiny catamaran.

Certainly, the Heavenly Twins 27 had plenty of room - two dedicated sleeping cabins (a double for us and a single for Blue). A decent galley and you could get five round the table in comfort. She even had a shower. The design dated from the early '70s but had gone through several improvements - lighter, faster, more headroom...

Admittedly "faster" didn't mean much because the only time the Heavenly Twins went fast was off the wind. They sailed to windward rather like a bucket. Geoff did warn us that this would be frustrating - even dangerous if we should ever find ourselves trying to beat off a lee shore. But, on the other hand, we had all the time in the world. We could afford to wait for the weather.

There was one for sale in Brittany – really cheap, because she was home-completed and moored on a canal somewhere near Lorient. The vendor sent photographs - but by the time they arrived in the post, Tamsin and I had wound ourselves up to a pitch of high excitement. More to the point, Tamsin had organised our visit to view the boat. This involved taking a week to drive there and back by a scenic and circular route, staying at interesting B&Bs along the way.

I remember it as the most wonderful week: We would wake up to coffee and croissants in some quirky farmhouse and set off on the road with me driving and Tamsin navigating to some interesting market town. There, we would stop for coffee and a wander, buying bread, cheese and fruit for lunch (already, we had a six-pack of red wine in the boot).

Next would come the search for a scenic picnic spot. Tamsin was very particular: It had to be deserted, far from a main road and with a beautiful view. By the time we found it, we were usually more than ready for a whole baguette and half a kilo of full-fat soft cheese.

It is well known that cheese is more easily digested if mixed with wine - so it follows that eating a lot of cheese for lunch requires a lot of wine. At least that was my understanding, and so Tamsin would drive after lunch while I slept.

I would awake with a start in the late afternoon as Tamsin demanded: "Which way?"

Opening my eyes, I would find us at a road junction somewhere in the Brittany countryside (having, of course, no idea where - and certainly not whether I should say "left" or "right".)

Still, if you want a quick decision, ask someone with ADHD.

"Right." I would snap instantly. (Tomorrow it would be "Left".)

For the next hour, we would argue as we tried in vain to find the way - always coming back to the fact that I had got us lost at the first junction.

Never mind; by the time we found ourselves again - and Tamsin's meticulous planning had rewarded us with another unusual and romantic B&B - we would walk into town to Madame's recommendation of *Le Meilleur Restaurant,* and all would be forgotten.

And this was fine - except that there was supposed to be a purpose to the trip - and the couple who were selling the catamaran were pinning their hopes on us. After all, if we were prepared to come all this way, we must be keen. They really needed to sell the boat because, after setting out to sail the world, they had been hijacked by a tumbledown French farmhouse. The money from the sale of the boat would pay for a new roof.

There was only one problem: Having taken a magnifying glass to the photographs they sent us, it became clear that all the bulkheads - the walls of the boat - were covered with some sort of orange carpet. Tamsin and I were not prepared to live aboard a boat carpeted all over in orange. If she had been for sale in Portsmouth, we would simply have cancelled the viewing - but then, we would have missed out on that idyllic week of picnic lunches and interesting B&Bs.

So, we arrived ready for a cursory look before saying we'd think about it and make a quick getaway for the next interesting B&B on the (circular) route home. But first, there was the smell of fresh coffee brewing (obviously, the vendors had read those books on how to sell your home by enhancing the viewing with homely touches).

We motored out into the centre of the canal to demonstrate the legendary manoeuvrability of twin props. We couldn't do a sailing trial because they didn't have the mast up, but there was lots of talk about the boat's admirable sailing qualities (as long as you didn't want to go to windward - but then, who in their right mind, wanted to do that?)

Then there was lunch - a proper casserole to demonstrate the galley. I have never felt such a fraud. Did they ever sell their boat? Did they ever get their roof fixed?

In the end, we found a nearly-new Heavenly Twins in Chichester. I had never had a new boat before – there wasn't a mark on her. But also, it meant that she was equipped with only the basics.

One other small detail: she was called *Das Boot* – German for *The Boat* and also the title of the celebrated film about life on a U-boat during the Battle of the Atlantic. Honestly, who calls a boat *Das Boot?* We tried anagrams and came up with *Bad Soot*.

It is considered very bad luck to change a boat's name - although, of course, racing sailors who rely on sponsorship are happy to change their boats' names to absolutely anything, no matter how absurd. Money talks.

We weren't asking for sponsorship - but at the same time, I did intend to write about our adventures, and somehow they wouldn't seem half so alluring in a boat called *Das Boot* (or come to that *Bad Soot).*

Also, I have a seafaring heritage: My great-grandfather on my mother's side ran away to sea at 16. Family legend has it that there was some trouble with an under-housemaid, and young George Warren made for the docks, telling the coachman: "You may inform the family that I shall not be returning."

In time, he built up his own shipping company, The Warren Line, plying the Boston-Liverpool route. My parents named one of their boats after a Warren Line ship, the *Joshua Bates*. Call me sexist, but I think boats should have girls' names. *Das Boot* became *Lottie Warren*. The original, named after one of George's daughters, was built in 1863 - 1,184 tons - and scrapped, for some reason, in 1879.

Years later, I discovered that George Warren did so well that he built himself a splendid house in Liverpool and called it Strawberry Field. Yes, that Strawberry Field. It became a Barnardo's home - and that was where a young John Lennon used to climb over the wall and sit in a tree.

We moved *Lottie Warren* from Chichester to the East Coast (cheaper, different and shallow water ideally suited to catamarans).

Also, I discovered that while I had been globetrotting, I had not been working a four-day week but a seven-day week. For instance, during the six weeks I spent in China at the time of Tiananmen Square, the newsdesk secretary had been faithfully logging three extra days every week. It turned out that this added up to an awful lot.

All this extra time could be translated into money - a nice pay-off when I left. Or I could add some of it to my regular holiday entitlement.

Yes, please.

That summer Tamsin and I took *Lottie Warren* to Holland for six weeks. The idea was that it was a sort of shake-down cruise. With six weeks, we could really find out what she was like to live aboard.

Also, of course, we could see how we managed together in a small space for an extended time.

I think idyllic is the word that comes first to mind.

Certain moments stick in the memory - like the photographs I have framed around the *Samsara's* cabin as I sit here on a windy February evening with a candle on the table and the charcoal stove banked up for the duration.

I remember Tamsin in a pink bikini running around the deck as we threw buckets of water over each other to cool down (we were moored right next to a restaurant at the time - the diners seemed to like the show).

I remember cycling for miles on the ancient Dutch bicycles with peculiar brakes we bought in Amsterdam - and finding a restaurant serving *mosselen frites* which were so delicious, we made a big effort to compliment the waiter - who promptly brought another huge pot, explaining that tradition demanded there was no limit to a serving of mussels.

I remember spending three days in the Kaag Lakes - a series of interlinked fresh-water lakes right in the middle of The Netherlands. Every day the sun blazed down. Every day we would lie on deck with our books, pausing periodically to dive over the side and swim to a buoy about 50 yards away for exercise.

At one point, Tamsin closed her book, pushed her sunglasses up her nose and said: "You know what would make this perfect? An ice cream."

Immediately, there was the sound of a bell ringing - not the ubiquitous Town Hall chimes which go on all through the night in every Dutch town - but a high-pitched "Ding-Ding" of a handbell - and there, motoring placidly towards us was the ice cream boat flying its ice cream flag from the ensign staff. Perfect.

Yes, we decided we could live together in a small space. In fact, we couldn't wait to get started.

Now that I knew when I was leaving the Standard, we could really make some plans. First of all, I was going to let my flat - that meant it had to be emptied of all personal possessions - clothes, 2,000 books…

Tamsin would be resigning her post as the nurse at Highgate School - and losing the flat that went with it - which had to be emptied of personal possessions, all *her* clothes and 2,000 books (although I think her beloved red silk suit may have gone into the back of her mother's wardrobe.)

This was long before Marie Kondo and her *Magic of Tidying*, so we didn't actually hold up each item and ask ourselves if it "sparked joy". But we did hold up each item and ask ourselves if we could live without it. No contest with the SodaStream or my leather bomber jacket, but we did have a problem with the 4,000 books. Books are heavy, and catamarans sail best if they're kept light. In the end, we packed the books into dozens of banana boxes for the car boot sale.

Writing that makes me appreciate my Kindle – my second (you didn't know you could wear out a Kindle did you? All that tapping the screen to turn the page…)

The boxes of books went into an empty room at the top of the Highgate School Medical Centre - along with our collections of LPs - after the favourites had been transferred to cassette tape. We allowed ourselves a hundred - but then cassette tapes don't weigh much.

Larger and more expensive items ended up in Loot, the free-ads paper. Everything else went into the car boot sale. We did a car boot sale every Sunday morning through the winter (in the summer, we were sailing).

Possibly because it was all in such a very good cause or possibly because anything we did together in those days was a total delight, we actually enjoyed those miserably cold car boot sales with the sleet going sideways and the people who would examine a frying pan as if it was a family heirloom - and then offer a quarter of the price (I used to allow them to haggle me down to half price. Then, without warning, I would start going back up again. Sometimes they didn't notice and followed me up - eventually paying more than the price we'd started at.

After a while, it became a routine: Load the car the night before - everything was already in boxes in the room at the top of the stairs. Then, get up while it was still dark and join the queue outside a vacant lot somewhere in Muswell Hill. The idea of getting there early was to set up before the hordes arrived. It didn't make any difference: Car boot sales attract the most peculiar people. Some of them would climb into the car and start rooting through the boxes as soon as we opened the doors. No amount of polite "Would you mind?" and "Excuse me, can you give us a chance to unload" would have any effect. They would root and scrounge and dig ... and invariably decide our stuff wasn't to their liking and rush off to attack the next car.

Since these were the same people every week, you would think they would learn that the little blue Citroen ZX never had anything they wanted. What did they want? I wish I knew.

Certainly, nobody wanted the SodaStream. But then a SodaStream is one of those features of all car boot sales - like old telephones and cassette players - and, in those days, boxes and boxes of vinyl LPs - how were we to know that in 30 years' time, they would become collector's items?

When things were quiet, we would take turns to wander round the rest of the sale. I picked up a few useful additions to the toolbox - but the idea was to get rid of clutter, not acquire more. That was why I was sometimes disturbed to see Tamsin returning with a plastic bag. But she would say, vaguely: "It's just something for Mum."

She was right up to a point (Tamsin is nothing if not truthful) - although, the whole truth was that she was secretly buying baby clothes which her mother hid away in a bottom drawer.

As lunchtime approached and the crowd began to disperse, we started to pack the display back into its boxes - a lot easier than it had been the previous evening. Heavens, we even had empty boxes left over! That was a good sign.

With the surplus stock back in the room at the top of the stairs, ready for next time, we emptied the takings onto the table and sorted it into bags for the bank - and, of course, calculated the day's profit. Here's the reason this was so important: If we made more than £100, we would go out for lunch - and then take Blue for a long walk on the heath.

You might consider that it was counter-productive to do a car boot sale and then pay for a meal in a restaurant. But, when we established this charming tradition, we were making £300 with no trouble at all. Towards the end - when there was not much more on the folding decorator's table than the wretched SodaStream, lunch was more difficult to justify.

Fortunately, by then, the savings account was looking very healthy. I had sold my suits and ties, the city gentleman's overcoat with the velvet collar which always embarrassed me…

And I moved into Tamsin's flat. It meant I could let mine to a tiny lady from Japanese Airlines who couldn't believe the size of a London mansion flat compared to a Tokyo apartment. More importantly, it meant an end to the continual driving backwards and forwards round the top left-hand section of London's North Circular Road. In two years, we had come to know the North Circular much too well.

To celebrate this event, Tamsin presented with me an "Advent Calendar": A greetings card with the number of days until our departure carefully marked, ready to be crossed off every evening when I came home from work. It looked a bit daunting - rows and rows of little "1's".

So, four days a week, I would put on my one remaining suit and drive into the Evening Standard to serve out my notice. I had about nine months to go. Also, I was in disgrace for not showing the required enthusiasm for the new efficient regime.

No longer did I find myself despatched to the other side of the world at a moment's notice. In fact, I have a feeling I was assigned the least important and most boring stories. However, largely for my own amusement, I did the best I could to make them entertaining, and quite a number of them got into the paper.

In desperation, the newsdesk executive who was in charge of these things put me down for the most menial task on the whole paper - this was to prepare the "News List" – a sort of jump-start device to get the day's news-gathering process into motion. It involved monitoring the morning radio and television bulletins and listing what it was they considered worthy of the nation's attention. At least we had some sort of starting point. Every morning, I typed this up and delivered copies to the newspaper's executives – all the way up to the editor (who always used to look at me for a second longer than necessary and give a little shake of his head).

Of course, what he didn't appreciate - what none of them appreciated - was that I had finished with being the big-shot Foreign Correspondent. I'd been there, done that, got the money belt. I was much more excited about the prospect of reaching the end of the day and getting home to Tamsin, carrying on making plans for the Great Escape.

Sometimes, of course, I couldn't wait. For instance, the Newsdesk needed someone to cover an unremarkable story about a new species of crustacean, which was devastating the delicate eco-balance in the ponds on Hampstead Heath. By the time I had finished with it, the event ranked with final proof of the existence of the Loch Ness monster. The news editor was thrilled. He even agreed to me getting a bit of lunch before returning to the office.

Of course, the nearest place to have lunch was the Highgate

School Medical Centre and what with one thing and another, it was getting on for five o'clock in the afternoon by the time I reappeared at the Evening Standard.

The News Editor was a good friend and a decent man. He really didn't deserve this: Somehow, he had to re-establish his authority. Put simply, he could not have reporters disappearing for the whole afternoon - and also, since I was now so unimportant, what was I doing swanning around with one of the newsroom's two mobile phones (and why had I turned it off?)

They found a new name for me. I became known as the "Rotting Corpse" - or, affectionately, to my friends, "Mr R Corpse". The management decided I was a bad influence. It was time to remove me. I was summoned to see the Managing Editor. The paper was prepared to pay me a lump sum equivalent to the salary covering the remaining four months of my contract. I would leave on December 22nd.

I agreed without a second's thought. The Manager Editor slapped his hand on the desk and cried:" Done!"

Clearly, I should have asked for more.

I went home to Tamsin and, without any particular comment, took down the advent calendar from the kitchen shelf and, as I always did every evening, crossed off one more day of those remaining "1's".

...and then crossed off another... and another...and another...until she said: "What are you doing?"

Then I told her. We weren't going in April at all. We were going on December 22nd. That night we opened real champagne. The fact that December 22nd is the shortest day of the year, somehow being forgotten in all the excitement.

Now the car boot sales went into overdrive. Prices plummeted. Even the SodaStream went (probably straight to somebody else's car boot sale).

And, of course, it was time to sell my old Brother portable typewriter. I did, for a minute or two, consider hiding it away in Tamsin's parents' attic along with the box of photographs and (unbeknown to me, the baby clothes). I opened the lid (repaired with marine epoxy) and looked at the scratches and the paper clip holding the casing together where the little bolt had fallen out. A lot of memories there…

However, I hadn't used it in years - reporters on the road had Tandys by this time - a sort of rudimentary laptop with an LCD screen containing about five lines and powered by endless supplies of AA batteries.

On Lottie Warren, I would be using the very latest laptop with the very latest black-on-white screen. Having written my Dogwatch column for Yachting World, I would print it out on a portable inkjet printer and then find a hotel with a fax machine to send it to the magazine. The magazine would forward a copy to Bill Stott, the cartoonist in Liverpool who never failed to find something funny to illustrate it.

Every three months, I was to write a longer piece about some place we had visited. This was to be called Passing Through and would be illustrated with photographs - 35mm photographs, of course - the film cassettes being sent in by post, naturally.

And this was the time to approach the Daily Telegraph. The editor, Max Hastings, had attempted to recruit me when I had been at the Daily Mail - the interview was at the Reform Club, I remember, and frightfully good for my self-esteem.

Max's problem when he took over the ancient and ailing paper was that its landmark building in Fleet Street was filled with very respected and highly-paid correspondents specialising in all sorts of esoteric backwaters of sport and science and whatnot… or, to be perfectly accurate, the offices weren't actually filled with these people since hardly any of them ever deigned to put in an appearance - at least not until the new and frightening young editor started taking a red pencil through the staff list.

Consequently, although he was very flattering over the Reform's gin and tonic, he wasn't able to offer much more than I was getting from the Mail. David English took great delight in putting the new upstart in his place by awarding me an instant and positively embarrassing pay rise and a new title (titles are a big thing in newspapers). I think I became Senior Correspondent or something. Anyway, I stayed.

But now it was time to go. I telephoned Max's office and said I had an idea for him. Might I come to see him? I didn't mention it, but Tamsin was coming with me - and so was Blue. The three of us arrived at Canary Wharf and came up against the security man: "Is that a guide dog?" he wanted to know. "No dogs except guide dogs allowed on the premises."

"He's got an interview with the editor."

We rode up in the lift. We were shown into the editor's office.

"This is Tamsin Rawlins," I said. "And this is Blue."

"How did you get him in here?" said Max. "I've never been able to get my dogs in here."

We explained what we planned to do. We were going to give up real life. We were going to sail off and live on sunshine and coconuts. It would be the ultimate escape – the sort of thing people dream about but never do. But we would do it - and the readers would be able to come with us … through a column I would write for The Telegraph…

"With the dog," said Max.

"With the dog."

He thought for a moment. He picked up a phone and asked someone on the other end to step into his office for a moment.

Twenty seconds later, a woman in her early 30s entered the room. She was wearing the sort of silk dress that goes with climbing the newspaper career ladder. She also had a beaming smile.

Blue appreciated the gesture and responded appropriately. That is to say that without a moment's hesitation - and before Tamsin or I could do anything to stop him - he jumped up and scraped his claws all the way down the front of the career-ladder-climbing silk dress.

I don't know whether this had anything to do with what happened next. The Travel Editor - as she was introduced - stopped smiling and explained that she had plenty of copy about sunshine and coconuts. What she was really short of was stuff about Britain. Would we consider starting the adventure with a trip round the UK instead?

We walked out with a deal for a monthly column together with a big "scene-setter" piece - and, of course, photographs to be paid extra.

Sitting afterwards over a very expensive lunch in a restaurant overlooking the Thames, it occurred to me that this was the dream come true: I would be going sailing, having adventures and writing about them.

The only difference between the new reality and the dream of the eleven-year-old boy was that I would not be alone.

But I could live with that. I could live with that very happily...

Chapter 11
Away

The room at the top of the stairs - once crammed with cardboard boxes (surmounted by the wretched SodaStream) was now empty. The last couple of banana crates full of paperbacks were in the Evening Standard's office in Kensington High Street - on the empty desk beside my own so that people could help themselves. In fact, they would flip through the titles before putting them back and ask (since this had been the real reason for stopping by): "You're not really going, are you? You mean, you just resigning?"

They thought I was mad. But at the same time, there was a distinct undercurrent of envy. I just breezed through it all. In my head, I had a ring-bound notebook with a page of poverty. Any time I liked, I could watch it blowing away in the wind. Something would turn up.

In the meantime, I brought in a big box of bottles to sit beside the books - all the peculiar liqueurs I had collected on my travels and which turned out not to travel well (most of them tasted like cough mixture). They proved rather more popular than the paperbacks.

We organised a farewell party and invited the sort of people we would have invited to our wedding if we were getting married. There is a photograph taken that night in front of me now as I sit in *Samsara's* cabin writing this: I look rather drunk, and Tamsin is gazing at me adoringly. It was a great night.

A few days later, I delivered the car back to the company garage, turned in my security pass and went to empty the last few items from my desk into the wastepaper basket. That was when I opened the second drawer. I had forgotten about this one. This was where I stored my old notebooks - all stacked in date order with the stories contained in them written neatly under the date. It was like the day the Head Librarian had delivered my "Corres" file - a whole life's work in the bin - well, the last three years, anyway. I found another bin for the overflow.

And then, on the morning of December 23rd 1994, Tamsin's friend Jan (the one who had helped sort the replies to the Lonely Hearts ad) came round with her leaving present: a day's rental of the biggest estate car she could find. We packed everything into it. Bearing in mind that for the preceding months, we had been gradually transferring everything we could down to *Lottie Warren* specifically in order to make this day easier, it was surprising to see how much you can get into a big estate car. I was the master car-packer, after all. Hadn't I served my apprenticeship with all those car boot sales?

Except this was no Sunday morning with the promise of lunch at Bella Pasta (the Standard was still doing its two-for-one voucher promotion and these were the days when Bella Pasta was much smaller and infinitely better). Also, this was for the rest of our lives. In the end, I had the dog on my lap. Tamsin was buried under a pile of all the open packets from the kitchen cupboards (well, she did insist on taking them).

We stacked it all in the cockpit under the canvas cover, and that night, as Jan drove back to London in the dark, we fired up the two fan heaters, opened a bottle of fizz and toasted our new life. Whatever lay ahead, we had done it now.

And so the new life began.

To escape on your own boat. To never have to get up to an alarm clock again in order to catch the train to work. Never again - come to that - to have to do anything if you don't want to; it's a dream for a lot of people. Just look at the adverts for pension providers showing silver-haired couples, their bare feet dangling over the side of a gleaming yacht, skipping along under a blue sky…

The reality is not always like that. We knew because we had read the warnings in all the books. When there is nothing that you have to do, it is necessary to find things you choose to do - even if you don't particularly want to do them…

This may sound like defeating the object of the exercise, but there are plenty of boats for sale in marinas around the Mediterranean because their owners just got bored. There are only so many beers you can drink in waterside bars. It can be tiresome having to escape the midday heat under an awning strung over the boom…

And Tamsin, being an organised person, had been working on this. For instance, every day, we would walk for two hours - we had a long-legged dog, after all. And here's the thing: We would walk for two hours even if it was raining. You have no idea how good it is to get back to a small boat, hang up the foul-weather gear in the cockpit and snuggle down in a superheated cabin with coffee and fruit cake.

Every evening we listened to the Archers. We had no television, and the intrinsically British radio serial about the everyday life of country folk in the imaginary village of Ambridge was something we could "get into". It would give a focus to the day, something to look forward to - something to talk about.

The fact that neither of us had ever listened to the Archers - and indeed had no idea who was who, might seem like a problem. But Tamsin's mother was a lifelong fan and had written a one-page crib sheet (Jill Archer: Matriarch, wife to Phil, mother to Shula and

Kenton...etc.)

Every evening after the seven o'clock news, we would sit opposite each other at the table, passing that sheet of paper between us as we caught up with a lifetime of something we never knew we had been missing.

After dinner, we played Scrabble. Tamsin was a big-league Scrabble player - she competed in National competitions, and we had a proper board with tiles that clicked into little slots and a swivel on the bottom so you could spin it round. We consulted the Official Book of Scrabble Words for things like *katti* (an Asian unit of weight) and *dacoit* (an Indian criminal) - but not the two-letter words like *ai* and *ba,* which every Scrabble player worth their salt knows are a three-toed sloth and a mythical Egyptian spirit. We even had a chess clock. In all the years that we played, I won only once.

We had the box of cassette tapes (home recorded from the CD collection because not only was it cheaper, but you could get more on them that way). And of course, we had books.

We were two months into the new life - first in Titchmarsh Marina at Walton, stowing everything from those cardboard boxes, and then in Woodbridge, tucked up in the mud under the Tide Mill - when Malcolm and Pixie came to see how we were getting on.

Malcolm was an Essex GP. Pixie was the practice nurse. I knew them from the Azores and Back race. They harboured the same ambition to sell up and sail.

It turned out that in the days after the leaving party in London, Pixie had started wondering why they had to wait until they retired. They had a large house with a beautiful garden in the Essex countryside. They had a business they could sell (the practice). Why did they have to wait?

Tamsin got out her biggest saucepan. I found a bottle of wine in the bilges that had a proper cork rather than a plastic cap. Lunch lasted until dusk fell outside the cabin windows, and we progressed to tea and cake. By the end of the day, they had decided they were going too.

And they did. In a Rival 41 (*Samsara's* big sister*)*, they crossed the Atlantic and spent three years in the Caribbean (dodging the hurricane season by nipping down to Venezuela) - and they discovered that it wasn't all sunshine and coconuts: Malcolm spent too much time sitting in waterfront bars, moaning about the Health Service with all the other retired doctors. Pixie sat under an awning with the wives and discussed how much they missed the grandchildren. In the end, they never did go through the Panama Canal and into the Pacific. Instead, they sold the boat and bought a flat in Scotland - to be near their daughter...

Mind you, it wasn't what we expected either. The first sign of this was a 2lb packet of sugar flying out of the aft cabin and exploding in the galley, followed by a volley of curses. Tamsin had discovered that the contents of her Highgate kitchen cabinets did not fare well in the damp atmosphere of the dog's cabin – I blamed all that dog breath.

I had tried to tell her that she should leave all this stuff behind - the boat was well stocked with victuals, and we had nowhere to put it. If we could have sold it at car boot sales, we would have done so. Alternatively, she could have distributed it among her colleagues - or the next school nurse would have appreciated it ... or, I could have put it on the empty desk at the office with the books and bottles...

But something I had not appreciated about Tamsin was that, although she had forced herself to sell all her possessions, she could not abide waste - for that's what leaving it behind would have amounted to. Tamsin, it turned out, was a closet hoarder. This would rear its head again later - much later.

Meanwhile, we began to settle into the liveaboard community. Woodbridge is a small market town eight miles up the River Deben. Frequently, it features in those newspaper surveys of the

"Best Places to Live". Apart from anything else, it has the Tide Mill. Waking up to see it out of the cabin window every day, with its Dutch-style roof and white-painted shiplap walls, I came to the conclusion that it was the most beautiful building in the world. It was the sort of natural shape that gave the early morning heart a lift - like seeing the Matterhorn from the *Casa di Diavolo*.

Other people thought the same. On one side, we had Dennis and Jane and their daughter Erika in a big steel motorboat which never moved. On the other, a mysterious old man living on a converted lifeboat called *Trimillia* - so called because she had rescued 3,000 men from the beaches of Dunkirk, ferrying them out to the ships anchored offshore. When the old man died, it was discovered that the boat was almost sinking under the weight of empty wine bottles and old racing papers - apparently, he had been a successful gambler in his time. At his funeral, three mystery women sat at the back - none of whom appeared to know about the other two.

Beyond Trimillia were Phil and Lil in an old RAF Air-Sea Rescue cutter. He was a brilliant jazz guitarist, having converted seamlessly from the trombone when he lost his front teeth. She was a marine biologist and lived with her work.

These people welcomed us (with the exception of the reclusive gambler) into their floating community, and the liveaboard lifestyle started living up to its promise.

Much of this was down to Tamsin - and this is one of the things I loved so much about her. She was so enthusiastic about everything: We would learn to dance, she decided after seeing a postcard advertising dance classes in the local shop. We went to a session. It turned out to be sequence dancing in the community hall - everyone else was over 70. We joined the choir (another mistake - at least on my part). We were first in the queue when the W.I. market opened its doors on a Thursday morning, and we changed our clothes to disguise ourselves when the supermarket imposed a "six bottles per person" rule for their 99p Bulgarian wine offer.

Finding copy for the Telegraph and Yachting World columns gave everything a purpose and, come to that, an excuse to introduce ourselves to interesting-looking strangers.

There was another side to it, of course - the dark side: the blazing row about whose fault it was when the "circular walk" ended with us tramping for miles in driving rain in the wrong direction down the hard shoulder of the A12.

And things didn't necessarily improve when spring came, and we untangled the web of mooring lines and anchors and set off on The Adventure.

This started with walking round Mersea Island. If you go back through the Telegraph cuttings, you will have the impression that this was another perfect day - oysters for lunch from The Company Shed. Wangling a bottle of chilled white wine out of the Yacht Club…

There is no mention of returning to find Lottie Warren high and dry on the mud - she had swung out of the channel when the tide turned.

I had this idea that you can run through mud. If you run fast enough, you don't sink. I'm not sure there is any truth in it, but I seemed sure enough to convince Tamsin. She would run on her own, and I would run towing Blue in the dinghy (we had seen Blue run through mud, and it always ended badly). Obviously, we would have to take off our shoes, otherwise we would lose them with the first stride.

This meant that Tamsin would have to accept the sensation of mud between her toes - which seemed perfectly reasonable to me but absolutely the worst thing in the world, according to Tamsin - who was, by this time, beyond the point of no return.

Pyefleet Creek is one of the more isolated parts of Essex, but I suspect her screams could be heard in Colchester.

Blue, meanwhile, was only too keen to feel the mud between his toes and jumped out of the dinghy within the first five yards, floundering for the boat with me chasing after him, trying not to let go of the dinghy.

When we arrived, all three of us were a sort of grey/blue colour from head to toe. I think we managed to laugh about it. Besides, it was worth it for the oysters.

And so, we progressed, stopping anywhere that looked interesting, giving ourselves every opportunity for adventure - or at least, readable copy.

I think that was how we managed to clean up at the pub quiz in North Fambridge. We won £5 prize on a tie-break (what do they call the Paris stock exchange - *La Bourse)*. It was only then that we discovered that, as winners, we were expected to set the questions for next week.

We were due to leave on the early morning tide for the passage inside Foulness Island. We sat up long into the night with the dictionary, compiling the questions. I remember one of them: What is the smallest number of people who may legally constitute a riot? (Three). We posted them through the pub letter box first thing in the morning. I still wonder how they got on with it.

The fiver was particularly welcome - after all, we were on a budget. This was not the poverty scenario I had been dreading. This was a carefully managed, modest lifestyle. We had five small incomes - two from Yachting World, one from the Daily Telegraph, the balance of Miss Japanese Airlines' rent after paying the mortgage and service charge – and we had *Going to Boarding School.*

Tamsin started her school nursing career with two years at Summer Fields, a traditional British prep school near Oxford - although, thankfully, not nearly as traditional as West Downs.

All the same, the new boys were plucked from their loving homes at just eight years old and thrown into what must have seemed to them a frightening world of timetables and bells and unsympathetic older boys.

Reminiscing about this one day, Tamsin recalled that some parents had asked if she could recommend a book they could give their sons to prepare them for this new world. It appeared there was no such book.

We decided we would write one - she would provide the words, and I would illustrate it (I had once taken a correspondence course in drawing cartoons). No, we would not approach a publisher with it - publishers take most of the money. Instead, we would sell it by mail order through the schools. All schools send a sheaf of advisory notes to the parents of new boys - the clothes list, where name tapes should be attached, the boy's school number, etc. All it would need was a paragraph recommending the book.

The reasoning went like this: The little chap's mother was suffering enough guilt about sending him away in the first place. She would hardly baulk at another £5.99 for something that might make the wrench a little less terrible - at least, not when you consider the thousands of pounds being blown on the fees…

We found a printer and Going to Boarding School, a tiny paperback (blazer pocket-sized) arrived in several cardboard boxes. We sent a copy to every prep school in the country. We touted it round the stalls at the annual Independent Schools Fair.

It sold surprisingly well. I would like to say it is still for sale – we have a few copies even now. However, it is hopelessly out of date in a world of mobile phones, emails and family WhatsApp groups.

In theory, we should have been able to survive on these "multiple streams of income" - although "survival" does not normally include meals in restaurants, something we liked so much that it really should have counted as a necessity. So, as well as Tamsin's carefully-catalogued accounts (every penny spent went down in her book), there was also the "treat fund". Any extra income we could get from whatever source went into the "treat fund" - and the prospect of sitting opposite each other over a red checked tablecloth with a candle in the middle made finding other sources of income very compelling indeed.

First, there were photographs. I had invested in a decent Pentax autofocus and wore it in a huge pouch on my belt like a six-shooter. One good-sized photograph in the Telegraph could pay for two lunches all on its own. Meanwhile, a £100 premium bond would set us up for a month.

And then there was the totally unexpected: We arrived in Brightlingsea to find a small freighter aground against the quay and the whole town embroiled in protests about it being loaded with live calves for export. There were people lying down in front of lorries and policemen losing their helmets - not at all the sort of thing you expect to see in Brightlingsea. Yet nobody else seemed to know anything about it. This was news.

I phoned the Evening Standard. It was just like old times - except suddenly, I was a freelance journalist stumbling on a story - or, to put it another way: Someone with a penchant for *excitement* who had been smacked over the head with it.

In fact, I made it sound so exciting the Standard despatched a staff reporter - our old friend Tom Leonard. He came for dinner and stayed aboard ... and ended up in terrible trouble for not checking in with the newsdesk - there being no mobile signal in the middle of Brightlingsea Harbour. Still, he seemed to get over it. Tom is now the New York correspondent of the Daily Mail.

As for me: I knew I'd done the right thing. No newsdesk executive would ever again be able to bawl me out...

This constant (if relaxed) search for something to write about worked brilliantly. It gave us a focus - something to do besides sitting in waterfront bars drinking beer ... which we couldn't afford to do anyway).

It meant that in Rye, we had an excuse to go and knock on the decks of interesting boats and ask people if they wanted to be interviewed - and of course, they did. This was not like tramping the streets of some industrial town in the dark and the rain, looking for the last corner of the vicar's love triangle. We found the new owners of Arthur Ransome's *Nancy Blackett,* and we found The Man Who Was Building The Ark.

That's what it amounted to - a massive skeleton of teak frames standing high on the saltings above the River Rother. From time to time, the man would come with his toolbox and do a bit of hammering. He had a lot of hammering to do - the thing was 80 feet long. Wisely, he had not appointed a timescale to the project. For all I know, he is still there, hammering.

And then, of course, there was the dog. By now, we had become used to people on shore exclaiming: "Oh look, there's a dog!" as if it was the most extraordinary sight - and I soon discovered that you could breathe life into any story simply by adding the dog.

Mind you, it took the customs man on the quay at Rye to prompt my only bit of fan mail. It was the wine that caused the trouble (I know, it usually does). But it wasn't the drinking of it that was the beginning of the downward spiral. It was the buying.

We had reached Dover - only 22 miles from Calais where you could get some really decent Corbiers for 99p a bottle (not the Bulgarian stuff - and with a real cork). The only problem was Blue. I don't know whether dogs could have passports in those days - anyway, he didn't - which meant that if he went to France, he couldn't come back without going into quarantine.

We were discussing this with the young man in the marina office when he came up with a brilliant solution. He would look after Blue for a couple of days while we nipped over to refill the bilges… he would love to…

And so, he did. We had two days in Calais, a few meals thanks to the treat fund and stocked up on enough wine and cheese to sink a lesser vessel.

Blue was delighted to see us on our return. It had all been a great success.

Until we arrived in Rye. Here is what I wrote from Rye:

> The Animal Health Inspector chose his words with all the care of an Old Bailey judge in the days when they still kept a black cap under the bench.
>
> "What we are talking about," he said, "is six months quarantine. We are talking about having the dog destroyed."
>
> Admittedly, the dog was not helping much. Ever since Lottie Warren sailed up the river to Rye, Blue had been looking forward to his run ashore. The Romney Marsh is home to 20 percent of the entire English sheep population, and there is still something in his rather complicated genes which tells him lambs just want to have fun.
>
> So, when the Animal Health Inspector came and enquired about the dog aboard the vessel, Blue hopped onto the quay, wagged his tail and sniffed the visitor appreciatively.
>
> The Animal Health Inspector's face registered alarm: "Please, the dog must not come ashore until I have verified the facts."
>
> Oh, very well. I called softly, and Blue sauntered back by way of a small boy carrying an ice cream at dog level. The Inspector swallowed hard.
>
> These were the anti-rabies regulations in full force, but we never expected to meet them head-on in Rye, a lovely little town immortalised as "Tilling" in the Lucia novels by E.F. Benson. From these

books, we knew it as an "ancient and enlightened town", and Tamsin had been reading hard in preparation.

So hard, in fact, that she had acquired something of the personality of Lucia herself, whose relations with petty officialdom bring to mind the phrase "withering scorn".

It was all my fault, really. I was the one who had filled in the harbourmaster's form about an animal aboard - and then mentioned by way of conversation that, from Dover, we had made a quick trip across the Channel to fill up with wine and had left the dog with the kindly man in the marina office. His own dog had died last year, I explained, and he had been reduced to going round to his mother's to play with hers.

None of which the Animal Health Inspector believed for a moment. The dog, he ordered, was to be confined to the vessel while he went off to telephone for verification.

This was becoming needlessly complicated. The harbourmaster's form had never even asked if we had been to the Continent with or without a dog. If I hadn't mentioned it, nobody would have been any the wiser – and besides, if we were going to lie about it, surely the first lie would be to say we had never been out of the country.

Meanwhile, the best of the day was being wasted. Quite apart from any walking, we would soon be too late to book a table for dinner at the Landgate Bistro.

So, when the Inspector returned and said that he had been unable to contact anyone and now required the animal to be confined below decks until further notice, there occurred what the court might describe as "an altercation". We refused. The dog needed a walk, and he was going to get a walk. He had broken no law. He was a free dog.

"Are you aware of the anti-rabies regulations?" demanded the Inspector.

Of course, we were. Why did he think we had left the animal in Dover?

It was at this point that Lucia entered the fray and called the Inspector: "You Stupid Man".

"Six months quarantine," replied the man. "The dog destroyed," he added for extra menace.

"Only if you can prove he's been abroad," I retorted.

At this point, a salient fact emerged: It appeared that the man - stupid or otherwise - had tried only one of the two phone numbers we had given him to verify my story. But we will never know how this might have influenced events because, at that moment, the dog decided to reassert his starring role in the drama. Seeing the Inspector about to walk off in the direction of the phone box - or possibly, the sheep-filled fields of Sussex - Blue jumped back onto the quay.

Or, at least, he jumped halfway. The Inspector caught him in a sort of headlock just as his back paws left the boat - but before the front ones connected with the quay.

The result was something like a Tom & Jerry cartoon where the dog remains suspended in mid-air, all four feet scrabbling at nothingness, and there is an agonising second or two when you know he is going to drop off the bottom of the screen.

That was not quite what happened in this instance. Instead, Tamsin leapt to the rescue and gave a final push which should have enabled Blue to scramble to safety. However, the Inspector, his mind still reeling with images of anti-rabies posters, pushed the other way. The fact that the dog did not end up in the water can only be ascribed to his powers of levitation.

After this, Tamsin had to stand outside the bistro and calm herself by reading aloud about leek and Roquefort tarte and steamed fillet of wild salmon with chive hollandaise.

She was still there when the Inspector returned, having finally verified what we had been telling him all along. With monumental awkwardness and mumbled assurances that we could each see the other's point of view, we shook hands. I am sure it made us both proud to be British.

* * *

I was rather pleased with that one, but I didn't expect the letter that arrived with the next bundle of post from our mail-forwarding service:

> To: Mr Charles Moore, Editor, Daily Telegraph
>
> Dear Sir,
>
> Please give John Passmore The Earth! Nothing, <u>nothing</u>, so convulsively funny has come my way since Gerard Hoffnung's Hod of Bricks and French Widow. Still - hours later - I have to sit down - or stand up -_rather suddenly after another serious attack.

I am, yours faithfully,

Betty Gibbs (Miss), Tunbridge Wells.

(Oh, the pleasure there is to be had in satisfying the **Desire for Approval**).

Chapter 12
Babies

Remember that first day on Hampstead Heath when Tamsin said innocently: "Did you ever think you'd like to have more children?"

And I said: "God, I'm not having any more!"

...and everything went a bit quiet.

Well, it didn't stay quiet. OK, so we all knew this was going to come up again - you picked up on the secret baby clothes-buying expeditions at the car boot sales? Obviously, this was going to come up again.

In fact, it came up at about the same time as I started thinking that my dream of living on a boat and sailing the world writing about it might become a partnership rather than a solo event - after all, why go on your own when there's a beautiful girl who loves you and wants to come too…

It was at about this time that friends started giving me knowing looks - and I overheard my father telling a family friend: "John's been caught".

I didn't see it like that. I thought I was the luckiest guy in the world. I wasn't going to be one of those sad old singlehanders. I knew all about them. Growing up on my parents' boats, I had been indoctrinated in the dangers of inviting a singlehander aboard - they drank all your gin and didn't leave until you heaved them over the side. If they were lucky, they landed in their dinghy - to row off into the darkness, still talking…

That first summer aboard *Largo*, cruising Brittany and the West Country, Tamsin and I had several "Baby Talks". To begin with, these ended inconclusively. But, of course, bit by bit, the balance began to shift. Anyone who knows anything about relationship dynamics will tell you something has to give. If it keeps on snowing, you're going to get an avalanche.

Also, as we know: **An adult with ADHD often has trouble in relationships, whether they are professional, romantic, or platonic. The traits of talking over people in conversation, inattentiveness, and being easily bored can be draining on relationships, as a person can come across as insensitive, irresponsible, or uncaring.**

Or, to put it another way, they get bored and agree to anything.

No, that's not true. Imagine what the children would say if they thought they were only here because their father got bored…

Or was I **saying "Yes" to requests because of a desire for approval?"**

Actually, I'll tell you what it was: It was the knowledge - even without the proper emotional understanding that everyone else seems to take for granted - that the surest way to make a woman unhappy is to tell her she can't have babies.

And I just couldn't bear the thought of making Tamsin unhappy.

So, it was agreed. We would have two babies - two little girls (how naive was this!) Girls, because I had two boys already and little girls sit and play quietly in the confined space of a small cabin.

Baby number one was going to be a "Millennium Baby". That is to say, she would be born in the year 2000 after we had crossed the Atlantic and explored the Caribbean.

Remember, we were making these plans in the early 90s - the year 2000 was so far off nobody had even thought about the

Millennium Bug, let alone the Millennium Baby.

As we now know, Tamsin and I moved aboard at the end of 1994. Six months later, we were wandering around Brighton Marina putting together a "Passing Through" column for Yachting World and were intrigued to discover that the pontoons of this fashionable marina development yielded a complete liveaboard community. Given the price of property in Brighton with its cosmopolitan vibe and excellent rail service to London, a lot of people opted to live on a boat instead - from the university lecturer sharing a tiny Folkboat with so much junk that he kept his defunct outboard in his bunk - to the couple finding they had so much room on a 38footer that they even had … wait for it … *a baby!*

"You see," said Tamsin, in the sort of studied matter-of-fact tones you expect from someone engaged in nothing more significant than journalistic research, "a baby on a boat is no trouble at all..."

I think I went a bit quiet.

And then we arrived in Hamble to meet up with the Packs - after all, they had been so instrumental in our getting away in the first place - and particularly, in a catamaran. Geoff and Lou-Lou took us to their children's school fete. They had four children - the youngest, Tilly, hardly more than a toddler.

The Brighton baby in Tamsin's mind's eye was now doing finger-painting at the chart table…

I, of course, was completely oblivious to what was going on. I was talking boats with Geoff - rolling down the trades with dolphins playing under the bow…

And so, a few weeks later, we ended up on the beach in Jersey, making the big decision. Was this planned? I don't think so - but what do I know…

Lottie Warren was sitting on the sand at St Aubin. This is the tiny drying harbour at the western end of the enormous St Aubin's Bay - at the eastern end is St Helier with its expensive marina and

Michelin-starred restaurants.

Not that expense kept us out. We had the treat fund. We walked back on that mid-summer evening well content and with the sun sinking ahead of us, turning the water and the sand into a lake of liquid gold.

Hand-in-hand, we splashed barefoot through the shallows.

"So, what do you think?" said Tamsin.

"About what?"

"*You know!*"

Honestly, I didn't. How can someone think of the same thing for all that time? I had thought a million different thoughts since then (why was the engine pinking? Would it be worth getting a longer endless line made up for the genoa - and, anyway, how could you make an endless line longer - it was endless, surely...)

"Well?"

Well, look at it this way: We were happy. We had managed to do something that a whole lot of people told us was impossible. We were making it work. And, as I said, we were happy - yes, we were definitely happy. The money was coming in - and that had been what worried me, mostly. Something always seemed to turn up...

"Yeah, come on." I found myself saying. "Why not now? Let's have a baby."

What was that about **continually starting new tasks before finishing old ones?**

And, besides, there are some women who are just made for having babies - and there is nothing, absolutely nothing, that makes them happier than doing just that.

And, of course, if Tamsin was happy, I was happy.

At this point in our adventure, everything came together in a sort of cornucopia of delights. The weather was perfect, strangers wrote in saying how much they admired us - Country Life sent a photographer for a feature they were writing about dogs on boats.

They paid us for the privilege, and it is still one of my favourite pictures - posed on the foredeck with Blue in his lifejacket and me pointing at the horizon (and Tamsin looking in a different direction because, actually, I wasn't pointing at anything at all, just following the photographer's direction…)

Maybe it just represents that moment when everything was perfect.

You see, the trouble with perfection is that you can't improve on it - and as soon as you make any changes - any changes at all - then life becomes less than perfect.

Of course, the secret to happiness is to change with those changing circumstances - to allow the new experiences to create a new sense of perfection…

All you need to do is change your thinking. I knew all about this - after all, I had Ultimate Power! I threw myself into the excitement of having a baby as if I was the first man ever to have a baby. Tamsin, of course, needed no encouragement.

Then, one morning in Plymouth, I woke up to find myself alone and the dinghy gone. Sometime later, Tamsin reappeared. She had been ashore to the chemist to buy a pregnancy test. The somewhat premature "Millennium Baby" became the number-one topic of conversation - the top priority.

Of course, this was never going to be a normal pregnancy. For one thing, we kept moving. This meant that Tamsin had to keep her medical notes with her - and take them to a new doctor wherever we happened to be when the time came for her next check-up.

Also, as anyone who has ever had a baby will be aware, there is a "home visit" to ensure the facilities are adequate for the new arrival. With us, this was no foregone conclusion.

Gradually we began to acquire more and more absolutely essential equipment - a baby bath (it just fitted in the bow locker on top of the water tank). A crib? We would do without one (we had a book advocating that newborn babies should be held by their parents all the time and sleep in bed with them.) We could manage that. Anyway, we had nowhere to put a cot.

At this point, I can imagine all those parents of small babies reading this and shaking their heads.

How about all the books and magazines and Planning the Birth? How about a water birth - doesn't that sound great? And don't forget to choose your music - most important that Baby pops out to something appropriate. Motorhead could cause serious psychological damage...

As a venue for the Great Event, we chose North Wales - there was a brand new hospital at Bodelwyddan, and wouldn't that look good as a "Place of Birth" on the passport? These things are important considerations - they're going to follow you through life. Besides, Tamsin was half-Welsh. Everybody we met seemed to be a relation of some sort.

The baby was going to be called Poppy (Pretty Poppy Passmore from Paddington Green) until the scan insisted she was a boy, so she became Charlie ... until we started thinking of the number of Americans we would meet on our travels and the way they would call him "Chuck". Anyway, he was going to be a Welshman. He should have a Welsh name. Instead of Charlie, he would be Owen. It was all going swimmingly well. Tamsin outgrew her foul-weather trousers. The readers of Yachting Monthly and the Daily Telegraph were informed of the forthcoming arrival of the small crew - indeed, the small crew took over from the dog as the standard source of copy.

And then, on Tamsin's birthday, when we had just bought some fresh trout for dinner, the doctor paused in the weekly check-up and looked across at the patient and said matter-of-factly: "You must go to hospital immediately. Do not go home. Do not collect any clothes. Take a taxi immediately. Or should I call an ambulance?"

Hold on, what was happening here? What about all our careful plans? It takes time to organise a water birth… what about the fresh trout?

This was a case of something called pre-eclampsia – about which I knew nothing at all but which is, apparently, very dangerous. You can be dead from preeclampsia in no time - mother and baby, both…

So, Tamsin spent her birthday and the following three days hooked up to all sorts of monitors in Glan Clwyd Hospital while I whizzed *Lottie Warren* through the Menai Strait to Conwy as fast as I could and skittered backwards and forwards on buses, walking Blue up Conwy mountain in the morning and sitting beside Tamsin's hospital bed in the afternoon muttering platitudes while wondering where everything had gone wrong.

And then, three days later, Tamsin's battery of monitors started spewing out all the wrong numbers, and somebody said: "That baby has to come out now!" and Tamsin said, "But he's not due for another five weeks!"

Naturally, nobody took any notice of the patient and just loaded her onto a trolley and pushed her at a run in the direction of the operating theatre. She remembers it as being like something out of *Casualty* - all banging swing doors and people thrusting pieces of paper in front of her to sign. "Where's John? Where's John?" she cried.

Actually, John was leaning against a bus stop reading a book.

I was resigned to this - after all, I was going to spend the next five weeks doing it. Blue had been walked up the mountain and down the mountain again. I had a rucksack with the inevitable items hospital patients demand when they have nothing to do but think of things they can't do without. The fact that there was no mobile phone signal at the bus stop was not something that I considered for a moment. In those days, most places didn't have a mobile phone signal – Wales even more so. I could wait. Tamsin wasn't going anywhere.

When it became clear that I had not just missed the bus, but I had missed the next one as well (there was supposed to be one an hour) it occurred to me that the thoughtful thing to do was to phone and leave a message. I had been delayed. The fact that I had to come to the conclusion that this was the thoughtful thing to do rather than just doing it in the first place, I now recognise as **coming across as insensitive, irresponsible, or uncaring.**

So, in the middle of Owen's birth by Cesarian section, at a time when I should have been at Tamsin's side, holding her hand and telling her everything was going to be all right, I was actually walking about on top of the hill next to the bus stop looking for a fleeting LCD bar on my phone. When, finally, I could get through to the ward, a breathless nurse told me: "We've been trying to get hold of you. She's gone to theatre."

I remember wondering why she had gone to the theatre. We thought twice about the cost of cinema tickets.

Here's where journalism training comes in: If you have to be somewhere *now,* you get there by any means available. On this occasion, it involved running into the middle of the road and holding up my hands - and asking the first car that stopped: "Can you take me to the hospital? It's an emergency."

The man behind the wheel was brilliant - and I hope he reads this: He had a newborn baby at home. He knew not just how to get to the hospital in double quick time - but how to navigate the usual labyrinth of car parks and ambulance lanes to get right to the front door of the maternity unit.

They took me straight to the Special Care Baby Unit - Tamsin was still being stitched up - and there they presented me with our son. I had never seen such a small baby before. Owen weighed just 4lb 2oz (1.87kg). They gave him the smallest baby clothes they had on the unit – and they were still two sizes too large. But he was perfect.

The experience was not so good for Tamsin. Owen was in the Special Care Baby Unit and couldn't leave it to see her. She was in the post-op ward and couldn't be moved to see him. Two days later, it was Mother's Day, and the hospital sent her a card with a polaroid photograph of her baby. She burst into tears.

I wanted to run into the middle of the corridor with my hands up and stop the nearest porter and say: "Take this mother to see her baby. It's an emergency." But you can't do that when everyone's being really kind and understanding - just not understanding enough…

Eventually, somebody stopped saying: "We're really busy" and said: "Don't worry. We'll find a way…"

And so, they moved Tamsin, with a good deal of wincing, into a wheelchair, and we took her up to see her little boy.

From then on, everything changed once more. If The Baby had been the main priority before, now he was the only priority. I bought a car - an ancient Mini Metro which smelled suspiciously of petrol and over the following three weeks, we lived at the hospital.

Really: Glan Clwyd Hospital had a wonderful innovation called *Ty Coeso,* which is the Welsh for "Welcome House". This was a bit like student accommodation but for the parents of sick children - and as soon as Tamsin was discharged from the maternity ward, we moved in there (and Blue moved into the car).

Gradually, day by day, gram by gram, little Owen grew. We doted on him, of course - the whole hospital doted on him. It was a terrible shock when a new premature baby was born - and usurped his position as everyone's darling.

After five weeks, we took him home to the marina - where, of course, he was considered even more special: Not just a tiny baby - but a tiny baby on a boat!

And, just as we had promised ourselves, there was nothing to it. We cradled him in our arms, carried him around in a sling, and at night, he slept between us and fell asleep sucking the end of my nose (which I found quite the most delightful sensation).

Family and friends came to visit and cooed over him. The health visitor clambered over the rail to declare his welfare up to standard - and I fitted special fastenings into the cockpit for his car seat. By the time he was two months old, we were ready to move on.

I found that I had become a bit more cautious about the weather - which is how we came to be stuck in Fleetwood for two weeks waiting for a free wind for the Isle of Man. Nevertheless, Owen proved himself a sailor - he was the only one who wasn't sick crossing the Irish Sea.

And so, we progressed - slowly, carefully - but at every stop, being celebrated by everyone we met - the whole world was captivated by the miraculous, tiny baby. It was only later that I realised all parents believe this to be the case.

Admittedly, this was when he was too tiny to make much noise - just a cute little mewing sound. By the time we reached North East Scotland, Baby Owen had developed the strength to cry lustily - a charming phrase which completely fails to convey the sheer horror of having a baby who cries throughout every waking moment.

Lunches on the Treat Fund were no longer the two-hour affairs we were used to. Instead, they became a race to finish before he woke up – although there was one in Fort William which involved us eating by turns - the other pushing Baby Owen up and down the towpath while he screamed relentlessly and people turned and frowned.

In Buckie, we entered him in a baby show (do they still have baby shows?) How we imagined this scrawny little premature mite was going to win a bonny bouncing baby show, I can't imagine.

But Tamsin, in particular, was terribly disappointed and had to be dissuaded from lodging a complaint with the judges.

Something else that we hadn't expected: I wasn't enough for Tamsin anymore. Not in her new role as a young mother. Suddenly - unexpectedly - she craved the company of other young mothers. When we arrived in Edinburgh, we would take the bus every day into the city centre, where mother and baby would disappear into the baby-changing facilities at Boots the Chemists - leaving me outside to inspect the 101 different cures for colic. Sometimes, they would be in there for an hour.

I asked why so long? Tamsin, it seems, had got talking to some other young mother - and carried on talking. In an hour, they would have swapped entire life stories. I have always marvelled at the way my mother-in-law can do this: meeting someone new and immediately questioning them about every member of their family - their names, where they live, who they had married, the names of *their* children…

The first time I witnessed this, I was amazed. After all, I had spent a lifetime interviewing people or - to put it another way - persuading people to tell me things they really should have kept to themselves. Why would anyone want to tell Tamsin's Mum - and, come to that, why would she want to know…

But, of course, that is to ignore the fact that not everyone is **self-centred and easily bored**.

You can see where this is going. We needed to make some changes. I was up for this – after all, it sounded just the thing for someone who **constantly scans the environment for more stimulation.**

The first change was to recognise that Blue had been downgraded to "bottom dog". He wasn't getting the attention and exercise he deserved - but we had some new friends who could offer him a home in his retirement: The Braithwaites had written to us as soon as they read the first piece in the Telegraph and found that our stories were uncannily similar: they had a Heavenly Twins catamaran. They had given up their high-powered jobs in London to escape to a better life. We should go and see them when we pass through Argyll. We stayed for a week.

Now, we asked if they would like Blue as a companion for their ageing Labrador, Julie. Sure enough, he jumped into the back of Chris's truck without a backward glance. He spent the rest of his life herding the family's pet sheep and proved a most devoted guide dog when Julie went blind.

But there was more to the changes than that. Summer was coming to an end, and Tamsin needed a break. She went home to her parents while I delivered *Lottie Warren* down the east coast in two giant leaps. I think we were both mightily relieved to get back to what we each considered to be real life. Maybe this was a glimpse of the future…

The little family re-joined me in Lowestoft, and we hopped down to Southwold.

If you look up Southwold, you will find that it is no ordinary seaside town. It has been so gentrified that it can be argued that half the houses are second homes and the other half, holiday lets. Out of season, it is a ghost town, but from April to September, with its beach and common, Adnams pubs and compulsively browsable shops, it is truly special. Also, it is home to the Southwold Beach Huts - a mile or more of brightly painted little sheds facing the sea.

So, guess what we did? We rented one for a day. It was a cold, grey day, but we bought a blanket from a charity shop to spread on the floor and a picnic basket for tea. We invited friends from Woodbridge. Anyone who could read behind the lines would have said that Tamsin was nesting.

But that would be someone with insight rather than someone who **comes across as uncaring.**

By the time winter set in, we were back in Woodbridge. Back

in the mud by The Tidemill - and Tamsin was back with all the friends she had made in our first three months.

But this time, we weren't sea gypsies about to set off. This time, we were a family coming home.

Chapter 13
Home

Well, the 27ft x 14ft patch of mud beside Woodbridge Tide Mill was the nearest thing we had to a home. I considered *Lottie Warren* as home wherever she happened to be. That was the whole point of the adventure: One day, it may be a patch of Suffolk mud; another, it might be a palm-fringed lagoon in the South Pacific.

But home means different things to different people. While Tamsin, as a school nurse blinded by love, might have persuaded herself to follow my dream - as a mother with a tiny baby, suddenly she was thinking very differently.

For instance, she was thinking of Mother and Baby groups. The first sign of this had appeared in Edinburgh when it seemed as though "home" was not the berth at Port Edgar Marina at all but the baby changing facilities of Boots.

And, of course, the mothers she met there had normal lives. They lived in houses - had husbands who went off to work in the morning and came home in the evening - who understood what it was their wives needed to hear when they came home (How was your day, darling... oh, no, really? How was that for you? Oh, absolutely... poor you... etc...etc...)

Not "put the head back on the broom and give it a bash on the floor."

Not someone who saw the winter as an inconvenient pause

before we could get going again.

We began to argue about my shortcomings - which, of course, I didn't see as shortcomings. Wasn't everyone like this? Or at least every man?

It had never really caused a problem before. Now we discovered that I could not complete what I had to say if Tamsin began to respond before I had reached the end. I called this "interrupting", but somehow Tamsin didn't see it like that. To her (probably to all women) this was normal conversation.

Listen to any group of women talking, and you will discover they all talk at the same time - how do they do that? I should have known this was going to happen, Tamsin's mother had always been able to begin a conversation by saying: "I don't like the colour..." or "She's right, you know..." and somehow, by some miraculous act of telepathy, Tamsin would know what she was talking about. As I say, how do they do that?

But, of course, they'd been doing it for 30 years...

Listen to men talking to each other (when they do talk to each other) and you will find they take it in turns. One says something. The other listens. Then grunts.

Since it seemed this was the only type of conversation I could cope with, we tried having managed discussions (or managed arguments). Taking a leaf out of Lord of the Flies, we really needed a conch shell to pass backwards and forwards across the table - transferring the right to speak. Instead, we set the kitchen timer.

It was a disaster. Tamsin couldn't get out of the habit of talking and listening at the same time, and of course, as soon as she started talking, I had to stop so that I could concentrate on what she said – except I didn't. I just bounced up and down on my seat, burbling: "Uh, uh, uh... buh, buh, buh...)

Or, to put it another way, **blurting out responses and poor social timing.**

As I say, it was a disaster. But, to give ourselves credit, we did try to do something about it. Thinking back, it seems absurd, but don't forget we were convinced we had such potential for happiness that we were prepared to try anything.

And we did. We tried Dr Bach's Flower Remedies. These are a range of 38 preparations made from flowers, the idea being that just a drop can change a person's mood - and (what the original Dr Bach was concerned about in the 1930's) relieve their physical afflictions.

We were perfectly healthy, but we both needed to control our moods. For instance, a drop of essence of Beech for Intolerance or Chestnut Bud for Failure to Learn from Mistakes.

Truly, the list is little short of an instant and rather charmingly English solution to all of life's problems: Clematis for "Dreaming of the future without working in the present" or (in extremis) Sweet Chestnut for "Severe mental anguish, when everything has been tried and there is no light left".

I regret to say that none of them did the slightest good. Tamsin still found me exasperating; I failed to understand why and carried on much as before - which led to further exasperation.

The only respite was when Mother and Baby went off to the Mother and Baby group and Father sat in front of the keyboard trying to concoct light-hearted and entertaining journalism out of the shambles into which the idyllic lifestyle seemed to be degenerating.

Meanwhile, Malcolm and Pixie turned up, ready to share in the what we still insisted in presenting to the outside world as the idyllic, etc...etc...

You'll remember that it was our naïve enthusiasm which prompted them to sell their medical practice and go off sailing, too. Now they arrived in the marina with their 41ft Rival *Matador*. They had spent a fortune doing her up, and the cabin was an interior decorator's delight - all blues and yellows with a stuffed parrot in the corner. Also, Pixie brought with her a tiny Jack Russell in place of a tiny baby. Of course, we couldn't keep our troubles from them. Indeed, they looked after Owen for an hour when we gave Marriage Guidance a try. That did not end well - but what is said in Marriage Guidance stays in Marriage Guidance (unless you're making a Hollywood romcom, in which case you put it right up there ahead of the opening credits).

Maybe this was no worse than the growing pains other couples experience. At times, it seemed to me to be just as miserable as my first marriage - no, actually, this was worse: This time, there was more emotion invested.

It's an interesting scenario - a "domestic" in a small boat. For one thing, anything thrown cannot go very far. Also, you have deliberately stocked the boat with things which will not break. Flinging a plastic cup to bounce off the padded bulkhead six feet away is not nearly as satisfying as seeing great aunt Mildred's teapot sail the length of the kitchen to smash into a thousand Wedgewood pieces on the ceramic tiles.

On the other hand, we were still at the stage where making up is so wonderful it almost makes the row worthwhile. Owen's first birthday came and went. We stuck to The Grand Plan - well, mostly. In the spring, we would be off again - however, not south to the sunshine just yet.

Remember, he was only Baby Number One. He was going to need a brother or sister - but neither of us could face the prospect of going through all the stress of his birth a second time - especially in a foreign language (Spanish had been mooted). Instead, we would award ourselves a summer holiday and then return in the autumn to the comforting embrace of the National Health Service.

We would restore our relationship by recreating that magical summer when we didn't have a care in the world except for using up my holiday entitlement. We would go back to Holland - only this time, we would keep going all the way up to the Frisian Islands. Tamsin could travel back for check-ups and - in between, she could visit the nearest Dutch doctor.

Parts of this went according to plan: Owen took his first steps in a park in The Hague. We bought him a little seat to go on the back of Tamsin's bike - a stately model designed for Dutch mothers who have one child on the front, another on the back, the pushchair attached to one side and the shopping on the other. In time, he even learned to sleep through the bells which chime out from every Town Hall on the quarter hour day and night.

The Telegraph - whose readers did not seem to have noticed we had spent six months in the same place - contributed picture royalties to the Treat Fund. Yachting World - bless them - were as loyal as ever…

And it was not just Tamsin who had to make flying visits home. My grown-up son, Oliver, graduated from Edinburgh University, and even estranged fathers have obligations. I checked the mooring lines on the canal bank somewhere in Central Flevoland and took the train to Schiphol.

It was only at the departure gate that it became clear that, possibly through some **lack of attention to detail**, I had Tamsin's passport instead of my own. The immigration officer was very good about it - as he could afford to be: After all, I was not entering his country, I was leaving it.

But, as he said: "You will have to have your own passport if you want to come back."

First, I had to get into the UK - if I didn't want to end up like Tom Hanks, living for the rest of my life in The Terminal.

This was what those 20 years of journalism had been leading up to - particularly the last ten and all the hours spent wheedling, cajoling (and bribing) my way across international borders - although I would like it noted that no money changed hands in the immigration superintendent's office at Edinburgh. It was enough to explain about the **lack of attention to detail.**

But that still left me with four days to find some way of getting the right passport to Schipol Airport for my return. Nowadays, with mobile phones, this would not be a problem. But in 1997, you had to pay for incoming calls when roaming abroad. We had sold the mobile.

I couldn't write because Tamsin wouldn't know that she needed to go and pick up a letter.

The good news was that her parents were visiting while I was away - and they had a car. Still, getting the passport to the airport was the easy part. Getting the message to them was the difficulty.

In between celebrating Olly's graduation, I exchanged a handful Scottish banknotes for a pocketful of small change and settled myself in an out-of-the-way phone box, safe in the knowledge that hardly anyone used phone boxes anymore. This might take some time.

Eventually, the duty officer in a small police station in central Flevoland received the following phone call: "Hello, do you speak English?"

"Of course." (Everyone in Holland speaks English).

"Can you help me? I am a journalist, and I am writing about my travels in your country, and I have returned to the UK but left my passport on a small boat moored to the canal not far from you. I need to get a message to my wife, who will arrange for the passport to be taken to the airport to meet me. All I need is someone to give her a message to call me. I wondered whether you would be able to do that?"

Some time later, Tamsin and her parents were sitting in *Lottie Warren's* cabin, enjoying dinner and watching the sunset when their view was blocked by two Dutch police officers.

The officers had what they called a "Small Emergency". We had spent some time discussing how the emergency should be described. Obviously, it had to be an "emergency", or nobody would take any notice. But the very word could have all sorts of unfortunate consequences for an expectant mother - so, a "small emergency" it was.

Sure enough, on the return journey, when I presented myself at Dutch immigration, I was ushered into a separate room and, with the utmost courtesy and understanding, reunited with my identity.

I had expected nothing less.

Tamsin's experience with the Dutch doctors was not so straightforward. We should have expected this from the first recommendation in Amsterdam - the doctor's consulting room was between the Erotic Sex Shop Discount Centre and ABC Big Collection (Video, Leather, Lingerie). We were slap in the middle of the Red Light district - and the doctor wore an earring.

Besides, why did this expectant mother want a check-up in the first place? Dutch mothers did not keep going to their doctors for check-ups. They just had babies. What was all the fuss about?

It was all good copy.

But Tamsin was getting bigger all the time. The baby was due in November. By the time we had explored the Friesian Islands and were edging towards Germany, it was time to turn round.

This was going to be our second winter "at home" in Woodbridge - and, remembering the arguments of the last one, we agreed to make life easy on ourselves and rent a house.

Lark Cottage was as delightful as its name - with oak beams and lintels for banging your head - an inglenook fireplace with a great iron stove. We moved in with all our belongings while *Lottie Warren,* empty for the first time in three years, came out of the water for some overdue maintenance.

We rented a television and Owen fell in love with La-La from the Teletubbies. We became, in short, a normal family living in a house. I wasn't quite sure how it had happened. Meanwhile, Tamsin blossomed: she had her friends around her again - and, of course, so did Owen.

In particular, there was a little girl with big blue eyes and blonde curls called Leah. For the first few days, Owen did not let go of Leah's hand for an instant. Everybody was happy – and if everybody else was happy, I was happy. After all, this was just a temporary pause in our plans. The lease on the cottage was for six months. We would be off again in the spring, wouldn't we…

As if to take my mind off it, Adlard Coles, the nautical publisher, asked whether they might have the honour of bringing out a volume of collected columns from Yachting World. I would select them, approve the cover, write an introduction… The fact that we were not actually sailing was somehow lost in the warm cocoon of **approval**.

Friends came to stay. I helped Owen build a snowman. Tamsin got bigger and bigger. Her regular check-ups with the doctor became regular check-ups at the hospital…

Finally, 19 days late, Owen's little brother Theo arrived. Now we were really in baby mode again: Play dates, sing-songs at the Church Hall (The Wheels on the Bus over and over again). Birthday parties… I had no idea the world was so full of small babies.

But gradually, inevitably, the snow melted, the days grew longer - and I started taking the bus into Ipswich to prepare *Lottie Warren* for the next stage of her adventure. I took sandwiches with me and at lunchtime, would sit looking out over the marina at the neat rows of boats with their halyards slapping and wind chargers whirring - and felt a thrill that soon we would be off again - and this time, we would keep going…

Of course, someone who was not totally wrapped up in his own dream might have noticed that the other party in these plans was not so enthusiastic. What I did not know was that while I was varnishing and polishing, Tamsin was telling all her friends how much she dreaded leaving them and the home she had made for us all - even the blasted wheels on the bus…

She didn't tell me this - after all, she knew how excited I was to be sailing again. I had hired a tiny car and made countless trips to the boatyard with all the belongings - meticulously stowing every pair of baby socks and plastic train set. Somehow, over the winter, the amount of "stuff" had multiplied to the point that, on the day *Lottie Warren* was due back in the water, I worked through the night stowing and re-stowing everything until every nook and cranny was filled to bursting - and heaven help us if we wanted something from the bottom.

And then we moved aboard. And then we set off. And if Tamsin was miserable and distraught, and her friends were rallying round and comforting her, how was I supposed to know? Nobody told me. I just thought they were saying goodbye.

Chapter 14
Departure

Tamsin decided to take the ferry across the English Channel with the little boys. I couldn't blame her - after all, she had stayed in bed for most of the crossing of the Thames Estuary - simultaneously feeding Theo and playing with Owen while I sailed the boat (secretly, rather grateful to be able to get on with it).

So, I looked forward to the crossing from Ramsgate to Calais without having to worry about anyone else. It seems extraordinary looking back on it over 25 years. Didn't I have any idea of what was going on?

In Calais I took the mast down - we could leave it behind and have it sent on to the Mediterranean by road. Of course, the actual mechanics of taking a mast down are best accomplished without the assistance of a two-year-old who hasn't yet learned the difference between a tool box and a toy box. This meant that every time I started doing any work on the boat, Tamsin had to take both children to the playground at the beach. They spent a lot of time in the playground at the beach.

But eventually, we passed through the lock into the canal du Nord and started the long progress south. Life settled into a routine. We puttered along between the fields. Occasionally a boat would come the other way and we taught Owen to wave. Every afternoon we stopped at some small town, hammering mooring stakes into the bank or maybe tying up to a municipal pontoon.

Then we would heave the double pushchair ashore and set off to explore. It soon became apparent that in every town there were two things we needed to find: The first was a playground. If we could find Owen a playground, we could find him playmates - and he delighted in meeting new children - the fact that they spoke French didn't seem to bother him at all: *"Se glisser, se glisser..."* he chanted while we sat on the bench - and, of course, Tamsin started making friends with the French mothers.

And then Owen met Nina. Nina was a little girl, just a couple of months older than him. She was with her parents on a tiny motorboat which they had navigated all the way from central Belgium – and they were going our way. We stopped in the same place for the night and the children played, while Tamsin and Nina's mother combined forces to provide a meal for all of us - and her father helped me investigate why the engine kept losing power for no apparent reason.

The following night we stopped again, mooring next to each other on the canal bank. Owen rushed to find Nina.

And the next night.

We stopped for lunch as well and they played some more. And so it went on for a week. Indeed, this was exactly what we hoped would happen – the cruising community in action. Then Nina's family announced that it was time for them to turn round and go home. They had three weeks holiday. Most people have to go home at the end of their summer holiday.

The children said goodbye to each other, gave each other kisses...

The next day, Owen said: "Where's Nina?"

"Well, Nina's gone home to Belgium, darling. But don't worry, there will be lots of other children for you to play with."

"I want Nina!"

... and a few hours later, it would be "Where's Nina?" ... and again.

It took him 500 miles to forget Nina.

Or, maybe, he didn't forget; he just stopped asking…

Meanwhile, we had to find the *Super Marché*. There was nothing that lifted Tamsin's spirits quicker than shopping. It wasn't that she was extravagant - indeed, it was the bargain-hunting that seemed to be the whole point of the exercise. What is it about women and shopping? Never mind, if it made her happy, it made me happy.

…at least it did until she found the plastic tractor. This was not a tiny toy tractor - we had plenty of those already filling up the toybox tucked into the corner of the saloon. No, this was a full-sized child's tricycle - complete with a trailer… of the sort that little boys of three-and-a-half might learn to ride in the garden. Owen was just over two - it would be more than a year before he could ride it - and in the meantime, where were we going to put it?

"It can go in the bow locker," Tamsin reasoned, reasonably.

The "bow locker" was a cavernous space above the water tank where I stowed all the bulky, lightweight stuff I couldn't put anywhere else - and, of course, because *Lottie Warren* was a catamaran, we had two of them…

"But he won't be able to ride it for at least a year. Let's wait and get him one then…"

And then she delivered the *coupe de grâce*: "But it's half-price."

It was too - incredibly good value at just £10 - and that little tractor went on for years. It's just that it had to spend the first year hidden away in the bow locker above the water tank.

At least shopping took our minds off the hunt for a launderette. We were always hunting for a launderette. A two-year-old and a tiny baby generate an astonishing amount of washing and this was not something that had featured very much in all the books about children on boats. The authors had been more concerned with how to rig netting round the guardrails to stop toddlers falling over the side and the best schedule for home schooling in the South Pacific. In her book *Children of Cape Horne,* Rosie Swale devoted far more space to turning a forward cabin into a padded playroom for rounding Cape Horn than she did on getting the laundry done.

The essential truth - which is very rarely mentioned in the cruising books - is that there are two ways to bring up children on a boat: One is as a family of happy-go-lucky water gypsies, content to sail a somewhat shabby but essentially seaworthy boat on a shoestring. The hippy lifestyle and sailing seem to go together: If nobody worries about convention, there's no need for a launderette – especially if you don't much bother with clothes in the first place.

However, I had always veered towards the second option. I took a pride in my boats: I grew up with my father swabbing the decks as soon as we arrived in port (when he bought a boat with windows that opened, it took him years to learn that my mother liked to open them at about the same time as he broke out the bucket. The resulting explosion from below was nothing if not predictable).

And Tamsin was determined to take pride in her children - after all, she had all those baby clothes gathered so surreptitiously at car boot sales. Theo could go through half a dozen changes of clothes every 24 hours - all of which ended up in the laundry bag.

And in due course, the laundry bag (or more accurately, two or three laundry bags) would end up jammed into one half of the double pushchair next to Owen. Theo would go on my back and off we would go on an expedition to find the launderette. I must say I grew to hate French launderettes: We would trundle the pushchair with poor little Owen bumping and jolting over the cobbles - only to find that the directions were wrong or the establishment was *fermé* for a public holiday, or a family bereavement - or merely because the proprietor was busy doing something more important.

If we did find one - and it was open - we would load the machines, fill them up with coins, and set out for the playground while the washing went round. Invariably the playground was on the other side of town so that, by the time we arrived, it was time to find our way back to transfer the washing to the dryer, which ran for about five minutes per Euro - which, in turn, meant that it might have been cheaper just to throw the clothes away and buy new ones…

Back in London when we took the brave and exciting decision to cut our ties with the land and go off in search of adventure, everything had promised to be so different: Where was the smart white yacht? Where was the deep blue sea? The taught white sails straining? Sunlight sparkling on spray…

And where, come to that, was the happy, smiling, wonderfully enthusiastic girl who loved me so much that I tore up my grand plan, threw away the best job in British journalism because I couldn't wait for the rest of my life to begin?

Neither of us seemed to be getting what we wanted. We began to argue again - not the short, sharp arguments, which had troubled us so much during Owen's first winter in Woodbridge (and which we fondly imagined would be solved with Dr Bach's charming but useless Flower Remedies). And I did look back fondly – at sudden outbursts quickly forgotten amid the delicious process of making-up. In France, the arguments went on all day. One of them, I remember, for several days.

The love that had seemed so powerful it could overcome any obstacle, now seemed unable to cope with an afternoon on the same boat.

We began to retreat into long silences. I don't know what Tamsin thought about while we weren't talking. But I know that I began to brood; it all seemed like the most terrible mistake.

Of course, as soon as I found myself starting to think like that, I knew what I had to do: I had to change my thinking. I had read *Ultimate Power!* I knew how this worked: You get what you think about. You create your reality by the power of your thinking... Thoughts are Things... etc... etc...

And then something happened which changed everything. At 4.40 in the morning, Theo woke up.

The next day, at about 4.30 in the morning, he woke up again.

Our little boy had graduated from being a newborn waking for his feed every few hours into a baby who slept through the night. It wasn't his fault that the night ended at dawn, which just happened to be at half past four in the morning - and the boat didn't have any curtains.

Also, he shared a cabin with his brother - what had been Blue's cabin. This meant that if Theo woke up and started crying, it was not long before Owen did the same. There was only one thing for it: If anyone was going to get any sleep, Theo had to be removed from the boat.

I leapt up and started throwing on clothes. I yanked open the cockpit canopy. I grabbed the baby backpack and threw it onto the towpath - and then took Theo from Tamsin who had been cooing for all she was worth, while Owen tossed and turned and thought about starting his day as well.

We got it down to a well-oiled routine: Within five minutes of the first whimper, I would be striding down the canal bank with my six-month-old son on my back, snuffling his way back to sleep with the motion. All I had to do then was to keep moving and find some way to fill the next three hours.

So, let's say we had tied up in some small town: There I would be in my polo shirt and shorts, shivering a little but confident that the day would warm up soon. I would reach back over my shoulder to check that Theo still had his hat on. This was important because, if it fell off, I would have no way of knowing - his head was directly behind my own and there was no one to tell me. Then I would retrace my steps and start looking for it. Actually, this was a very good way of filling the time. Sometimes I had to back-track for miles before I found that little blue hat on the grass verge.

Meanwhile, hat on; the next question was which way to go? I would look this way and that. The decision was fairly pointless because with all that time I had to fill, I was going to end up walking both ways…

There would be the church, of course - and some shops, some bars… a restaurant with its menu fixed to the railings. I could spend a good five minutes reading a menu (although, of course, the treat fund did not allow for restaurant meals on a whim).

Eventually, I would set off on the road out of town. I had three hours to go before I would see *Lottie Warren's* canopy unzipped – the signal that Tamsin was up and ready to begin the day.

In small town France, all roads lead out of town. This is the region they call Picardy - and you cannot walk far down any road out of town in Picardy before you come to a First World War cemetery. We have all seen the pictures of those endless rows of identical white headstones - thousands and thousands of graves of young men who died in seemingly endless and certainly pointless battles between 1914 and 1918.

But the enormous cemeteries are only a part of the story. What I had not realised was the number of small ones scattered around among the fields and lanes. Sometimes they would be on the outskirts of the town - or even the smallest village. Sometimes they would be in the middle of nowhere. It all depended on where the front line had been at the time and where the burial parties could dig in relative safety. I would be walking along with the sun in my eyes and my baby on my back and suddenly there would be another one - perfectly maintained by the War Graves Commission: The grass trimmed, the flowers perfectly ordered, the names clearly legible.

And just as I would read restaurant menus from *hors d'œuvres* to *dessert*, I would walk up and down the rows of graves and read the names. It became a compulsion to get round them all; not to leave anyone out. I felt I owed it to all these poor dead young men - and they *were* young; so very young - hardly any of them over 30 and the vast majority between 18 and 25.

It passed the time but also, it began to feel like a duty. The way I looked at it, I was 45 years old. I was standing in front of these gravestones with my baby son on my back - my fourth son, that is - and these young men had died, most of them, without ever having families… almost all of them, I suspected, without being married. Come to that, without ever having a relationship which amounted to more than "walking out" with the girl from the corner shop back home.

The way I saw it, these hundreds and hundreds of young men had never had the chance to live much of a life at all … and here was I, already into my second family, having had a successful career and now with the freedom to decide how I wanted to live the rest of my life - something that none of them could have imagined. It made you think...

No, it did more than make you think. It made you stop and stand there with the tears running down your face and it forced you to remember that whatever troubles you thought you had, none of them amounted to so much as a temporary inconvenience when compared to getting up in the morning and being ordered to walk into machine gun fire.

As I made my way up and down the rows, reading the names and the ages, something very peculiar happened. I began to experience a very strong sensation that in some way these young men were crowding round me - not in a disturbing way, not as if I was beset by a host of ghouls. But with their everyday names and their universally young ages, their junior ranks, it was easy to image them from the archived films, grinning under their helmets and giving the thumbs up.

The more I walked with my sleeping son on my back, the more it came home to me that these young men had a message for me: From now on I would not be living just for myself. From now on, I would be living for them too. It was my job, now, to live as good a life as I possibly could. To do the right thing at every turn, just as they would have done the right thing if only they had been given the chance.

Everyone has a defining moment in their life: A point at which, unexpectedly, something happens, some decision is made which changes everything. Day after day, in those early Picardy dawns, walking the rows of those poor dead soldiers, I came to realise that things would never be the same again.

I found that I couldn't help but compare my situation to that of my new imaginary friends. For instance, when I was guilty of some domestic misdemeanour – typically putting too much Marmite on Owen's toast soldiers (I happen to like Marmite), I had a choice in how I would react to the resulting explosion of criticism.

I might think that too much Marmite (and anyway, was it really too much?) was fairly insignificant in the grand scheme of things. But then, before I opened my mouth to argue, I would find that, suddenly, it was the easiest thing in the world to accept Tamsin's view. As I told myself, it was better than walking into machine gun fire.

An unusual peace began to blossom aboard the little boat as we moved from the Canal du Nord to the Oise, through Pont L'Eveque and Chalon-sur-Soane. Besides, we had Paris to look forward to.

We were going to "do" Paris - and with two little boys, what did that mean but Disneyland?

First, though, there was the Eiffel Tower - little boys love big things and we found a spot to moor right next to it. In fact, we were so close that I contrived to take a picture from the Pont de Grenelle. How lucky to find such a perfect spot, tucked in as close as we could get to the stern of an enormous barge, only protruding by a few centimetres into the "réservée" space behind it…

The way I looked at it, this was the equivalent of parking an inch over a yellow line. I mean, you'd have to be a pretty pedantic traffic warden to worry about that, wouldn't you? Anyway, we were off to Disneyland for two whole days - we were going to stay in a hotel!

Alright, we were going to stay in the cheapest hotel, furthest from the park; but we were going to be on holiday! We were going to see Mickey Mouse!

And we had a wonderful time. We saw the parade. We went on all the little rides (until we were heartily sick of singing *It's a Small World After All*). The sun shone. We shelled out for a Mickey Mouse - and in the evening of the second day, weary from all the fun and the long journey back into the city, we arrived on the river bank to find *Lottie Warren* just as we had left her, tucked in close to the stern of the barge.

As so often happened, there were people admiring her - or at least marvelling at something so small amongst all the commercial traffic.

As we got closer, it appeared the people were in uniform. I think I nodded a *Bonsoir* as you do and prepared to get the by-now sleeping children aboard.

"Is this your boat?" said one of the uniforms. Of course, he said it in French so the conversation was a little more halting. But essentially, it proceeded like this:

"Yes, it is. We have come from England."

"But you must go. You must go at once."

"But why must we go? This space is not reserved. Only that space. Is it not so?"

"But Mister, you are in that space, also."

"It is only a small piece we are in that space. We will depart in the morning…"

That was when it was explained that if we did not move at once - *tout de suite* - the River Police would move us, and our vessel would be impounded.

Well, really - all because we were a few centimetres over the line…

I think that by now, I must have mastered the Gallic shrug because the Frenchman, who seemed to have swelled with indignation and the full force of the law, flung out his arm and announced: "You must go because this is coming!"

I looked, and there – stationary in the middle of the river - was possibly the largest, longest river cruise ship I had ever seen. Maybe because it was so low (so as to fit under the bridges) it looked even longer. In fact, it looked every bit long enough to fill up every single centimetre of its officially-reserved space.

We bundled the children aboard, I cast off the lines, and we were off again at seven o'clock at night with not the slightest idea of where we were going to go. After half an hour of wandering up and down, we found a deserted barge to moor alongside - hoping at least we could stay until morning.

Later, we discovered that the cruise ship had been loaded with Americans who were all due to be decanted directly into the Champ de Mars to hear the Three Tenors who - at the very moment we reappeared - were already tuning up.

I seem to remember hearing that on this particular evening, the start of the performance had been delayed - but maybe my imagination is awarding us more importance than we deserve.

But what it did, of course, was to start us off on the next stage of the journey with the impetus of the unexpected - in other words: **Excitement.**

Chapter 15
Turmoil

If I were to tell you about our travels down through France, chugging along dead-straight canals interspersed with more little towns, more playgrounds and launderettes - more supermarkets (and the thrill when one of them turned out to be a hypermarket) and my occasional solitary excursions to buy petrol ... then this would become a very dull book indeed.

Maybe it wasn't really dull at all. Maybe my memory has been coloured by what happened next. I have a picture in front of me now - Tamsin and the two little boys on the foredeck - the paddling pool. Sunglasses and sunhats. The French flag tied to the pulpit...

But looking back over more than 20 years, all I see is how different it was from the grand plan - and how those differences crept in, one at a time, so that they became part of our daily existence. Surreptitious is a good word for it.

In the same way that I had put my worries aside when they had crowded around me before we left London, I could do the same when I returned from a petrol-buying expedition to see *Lottie Warren* without her mast, with dirty fenders and old tyres dangling down her sides, the muck and filth of the canal accumulating on her topsides because there was no point in cleaning it off if there would only be more of it tomorrow...

I could ignore all of this. I could rip it out of my mind using the same Tony Robbins technique because this was temporary.

When we emerged from the canal system and burst out into the Mediterranean, everything would be different. We would summon the mast from Calais, clean the hull, hoist the sails... everything would be different.

Meanwhile, pin on a smile. Play with the little boys. Rumble-tumble...

Rumble-tumble?

Yes, that was when the confines of the little cabin turned out to be not enough for two energetic small boys. Whenever Owen and Theo began to grizzle, we could always rely on Rumble-Tumble.

I had rigged up netting in their cabin to stop them falling out of bed. Rumble-tumble involved the three of us climbing in there and rolling around to shrieks of laughter and over-excitement. It was a way of letting off steam - and, for me, a way of imagining that everything was going to be all right after all.

The whole expedition had become a compromise: If I was burying my nagging doubts about whether this was really what I called living on a boat, then Tamsin was very likely burying her own feelings of isolation from her friends - her network of mothers back in Woodbridge.

I don't remember us talking about it. We had tried talking, but it hadn't been a great success - the usual thing: I couldn't martial my thoughts while Tamsin was talking, and she couldn't understand why not. Better, perhaps, to keep our heads down and make the best of things. Everything would improve when we reached the Mediterranean. Already, Theo was sleeping until a reasonable hour. Owen had forgotten about Nina. Everything would be alright.

Well, we assumed Owen had forgotten about Nina - but he had changed. No longer did he rush into the playgrounds (*"se glisser, se glisser"*). He didn't seem to want to play with the French children anymore. We put this down to the fact that he now had a ready-made playmate. Theo was nine months old and becoming really interesting to an older brother. Owen liked nothing better than to teach him to play with the train set and pour water in the paddling pool - and as for mealtimes... it was a great help to have someone else to ply the plastic spoon.

Then something happened which changed all our lives in an instant - one of those turning points to which you can trace an entire family history. Everything was different after Sète.

* * *

Like most momentous events, it happened with no warning at all. Sète is right at the bottom of the canal system. You can walk across the road and swim in the Mediterranean. In a few days we would be out. I would telephone for the mast, and the next phase (the real thing) would begin...

Really, we were that close.

And then Owen met Clara.

Clara was a pretty little girl with big blue eyes and blonde curls. Being French, she was beautifully dressed and being precocious, she completely ignored Owen's reluctance to play with her. In fact, she started playing with him as if he was an inanimate doll. I'm sure she began by doing his talking for him – a one-sided dialogue: "Allo Oo-en, you will play with me? Yes, I will play with you. You will be my friend? Yes, I will be your friend. That goes. We will play on the slide. Do you like to slide? Yes, I like to slide. That goes also..."

And gradually, grudgingly, Owen began to respond. If she had asked him, he would have said "Non". If the grown-ups sitting on the bench had cajoled him, he would have shaken his head and stuck out his lip. But there was no denying Clara, and sure enough, he began to play. He began to talk. His French came back.

And Tamsin and I looked at each other with a combined sense

of relief that was almost physical. It was OK. Everything was going to be alright.

"I told you so," we seemed to be saying to each other.

And Tamsin fell to talking to Clara's mother - that sort of mothers' conversation which had meant so much to her in the changing room of Boots in Edinburgh. Within 15 minutes, both women knew each other's life stories, had filed away all the names of children and siblings and marriages - and thereby cemented their place in the grand network of human relationships.

I wheeled Theo about the park until he fell asleep - and then wheeled some more since I knew that I had no interest at all in some stranger in a park in Southern France - but never thought to wonder why I should have no interest and why Tamsin should have such a compulsion to know everything...

By the time I had done a circuit of the park (and possibly another one) and Tamsin and the French mother had exhausted immediate family and were on to child development, ailments and eating habits, it was indeed getting on towards lunchtime and Clara's mother looked over towards the children who were now engrossed in the sandpit and said: "Come along, Cherie. Time to go. Say au-revoir to Oo-en"

Clara gave him a kiss and said "au revoir" and, without a second thought, trotted off with her mother.

Owen looked at her departing back and saw her chattering away to her mother - no doubt recounting all they had done and what they had built in the sandpit and how fast they had whizzed down the slide...

And Owen seemed to shrink before my eyes. He had taken a few paces to follow his new friend, but when she didn't turn back, he stopped and leaned against the wire mesh of the tennis court in an attitude of such despair and dejection that my heart turned over.

There were no tears. Not a word of complaint - just the unspoken acceptance that friends departed - nothing was permanent. Happiness did not endure.

And his mother and I looked at each other and, without saying a word, we knew we could not do this to him. This was not right - and yet this was the childhood we would be giving him - or rather, the childhood we would be stealing from him. There was no discussion. There didn't need to be. This was wrong, and both of us knew it.

We walked back to the boat in silence. We spent the afternoon each alone with our thoughts, and then, after dinner, with the children asleep and our "grown-up time" to ourselves, we talked it through.

It wasn't an argument. There was no need for the kitchen timer. This time, there didn't seem to be any other choice. For a while at least, we would have to rejoin the conventional world. For whatever reason - whether it was just us or just Owen or whether the whole plan had been fatally flawed from the beginning, it was time to face reality. This was just not working.

Besides, it was quite clear that Tamsin had never wanted to leave in the first place - she had said so to her friends - although not to me because a promise was a promise, and our whole life together had been gearing up for this. But if she was not happy, then I was not going to be happy. Clearly, Owen was unhappy. In fact, Theo was the only one who seemed oblivious to it all - but then who could say how he would feel when he got to a year old or certainly by the time he was Owen's age and went through the same heartache which his own Nina or Clara or whoever.

I got out the charts of the Inland Waterways of France and began to plan our return. The priority now was to get back to Woodbridge as quickly as possible.

Once the decision was made, Tamsin seemed to come out from under her cloud. The next morning, she found a phone box and broke the news. I imagine that by lunchtime, it was all over town. Her mother, too, would have relayed it to the farthest reaches of the family – all those Welsh cousins...

And if I was disappointed, nobody would have known it - after all, this was a change of plan. This was something **new and exciting.** And, of course, I had a new project: I had to work out how we were going to do it. The answer seemed to be to turn right into the Canal du Midi and leave the boat at Toulouse where we could take a flight back. Once everyone was settled in Woodbridge again (a friend was looking for a house for us to rent) then I could return for *Lottie Warren* at leisure.

And for a few days, everything was rosy.

We had about 200 miles to go - at our 20 miles-a-day average, that meant about ten days. Ten days on the Canal du Midi, which is one of the most picturesque waterways in France – dead straight and with trees planted at regular intervals all the way along both sides. We took it in turns to drive the boat or wheel the children down the towpath.

I remember it being the longest 200 miles of my life. Every step - every identical tree that slipped past - seemed to represent a defeat. The worst part was that everyone had told me this would never work. Of course, I ***hadn't listened*** - any more than I listened to anything else anybody said.

We were going back to live in a house in a small market town on the East coast of England. More than that, we didn't know. We would decide once we got there. What I did know was that if, before leaving London - if, when Tamsin and I had met on Hampstead Heath - when Lois, the medical correspondent, had suggested I answer a Lonely Hearts Ad in Time Out – if at that time, anyone had told me it would all end in a house in a small market town on the East coast of England - I would have run screaming for the exit.

This, as I told myself again and again with every tree that went past, was exactly what I did *not* want.

An image came to mind from years ago, when I had just been

making my mark in Fleet Street and was walking with the girlfriend of the moment down to the river at Chiswick for an evening drink in the pub overlooking the water. As we walked, hand-in-hand, we passed house after house with the windows open and the sounds of family life spilling out into the street.

These were the homes of successful young families. "Yuppies", was the term in those days - Young Urban Professionals (who else could afford a three-bedroomed house in Chiswick - even in those days?)

It was only too obvious that the pretty girl at my side could see us in one of those houses in a few years' time (probably three years, I suspect she calculated). But I had already been there. I had a family, and for reasons that I never fully understood, I knew that whatever happened, I didn't want to go back there - back to the claustrophobia, the routine, the responsibility… whatever you cared to blame for the **boredom**.

Which, of course, was entirely selfish - it wasn't the girl's fault. All she wanted was what every other woman wanted. Why didn't I want the same? But I didn't. I knew I didn't.

I knew what I did want. I knew exactly what I wanted - and on the towpath of the Canal du Midi, I was walking away from it with every step.

So, what were my options?

Well, one option was to abandon my family. I could sit down and tell Tamsin it was all over. She could go back to England, but I was carrying on.

She and the children could rejoin me later - maybe in some tropical paradise in the Pacific…

…or we could just leave it here.

…or I could take them back to England and turn round at the airport. No warning. Just walk away…

Believe me, the options which kept churning around in my head as I walked that towpath knew no bounds - no bounds of feasibility. Certainly no bounds of decency.

In the middle of it all, two images kept reappearing in my mind: One was from a small harbour somewhere in Brittany during that first year's cruise with *Largo*. Tamsin and I had just reached that stage in our relationship when my explosion on Hampstead Heath of "Children? I'm not having any more!" was beginning to resurface like an echo. It seemed that Tamsin had filed it away but certainly not forgotten about it. This was something to be dealt with later and, sure enough, the right moment had arrived.

Without my being aware of how the subject had come up, I found us discussing the prospect of children much more calmly. Tamsin felt that, deep down, I did want more children. It never occurred to me that possibly this might have had something to do with the increasingly obvious fact that, more than anything, Tamsin wanted children - everybody wants children. It would be alright. We could have children on a boat. Other people had children on boats...

And then she added - and this is what I had filed away - she added: "If you don't like it, you can leave us."

Of course, I filed it away - in a locked box with other shameful memories. Of course, it was never an option. No decent person has children on the understanding that they can abandon them if it all turns out to be not as much fun as advertised.

But all the same, the option was there, locked away, dismissed out of hand. Just... still there.

Remember that telling scene in Love Actually? The one with the character Mark, played by Andrew Lincoln; the one who is secretly in love with his best friend's new wife, played by the gorgeous Keira Knightley? She doesn't know – and, of course, he can't tell her. Instead, he walks out into the street but then changes his mind and turns back – but then heads once more towards the street – and turns round again...

This happens three or four times before he drops to his knees, clutching his head, berating himself, indecision bursting out of every pore - because the inner turmoil has now grown bigger than just all-consuming.

This was me walking the towpath of the Canal du Midi in the shade of those thousands of regularly-spaced trees, my whole life and the lives of three other people all at a turning point - the need to make a decision growing closer with every step.

I made lists in my head: pros and cons. I played out scenarios. What could I do? Could I go back to the Evening Standard and beg for my old job back? Oh, the humiliation! Would they give it to me, anyway?

I made lists on paper (because my head was so full of indecision, it couldn't hold any more pros and cons). I hid the pieces of paper. After all, the decision was made. Tamsin was receiving regular reports of the house-hunt-by-proxy. Did we need to be in Woodbridge itself? Would Melton do? It was only a mile away. How many bedrooms? When could Owen go to nursery school? Domesticity… Roots… Everything Tamsin had always wanted… Everything I dreaded…Oh God, what a mess!

And still, I didn't talk about it. What was the point? The decision had been made. The time for talking about it had been 50 or 100 miles back down the canal, the night after the painful parting with Clara.

Why had I agreed to go back? Why hadn't I told Tamsin there and then what I was telling myself now, halfway to Toulouse?

There's a good question - to which, I now realise, the answer – like the answer to everything else, is right there in that list of symptoms: **Saying "yes" to requests because of a desire for approval.**

So, what now?

To my shame, I remember considering delivering Tamsin and the children to her parents at the airport in England - and calmly turning round and flying back to France and my boat.

Of course, I couldn't do it. I was 49 years old. I had one broken family behind me already (coincidentally with two boys). Having made a mess of it once, was I going to make a mess of it again?

So, I walked on. At night I lay awake. In the morning, I woke to another day still with the same secret turmoil - and nobody knew. Tamsin was happy again. The children were calmer. The weather improved. With less commercial traffic, even motoring down the canal between the trees seemed like a holiday.

If you are of a religious turn of mind, you will say that when the soul is wanting, help will come. That's as maybe. All I can tell you is that at a time when I was more troubled than I can say - when there was no one I could talk to, I found myself walking among friends.

You may laugh at the presumption - and I must say I am embarrassed to admit it now. But don't forget that I have a tendency to **share inappropriate personal details.** So, maybe it is not surprising that I feel this compulsion to explain that, walking along that towpath, pushing my two sons in the double pushchair, I became convinced that all those poor dead soldiers from the cemeteries of Picardy were walking with me. It was the strangest sensation - sometimes it seemed they were crowding me; hundreds of them… thousands…

Of course, I remembered only too well how young they had been: "Aged 18 years - aged 21 years…"

They hadn't even started their lives - hardly any of them could have been married. So many would have died without even a girl's picture in their breast pocket. And yet, here I was, aged 49 years, already with one family behind me - and now, in my darkest, most selfish moments, thinking I could abandon another.

I walked with the tears running down my face – again.

Nobody told me to pull myself together. Nobody said: "Get a grip", or told me that I had nothing to complain about, for heaven's sake...

Instead, I knew that there was only one thing to do - the right thing. It was obvious what was the right thing to do - the decent thing. I didn't need anybody to tell me to do the decent thing. Gradually this thought – this image – took over from the airport scene: The shameful turning back in the arrivals hall.

Once the decision was made, it was as if a great weight had been lifted from me. Best of all, I knew I was not alone. Whenever the going got tough, help would be at hand.

And the strangest thing is that, from that moment on, I have always felt that presence. I feel it now.

It is my imagination, of course.

At least, that is what I tell myself.

Chapter 16
Return

All the agonising from the towpath of the Canal du Lateral evaporated as soon as we landed in England. Here was a new chapter in life - new and, therefore, **exciting.** So, it was no surprise that now, with my doubts behind me, I threw myself into our return to the UK with all the enthusiasm there had once been for leaving.

It was exciting. For one thing, we were going to be living in a house we had never seen. A friend had checked it out, and we signed the lease by post. For six months, we had a three-bedroomed house in the village right next door to Woodbridge. We moved in straight away.

Tamsin re-connected with her network of mothers and toddlers - and, of course, that meant Owen had friends again. One friend in particular: He only had eyes for Leah.

Leah had blonde curls and big blue eyes, and they had been playmates when he left, and now they were playmates again. Actually, Leah was a lot more than a playmate. Leah was Owen's link to a secure childhood when friends were permanent - not like Nina and Clara. For three whole days, Owen did not let go of Leah's hand. His face lit up when he saw her in the morning and - as long as we assured him over and over again that he would see her again tomorrow, he would go to bed happily, saying: "Leah tomorrow!"

Tamsin was happy too. Her friends welcomed her home - and it was home. We bought a car and took it to IKEA to buy pictures and laundry baskets. The toy tractor saw the light of day. *Lottie Warren* was laid up in the boatyard while I threw myself into the new and captivating business of home-making. Boats, suddenly, were not a priority.

We revelled in the amount of space. Owen ran from room to room. Theo crawled everywhere without us having to worry about him falling down the steps into the hulls. We had a garden. We had a washing machine!

Every day we walked into Woodbridge just as we had walked into whatever little town we had arrived in with the boat - only now, people came up and greeted us. Tamsin knew who they were. I nodded and smiled. I found nothing odd in this - I had always been awkward with people I ought to know - that is to say, people whose names I should remember but in fact are complete strangers to me.

We started going to church. The church was just round the corner and had a charismatic young vicar. In his former life, he had been a head-hunter in the City of London, finding high-flyers for top jobs. Now, as he put it, he head-hunted for God. He did things like getting the congregation to join hands in a circle - and then point out that we were all facing inwards rather than outwards – a clever trick. He must have been good in the world of business. We joined in with it all. We sat in the front pew. You might think we had been there for generations.

Tamsin had the background: Her mother had grown up going to Chapel in North Wales, and she had once belonged to a church youth group and, like everything else she did, she had thrown herself into all the activities (and ignored her father, who insisted on being a convinced atheist). For my part, aside from skipping chapel at school, my religious upbringing involved looking out of the car window on Sunday mornings as we drove past the "stuffy old Church".

But now, since my profound experience in the cemeteries of Picardy. I was ripe for a bit of belief. Besides, it was a good grounding for the children...

All of this gave our lives an air of permanence. Of course, it wasn't permanent at all. It was just a rented house for six months while we worked out where we were going to live. After all, we could live anywhere: Part of my deal with myself - my pact with my new imaginary friends - was that I was not going back to my old job in London. Quite what I was going to do seemed rather vague, but I still had my Yachting World column - although the Daily Telegraph now had a new Travel Editor - a new broom - and my column was the first pile of old rubbish to be swept away.

Never mind, something would turn up - as long as I did the "right thing", I told myself, "Everything would be all right."

On the strength of this, I bought a huge desktop computer - it seemed that whatever I was going to do, I couldn't go wrong if I started with a computer. I bought the biggest screen I could get. That would be good for graphics (what I was going to do with graphics, I have no idea).

And so, once life had settled down and begun to achieve a routine, we started to plan the next phase: Once the little boys were bathed and had listened to their bedtime stories - when all the cuddly toys were tucked up in the right order, Tamsin and I would settle down to "grown-up time" - and, of course, we began to wonder "what next?"

There is a film with Will Smith called "The Pursuit of Happyness" (and, yes, it's supposed to be spelt wrong). This is Hollywood's version of the autobiography of Chris Gardner, an American stockbroker who pulled himself up from being broke and homeless - all the while looking after his small son. It contains the line: "This part of my life is called Being Stupid."

And, looking back over 20 years, I know what he means. Yes,

this part of my life is called Being Stupid.

Up until now, while the decisions might not have been the most sensible (remember how colleagues at the Evening Standard had accosted me in the corridors and tried to talk me out of it?) at least they had logic on their side: We had been living the simple life on a boat - which in turn had produced a steady stream of copy. Meanwhile, the agent renting out my London flat sent regular payments to the bank – and that was all without taking into account the treat fund. We lived modestly, but we were solvent.

Now it was all rather different. Now we were paying rent and running at a loss - and where we had agonised over buying a £10 plastic tractor in a hypermarket, now we were going to IKEA and buying pictures - and, for Heaven's sake, a computer (with the biggest screen in the brochure).

Did I worry about this for a moment? Certainly not. Did I give a second's thought to Mr Micawber's famous recipe for happiness: "Annual income twenty pounds; annual expenditure nineteen, nineteen and six: Result happiness. Annual income twenty pounds; annual expenditure twenty pounds ought and six, result misery."

Did I give a thought to Father's oft-repeated dictum: "Only spend income. Never spend capital"?

Absolutely not. You see: Everything would be alright. Something would turn up. If I had a moment's doubt, I knew I had thousands of poor dead soldiers walking with me. In the same way that I had dismissed my worries with Tony Robbins' Ultimate Power, now I dismissed any fears that anything could possibly go wrong.

The great majority of people would recognise this as a recipe for disaster. The ADHD mind just finds it **stimulating**.

Meanwhile, we had been living in our rented house for three months. The daily walk into town, living with enough space to walk around, not having to go and hunt for a launderette... all of these excitements had now become routine - and what do we think of routine? Routine is **boring.**

It was time for something new, something **exciting…**

Try asking: "Where do we want to live?" Tamsin would have been happy to stay in Woodbridge - after all, it was a lovely little town – it invariably features on those lists of the Best Places to Live. Slap in the middle of an Area of Outstanding Natural Beauty. Woodbridge was within commuting distance of London and full of characterful pubs and good restaurants. It had the river, it had an independent cinema where people knew better than to rustle their sweet packets; a lot of them even sat through the credits at the end - and for the real enthusiasts, on the first Monday of the month, there was the film club with incomprehensible works of art with subtitles.

Nevertheless, we started looking at houses in the West Country. Although it was not something that had been discussed at any length, there seemed to be an understanding that if Tamsin was to have her home and her friends and her settled life, then I was to have my sailing.

So, if we were going to settle down, the West Country would be the place to do it: In Salcombe, for instance, there was deep water for a "proper" boat (something like Largo, I mused) and, of course, easy access to the Atlantic and long-distance voyaging.

And so, I called the letting agent in London, said that I wanted to sell the flat. Every post brought a heap of estate agents' bumph. Life had become **exciting** again.

The fact that we would now lose a significant income and, at the same time, start paying for buildings insurance and repairs and council tax and all the other hundred-and-one expenses that the home-owner is heir to – all of this somehow passed me by. Something, as I knew deep down, would turn up. In the meantime, I had lots of savings. There was nothing to worry about. Have a little faith…

In fact, have a lot of faith. Believe that everything will be all right - and believe it with such certainty that reality has no choice but to bend to your will...

Why would I think any different? Everything was going well. Coming back and throwing myself into this new chapter of my life had, indeed, been the right choice. Seeing Owen with Leah, Theo making his first friends at the baby and toddler group, Tamsin back to her old, loving self: How could I have contemplated abandoning them?

In fact, I think that from time to time, I may have said as much to the poor dead soldiers who accompanied me at every step, encouraging and silently nodding their approval – that signature thumbs up.

So, if we were going to settle down, if we were going to buy a house together, why didn't we get married?

This was never something we had discussed. Tamsin's priority had been to have children. Then, when it became clear that bringing up children on a boat was a non-starter, the next priority became a house. If marriage featured on her radar, she never gave any indication of it. In fact, I am sure she would have been quite happy to carry on as we were - cohabiting, living in sin, or whatever you want to call it.

The way I looked at it; if we were going to buy a house together (and the idea of buying in my name alone just seemed wrong) then we had reached the point when marriage was the logical next step.

Besides, the idea of surprising her with a ring was just too thrilling to pass up.

In secret - well, having explained to Owen that this was a surprise for Mummy (he was good at surprises) I took him and Theo to the jewellers and picked out a ring - Theo, I hoped, was too young to realise what was going on.

Then we went to Salcombe to look at a house. Getting married and buying a house! How exciting is that?

Since Salcombe is at the other end of the country and Tamsin's parents lived in Rugby which is more or less in the middle, it made sense to stop there for a night, drop off the boys and carry on for a crafty night away. I had booked a room in the Salcombe Harbour Hotel - a room overlooking the harbour, which came at a premium even though, on the day, there was thick fog outside the window and we couldn't see a thing. Never mind. It was all very romantic, and Tamsin was suitably surprised and didn't say she wanted to think about it. We went down to dinner convinced that this was the beginning of yet another new chapter.

After all, we hadn't come all this way without being fairly certain we had found the house of our dreams. The pictures were wonderful. The owners had decorated it like something out of Homes & Gardens. There was even an antique gramophone in the hall, with a big horn like the one on His Master's Voice.

By now, you can guess how impractical we were being - egging each other on without an ounce of common sense. In fact, behaving exactly as we had when deciding to give up our lives in London and go off and live on sunshine and coconuts...

Once again, we were living in a bubble of our own making - too happy with each other and our exciting plans to allow reality so much as a toe in the door.

Thinking back on it, here is one small slice of reality which I remember brushing aside: The dining room was so small that, if somebody was sitting at the table, there was no room for anyone else to walk behind their chair. Can you imagine living in a house like that?

Here's another one that I hadn't noticed: The estate agent said: "Come to my office. The house is only round the corner, we can walk there…"

How lovely, how convenient…

It took the surveyor to point out that the access to the house was down a short passageway between two other houses - a passageway which dated from the time the houses were built, sometime in the mid-1800s - in other words, when passageways between houses only needed to be wide enough for a horse and cart.

"In order to reach the house by car, it was necessary to fold in both wing mirrors. Even then, great care was needed," wrote the surveyor.

Put that one down to a "lucky escape". Where else would be a good place to keep a boat? Well, of course, there was the Isle of Wight - after all, Cowes is the world capital of sailing.

We looked at the Isle of Wight - and discovered something quite extraordinary: I was vaguely aware that Queen Victoria was very fond of the island - in fact, she built Osborne House and died there. You can see it if you anchor in Osborne Bay. Obviously, if she spent so much time on the island, then the nobility would want to be near her - and so they built houses there too - not quite as grand as the Italian Renaissance-style palazzo that Prince Albert designed, but substantial piles all the same.

Of course, these are plainly impractical for modern families, so we dismissed them. Instead, we went to the island to look at a converted church.

Well, it was the church that persuaded us to go for a week, rent a cottage and combine a holiday with a bit of house-hunting. It would be fun. That's the joy of not having a job - you can just go… especially if you have lots of savings and are happy to spend them because "something will turn up" (Mr Micawber again).

The church was a disaster. It had been renovated in the style of a Marriott Hotel - acres of fitted carpet and pale woodwork - all hopelessly out of keeping with the Georgian stone. Also, all the windows were three metres high and 30 centimetres wide, so it felt like being in prison.

Never mind, there were lots of other houses for sale on the island - and at very reasonable prices, too. The reason for this was that, mile for mile, the Isle of Wight ferries are reputed to be the most expensive in the world. Of course, that didn't matter to us: We wouldn't be going anywhere…

In fact, just driving around the island, it was surprising how long it took to get from A to B. Even so, by the third day, we had exhausted all the houses on the list - except for the ten-bedroom wreck outside Newport. Well, we assumed it must be a wreck - it was certainly cheap enough…

It must be worth going to look at it – if only because the little boys liked nothing better than house-hunting (this is my room…this is my bed…)

And, once again, of course - faced with a crazy, romantic project - Tamsin and I started egging each other on. On the top floor, up a rickety staircase, there were four equal-sized single bedrooms. Wouldn't that be great? We could have four children to put in them…

There were four reception rooms - an enormous playroom - a study overlooking the garden where I could write best-sellers - a big dining room for huge, chaotic meals. You could open a launderette in the utility room and, come to that, there was a coach house which could be converted into holiday accommodation.

Before we knew where we were, we were dreaming and, as I should have known by then, there is nothing quite so wonderful – nothing quite so dangerous - as dreaming. By the end of the day, I had persuaded a local builder to come and look round the house and suggest a "ballpark figure" for fixing it up.

We got on well, me and the builder. He understood that we didn't really need a house that size - but on the other hand, if we could get it cheap enough to make doing it up a practical proposition, then maybe…

The builder crawled into the attics and stuck his penknife into bits of wood. He thumped on walls and squinted at what should have been right angles. He went home and consulted the books. Actually, I think he put quite a bit of effort into this - presuming, I suppose, that if we did go ahead with it, there would be months of work in it for all his staff and probably a few jobbing tradesmen as well.

He came up with a figure.

It was huge. You could have bought a starter home for the cost of the builder's renovation. Never mind, it was a good deal less than the purchase price. We simply deducted the one from the other and - with a perfectly straight face (I was on the phone), put in an offer.

The agent said: "I will contact the owners." He sounded doubtful. Sure enough, the owners turned us down out of hand.

As I remember it, we were having a pub lunch at the time - somewhere overlooking the sea. There is nothing that is quite so much fun as eating seafood in the sunshine and buying houses at the same time. We decided to let them sweat. I had told the agent we would get back to them. All we had to do was wait.

Interestingly, the vendor decided to do the same. They knew we had gone back a second time with a builder - so we must be serious. All they had to do was make us sweat.

Of course, we weren't sweating at all. We didn't really want a house that big. We were just dreaming and having fun - if it fell into our laps for a song, wouldn't that be great?

We returned to Woodbridge and more piles of estate agents' bumph.

So, we had decided we were going to live somewhere with deep water where I could have a "proper" boat and sail long distances single-handed. We had tried Salcombe in Devon. We had worked our way eastwards along the coast, flirted with the Isle of Wight - and the only thing we could be sure about was that Woodbridge was a non-starter for the simple fact that twice a day, it ran out of water completely. In fact, at low-tide springs, you can walk across the river if you don't mind getting muddy. No, Woodbridge was out.

Then Tamsin returned from shopping with a glossy estate agent's brochure for a house overlooking the river. In fact, they hadn't even bothered to put a picture of the house on the cover - just the view.

It was absolutely stupendous. Probably one of the best views from any house in the town. From the living room - from the sunroom, which would be my study… from the terrace (big old flagstones for big barbecues) you could look right down as far as Methersgate Quay. When the moon rose in the South and reflected on the water, it was absolutely magical (as the vendor pointed out).

And, of course, there was the acre of garden and a ride-on mower which came with the sale. On top of everything else, four bedrooms and a huge, unused attic room which occupied virtually the whole floor area.

And because it was only half of an even bigger house, it was just about affordable. We met the neighbours, an elderly couple who explained that when they came to sell, they would give us first refusal - imagine that: Having the whole house! Of course, that would be years in the future - by which time we would be able to afford it because… well, I was sure we would be able to afford it somehow…

In the space of a week, I celebrated my 50th birthday, bought a house and got married. How exciting was that!

Chapter 17
First

By the end of the year, we had moved in, developed a taste for IKEA meatballs, embarked on a flurry of curtain measuring and carpet fitting, built an en-suite bathroom ... an absolute flurry of activity and excitement.

I was still writing my *Dogwatch* column for Yachting World, dragging out old stories from the distant past ... and some from my father's distant past. However, *Passing Through* had fallen by the wayside for the very good reason that the boat was ashore and not "passing through" anywhere.

It was time to do something interesting - if only to produce some copy.

You may remember the original plan in which I was going to retire at 55, buy the "ultimate boat" and sail around the world going in for all the classic single-handed races. Obviously, this would have generated all sorts of knockabout pieces for Dogwatch - and, no doubt, some longer and much more serious analysis of weather and seamanship.

In amongst this, I had always been aware that in all the annals of record-breaking voyages, the first single-handed non-stop voyage around the British Isles seemed to have been forgotten.

Oh, Joshua Slocum had gone round the world singlehanded, and Robin Knox-Johnston had gone round the world singlehanded and non-stop. But nobody had navigated around the British coastal waters all by themselves and all in one go.

There might have been a good reason for this - for one thing, the closer you are to land, the more traffic you are going to encounter - fishing boats, coasters... other yachts, for that matter. Also, the closer you are to land, the more chance there is that you might inadvertently bump into it. So, keeping alert and managing to sleep in very short snatches is vital - and this was something on which I had always prided myself. Of course, I hadn't done it for a good many years - my last long trip had been in 1991, and here we were in 2000, but surely it must be like riding a bicycle: I would soon get back into the swing of it.

The more I mulled over the idea, the more attractive it seemed. It would kill an awful lot of birds with one stone: It would give me something exciting to do. It would give me something interesting to write about. I could probably find a newspaper to pay me for regular updates (I could show them what I had produced for the Evening Standard during the OSTAR). If I was going to be generating all that publicity, surely marine suppliers would give me stuff. I might even get a supermarket to supply the food - public relations people all knew the (possibly apocryphal) story of Tony Bullimore, who survived for four days in the hull of his upturned boat in the Southern Ocean with nothing but a bar of chocolate. All the confectionary companies hoped it was their chocolate, but the canny sailor refused to say - at least until his agent had agreed a contract with the highest bidder.

And, of course, it would get *Lottie Warren* back in the water.

I was well aware that the caravan-like catamaran was not the natural choice for such an undertaking: The course is 2,000 miles, and the Royal Western Yacht Club, which organises the Round Britain and Ireland Race every four years, recognises that it is so tough, they insist the boats are double-handed and stop five times on the way.

I would be going on my own in a boat designed for family cruising and without stopping.

However, people had sailed round the world in Heavenly Twins catamarans. They might not be the fastest to windward but, properly handled, they had been shown to survive anything the ocean could throw at them - and, of course, now that I had decanted the ton of Lego and got the tractor out of the bow locker, she would go a lot faster. I began writing letters to potential sponsors.

Once the Daily Telegraph was on board with the offer of a weekly column - for what seemed to be great money (until I worked out that the faster I went, the fewer columns I would be able to sell them), other companies decided "what the hell", and piled in too. Tesco sent me enough vouchers to feed a family for six months, a marine supplier (to my chagrin, I can't remember which) lent me a liferaft. The local mobile phone shop arranged for an aerial to go on top of the mast. Casio sent me the most enormous "wrist chronometer" accurate to a millisecond and waterproof to 150 metres.

This last was necessary because I had decided I was going to be navigating by sextant and compass. The logic dictated that I had done it before - across the Atlantic - and felt a certain pride in maintaining the ancient art. But also, I knew I wasn't going to be getting round very quickly - Lottie Warren's windward performance would see to that. But there was another consideration, too: Being the first is a record that nobody can take away from you. It's as permanent as Robin Knox-Johnston's. But no sooner had he stepped ashore in Falmouth than Chay Blyth started making plans to go round the other way, against the wind.

Going round Britain clockwise or anti-clockwise wouldn't make a great deal of difference. But how about going round without any modern electronic aids? Now, that would be something different - rather as the Golden Globe Race has since captured the imagination of the sailing public by recreating Knox-Johnston's feat 50 years on...

So, partly because I didn't have a GPS to fix my position, but I did still have a sextant, I resolved to go low-tech. Besides, being slightly lost has always produced good copy.

At the last minute, the company supplying the liferaft asked about my EPIRB. This stands for Emergency Position Indicating Radio Beacon: When you press the button, it sends a signal up to a satellite, which is then redirected to Falmouth Coastguard, who coordinate a rescue operation. In other words, if I needed rescuing, someone would come and get me.

I wasn't at all sure about this - after all, it was hardly low-tech. But the man on the phone would have none of it: "I think you really should," he said.

Ah yes, there is something else I should mention: Amidst all the preparations, Tamsin said: "I have something to tell you. But, before I do, will you promise me you'll still go? It won't make any difference to your plans?"

Well, the plans were so advanced by now that it would be darned difficult to change them...

"I'm pregnant," she said.

She would be five months by the time I set off. Later, I was to discover that this was no accident. A doctor friend came up with some research about timing which should ensure this baby was a girl – and, come November, a little girl it turned out to be. Meanwhile, this seemed to be another good reason for taking an EPIRB along: I had already missed one birth by being stuck at the bus stop. I didn't want to miss another sitting in a liferaft waiting for a ship to come by.

The local paper and television station came to see me off, and the Telegraph had me write the whole front page of their Weekend section. The representative for the World Sailing Speed Record Council was there at the river mouth to time me crossing the start line.

And everything went rather well to begin with. It was wonderful to be back at sea on my own. The little boat seemed to appreciate it, too - skipping up the East coast unencumbered by a ton of domestic paraphernalia. Somewhere off Yorkshire, I set up the laptop - about the size of a briefcase in those days and put together a light-hearted and generally encouraging despatch - and then had to work my way back to the coast of Scotland in order to send it over the mobile phone network.

It was only then that things started to go wrong.

This was the beginning of June. It shouldn't be too much to ask for good weather in June, should it?

I was off the top right-hand corner of Scotland, heading offshore towards the Shetland Islands, when Radio 4's Shipping forecast mentioned a "vigorous low" tracking across the Atlantic. Well, if I was going to be at sea for a month, I would be very lucky not to come across one gale somewhere along the route.

However, the next forecast, which included the outlook for the following 48 hours, mentioned a "severe gale". At this point, I started considering options: The obvious (the sensible) thing to do would be to take shelter in one of Shetland's many sheltered inlets, but that would mean sailing into the rising wind - which was not the Heavenly Twins' strong point. Besides, when I got there, I would probably have to use the engine, which would mean disqualifying myself from the record attempt.

On the other hand, I could continue up to the top of the islands - to the wonderfully named headland, the Muckle Flugga, and then see which way the unpleasantness was going to come from. If there was any North in it, I could duck back down the North Sea and have all the sea room as far as the Dutch Coast to ride out the gale. If it was to come from the south, I could do the same all the way to Norway.

The suggestion that *Lottie Warren* could not cope with a gale did not occur to me. I had the designer's notes on storm management for Catamarans: Pat Patterson had sailed round the world in his Heavenly Twins and found that if he trailed a long rope in a big loop from the bow to the stern, the boat would lie sideways on to the wind and drift with the breaking seas - something a monohull with a deep keel cannot do without turning over. Only when the impact from the waves became "shock-like" and there seemed to be danger of the boat sustaining damage should you run from the storm, trailing the rope from the stern of each hull. I hoped it wouldn't come to that.

In due course, I found myself North of the islands with a forecast of south-westerly Force Nine. I put out my ropes with two motor scooter tyres from bow to stern. Gradually, the little boat took up an attitude sideways on to the wind. Time ticked past.

A fishing boat came and looked at me. Watching him through the tinted windows, I wondered what he must be thinking - was this an abandoned yacht? Might there be some salvage here?

I stuck my head out and gave him a wave. He revved up his big diesel and departed.

The phone rang. A friend wanted to know how I was getting on. I told him I had stopped and was waiting for the gale. If he had reservations about this, he was too good a friend to say so.

Gradually, the wind began to increase. The little boat bobbed gamely. With all sail furled, I pottered about, housekeeping, stowing things for when the weather became really lively. It was remarkable how calm it all seemed down below - the fruit bowl on the table staying put just as if it was in the kitchen at home. I made myself a meal. I thought of putting on my thermal underwear. Would I need it? I'd washed it on the way up the East Coast (heaven knows why - there was no one else to smell it). Anyway, it still wasn't dry. I pulled on my very splendid (and free) Dubarry boots and Helly Hansen trousers in readiness.

It was at this point that I picked up a garbled coastguard safety broadcast. I could have sworn they mentioned "Storm Force Ten". Still, it was too late now. All the same…

All the same, what? All the same, worrying? All the same, frightening?

Actually, all the same, **exciting**. I had never been in a Storm Force Ten before. Come to that, I wasn't sure I'd ever been in a Force Nine sustained for any length of time.

When, later, someone asked me if I was frightened at this point, it seemed vain to say that I wasn't. Now, of course, I can recognise this as **Taking risks in activities with little or no regard for personal safety.**

Daft, really.

Eventually, the breaking seas started hitting the boat like a car crash. Two or three times, there was an almighty bang, and everything shook before the cabin filled with a rushing noise as *Lottie* skidded sideways in a cloud of foam. Finally, a pot of light bulbs shot across the cabin from one side to the other. Time to re-arrange the ropes. Time to run before the storm.

Wrapping up in full foul-weather gear, I crawled up to the bow and tied a light line to the rope. Then, crawled back to the opposite stern and made it fast to the other stern. All I had to do then was release the heavy one from the bow. Sure enough, the boat turned through 90 degrees and set off at the most tremendous speed to the North East.

Standing at the wheel, I watched the log hit 13 knots - then 16. Looking behind, two white wakes stretched out astern with the tyres kicking up plumes of spray - and then, behind them, the crest of the wave. It was high, of course, but it was a long way behind, so it didn't seem particularly threatening. Meanwhile, the little boat continued to track dead straight downwind. I engaged the autopilot, and she thundered along, straight as an arrow. Of course, the wind had her hanging on the warps just as surely as a flag will fly straight in a gale. In fact, the more I stood there, marvelling at the scene, the more it became clear that this boat didn't really need me at all.

I started to enjoy myself. I got out the camera and took pictures of this wild and desolate seascape. It seemed to be white all over, with the sun shining out of a clear blue sky. It was while I was doing this that the boat gave a lurch, flinging me from one side to the other so that I landed painfully on top of the lumpy EPIRB mounted on the starboard bulkhead. Still, I hadn't let go of the camera. I carried on taking pictures – although I couldn't understand why the flash kept going off. It was supposed to be automatic, and there was plenty of daylight. There was daylight 24 hours a day up here.

But it wasn't the flash. It was the strobe light on the EPIRB - which meant that the EPIRB was switched on. I must have activated it when I sat on it. Now it was firing off distress messages to the satellites. When this happens by accident, you're not supposed to switch it off - that just confuses everyone. On the other hand, if I didn't switch it off now, I would find myself the focus of a full-scale search and rescue operation. I don't think I could have lived with the embarrassment. I switched it off.

It was too late. At home in Woodbridge, Tamsin received a phone call from Falmouth Coastguard. They said they received one "ping", but then nothing. They wanted to know if she had heard anything. In the end, they said they would treat it as a false alarm. If it happened again, they would act.

Of course, I didn't know any of this. Certainly, I didn't need rescuing. The little boat was running dead straight downwind in brilliant sunshine with excellent visibility. In due course, there would be some oil rigs to watch out for, but an oil rig is a very small target in a very big ocean, and you have to be incredibly unlucky to run into one by accident.

All the same, I was doing more than 12 knots, so I wouldn't get much warning. Maybe I ought to get some rest. I looked again at the compass, at the wake, cast an eye round the decks and cockpit for anything coming adrift. It seemed very clear that I could afford to get my head down for a bit. For the time being, I was surplus to requirements.

I ducked down into the cabin, shut the doors and lay down with the kitchen timer right by my ear. I set it for ten minutes. When it went off, I could just lift my head and look straight out of the window in front of me.

And so the storm raged, and *Lottie Warren* rattled on in the direction of Bergen or Tromsø or somewhere, and I slept and woke and slept and woke again. In a strange way, it was remarkably peaceful: The wind in the rigging, the rushing noise of the boat at hull speed - and more on occasions, as she seemed to lift out of the water - but all the while dead straight downwind.

A couple of times, the smooth progress was disturbed by a slight jolt. I took this to be the warps taking up the slack and pulling one of the sterns back on course. It seemed reasonable. I put my head down again.

How much time passed after that, I cannot say. Certainly, the alarm woke me a couple of times. I looked out, and all was well. But then I woke to the sensation of going up in a high-speed lift. The first thing I saw when I opened my eyes was the fruit bowl tipping over, spilling apples and oranges across the table.

Out loud, I said: "She's going over."

And she was. The whole cabin rotated - quite slowly, it seemed - and I found myself on the ceiling. Water squirted in around the door. All sorts of loose objects were floating about - sloshing back and forth as the boat now bobbed up and down as the waves passed under her.

If she had been a monohull, by now, she would have been coming up as the weight of the keel took over. With *Lottie Warren,* there *was* no keel. She was completely stable upside down - more so, in fact, now that the mast and sails were pointing at the bottom.

This boat would stay upside down indefinitely.

So, the first thing to do would be to activate the EPIRB. I opened the doors. Hardly any more water came in. I plucked the beacon from its bracket and brought it back inside, pressed the button, and the strobe began to flash again. Now, it would have to go in the water, floating alongside the boat with a clear view of the sky and the satellites. I thought about the cockpit, but that would mean negotiating all the ropes that were washing about there. Better if I could just push it out of the galley window - yes, it would fit. I tied the tether to the freshwater pump and pushed the rest out of the window.

Now what. The boat would float forever - for weeks, at least - that was the theory. She had buoyancy chambers fore and aft - as well as all the air trapped inside. All the same, maybe I ought to check the liferaft - get it ready just in case the boat decided to go down suddenly. The liferaft had been lent to me by the same people who supplied the EPIRB, and I had stowed it on the double bunk in the starboard aft cabin. Of course, now everything had fallen to the deckhead - and that included all the clothes stowed in the lockers under the bunk because multihull sailors don't need to secure their lockers against a knockdown or a capsize because once the boat is upside down, stuff falling out of lockers is the least of your worries.

All the same, rooting through the underwater mess, do you think I could find the liferaft? It did occur to me that the hinged hatch to the aft cabin was hanging open. Was it possible that it had dropped out? No, they're designed to float, even before you pull the lanyard to inflate them.

After a bit, I gave up looking. For one thing, my eyes were stinging every time I put my head underwater. That must be the battery acid leaking. Nothing to do but wait, I suppose. Wedging myself mostly out of the water on what used to be the top of the wardrobe locker, I wondered if anyone was on the way to rescue me.

Was someone in the Coastguard Centre at Falmouth at that very moment saying: "Distress Message from *Lottie Warren*? No, don't worry about that one. That's a false alarm. We had that a couple of hours ago."

Meanwhile, was there anything I could do to help myself? If there was, I couldn't think of it. It is only with hindsight that I consider warm clothes. Maybe a lifejacket…

Instead, I reached out for an apple floating by and bit into it. It turned out to be an orange.

I can't tell you how long I stayed like that. The water sloshed back and forth, taking with it plastic cups, a bottle of ketchup, my sunhat. I wouldn't need that...

Honestly, you would think, in a predicament like this, that I would consider what else I could do to help myself or those who were on their way to rescue me if, indeed, they were. Instead, all that time in the hull - and I have no idea how long it was - I am sure I became very philosophical about my fate. More interesting, of course, was finding out exactly what that fate might look like - the unknown. It was – and I find it absurd to say so – **really exciting.**

It might have been that this was the beginning of my muddled thinking. With a flash of recognition, I realised I was becoming confused - I was wading through deeper water now. Presumably, the boat was settling - which meant that there was less air - and anyway, that air was being used up as I breathed it in and out. One way and another, if I wasn't thinking straight now, nothing was going to become clearer by waiting. It was time to get out.

I had two options: The companionway doors or one of the aft hatches. The companionway would land me in the middle of the cockpit, and the last time I looked out there, it was a complete tangle of rope with sheets and control lines slopping back and forth. If I got tangled up in that lot, I might never get out - in which case, I would drown. Not an option.

The aft hatch, then. All I had to do was make sure that I turned in the right direction - away from the cockpit. Since I was in the hull with the galley - the port hull - I would turn right to face away from the cockpit. No - that wasn't it; in order to climb up the steps, I had to face forward. So, I should turn left…

But now the boat was upside down, so that meant turning right… although, because I *was* upside down, I wouldn't need the steps … which meant I would be facing aft after all … so… that meant turning left. No, right. Hang on, which way would I be facing?

The more I thought about it, the more disorientated I became. Whether this was because my brain was being starved of oxygen or because my brain is not very clear at the best of times, I couldn't say. One way and another, matters would not be made any clearer by waiting. It was time to go.

In fact, I think I said "Go" - and went. I dived down into the water, found the hatch, slipped through it into the bright, sunlit underwater world below and then, without another thought and certainly, without any apparent effort, found myself at the stern looking at the name I had stuck on so laboriously back in Chichester. It was upside down. Putting both hands on the bottom (what had been the bottom), I pushed myself up, and suddenly I was out of the water and standing up, holding onto one of the stub keels. I had lost my beautiful boots.

Chapter 18
Rescue

It was a different world standing on the bottom of the boat - and one I much preferred after the waterlogged confusion and stifling atmosphere of the cabin. Once again, there was the brilliant blue sky and the sea, a deep blue that you only get from an ocean in bright sunshine. And white, of course - white from the breaking waves all around and the long streaks of blown spume. In fact, there was a good deal of water in the air as well, flying off the breakers and hitting me in the face like hailstones. I didn't mind. It felt warm, and this really was the most fantastic scene.

Then a wave broke over the boat and washed my feet from under me. Of course: I had lost my boots, and so my socks slipped on the smooth gelcoat like fried eggs in a pan. This left me horizontal in the water, holding onto the keel for dear life.

The water drained away, and I stood up. The keel was about the height of the back of a dining-room chair - quite convenient. All I had to do was hang onto it. I let go and walked over to the other side. This was the windward side. The boat had taken up an attitude of 45° to the wind, and now I had it in my face. I walked back to the lee side again. I must say I felt very safe up there - there was plenty of room, and the bridge deck was bounded on both sides by the hulls like a big playpen. It was just the bow and stern I needed to be careful not to fall off.

Then another wave came along.

In fact, at regular intervals, a succession of waves came along. Each one washing me off my feet and then draining away over the bow before I stood up again. All I had to do was keep on standing up. I could see the tiny yellow EPIRB floating off to leeward, its strobe light flashing impotently in the sun. Presumably, it was sending out its coded distress message to the satellite, and that was being beamed down to Falmouth.

And what were they doing about it in Falmouth? Launching a full-scale rescue operation? Dismissing it as another false alarm?

If I had been in a monohull, by now, I would have been hard at work clearing away the mess and getting the boat secured ready for the time the wind would abate, and we could make sail again - even under jury rig. A monohull doesn't stay upside down. I hated the feeling of helplessness - just standing there waiting for someone to come and rescue me. In a monohull, I wouldn't even have activated the ERIRB - not unless I was actually sinking.

How long I stood there on the bottom of the boat in the middle of the storm, getting knocked down and getting up again, I have no idea. Time didn't seem to have any meaning. It never occurred to me to look at my big, chunky, shockproof Casio wrist chronometer (waterproof to 150 metres). But eventually, I realised that I could not stand there forever. Eventually, I would get tired. Eventually, when a wave came and washed my feet from under me, and I lay horizontal in the middle of the breaking crest, I would let go of the keel. Then, I would disappear over the bow as quickly as a child's sandal off a Cornish rock when the tide comes in.

And that would be the end of me. The chances of swimming back to the boat would be pretty slim. I wasn't wearing a lifejacket, but even if I had been, that would just have prolonged things for an hour or two.

Of course, this was not the way to be thinking at all. If I had learned anything from Tony Robbins and his Ultimate Power, it was that you get what you think about - thoughts become things...

If I was going to dwell on drowning, then the likelihood was that I would, indeed, drown. So, I had to think about not drowning - not dying. After all, I had a family at home. Tamsin and Owen and Theo were counting on me coming back - and there was the new baby on the way - a little girl. Besides, if I got back in time, I would be there when the cat had her kittens and for the church fete...

So, under my breath, to myself, so I would not be embarrassed by anyone overhearing, I said: "I won't die."

"I will not die."

I gave it some emphasis – put an exclamation mark on the end. I lifted up my head and shouted it. It felt good. It gave me strength in my hands – which was just as well because another wave came along and, sure enough, I hung on until it drained away over the bow, and I stood up and shook the water out of my eyes and shouted at the sky: "I WILL NOT DIE!"

And somewhere in the middle of all the drama, a small voice crept in and said: "You know, this is bloody good copy!"

The day wore on, but up there in those high latitudes, it never gets dark in June, and so it was difficult to recognise the passage of time. The waves kept coming, the wind kept blowing, and I kept picking myself up and shouting again.

Until something made me turn round. I don't know what it was – who can say what makes you notice something without sight or sound of it? Just a presence, maybe. After all, I hadn't seen anything of civilisation since the fishermen came to inspect me. How long ago had that been?

But for some reason, I looked behind me and there, hanging in the sky above my head, was a beautiful big helicopter with black and yellow stripes painted all over its underside. It was just hovering there.

I took a hand off the keel and waved. Now it would come

down and get me. I would be saved! I wouldn't have to hold onto this keel anymore. No more being knocked sideways by every wave...

Except that the helicopter stayed where it was – just hovering stationary above me. What was it playing at? I mean, they'd come all this way to get me. Surely, they would want to get on with it and go home for tea.

So, I waved again.

And again.

"Come on, what are you waiting for?"

And still, it hung in the sky.

Doubts began to creep in.

Of course! That was it. There wasn't a helicopter at all. This was an hallucination. Extreme stress and the mind-altering effects of exposure had caused my mind to play tricks – pretty cruel tricks at that: I wasn't going to be rescued. The EPIRB wasn't working; the signals were garbled; Falmouth Coastguard had put the whole thing down to malfunctioning microchips. I was going to stay on the bottom of my upturned boat until "my hands can't feel to grip; my toes too numb to step" (who said that? Bob Dylan?) Yes, that was it; now I was definitely hallucinating...

And then, a small black dot appeared below the helicopter. It dropped fast and evolved into the shape of a man on a wire, dressed all in fluorescent orange. He swooped down like a big bird, splashed into the sea next to me, whooshed up again and then down, falling across the hull. I grabbed him by the legs.

"OK?"

I couldn't hear a word he said. I nodded vigorously.

He put a strop over my head and pulled it under my arms, and we were off. I looked down, and already the sea was far below, another wave sloshing over Lottie Warren.

And then everything went warm and dark. I wasn't even in the helicopter yet – but I knew I didn't have to worry anymore. I didn't have to fight anymore. I didn't have to shout: "I WILL NOT DIE!"

... although it would make bloody good copy...

* * *

I was in a bath. The bath was in the middle of the room – which is an odd place for a bath. Usually, a bath is in a corner, but this one was in the middle of a large grey room with a counter like a kitchen.

At the counter, on a high stool, sat a young man with very short hair wearing a T-shirt.

"Hello," he said.

I said nothing. Best to work out what's going on before committing myself.

The young man got off the stool, advanced towards the bath and said: "Open up."

Then: "I need to take your temperature."

I opened my mouth as I had when I was eight years old, and the whole school had its temperatures taken twice a day for the first three weeks of term – only this thermometer didn't taste of methylated spirit.

"You've got hypothermia," said the young man. "Need to warm you up slowly."

He examined the thermometer, looked at another one floating on a string by my knee and added some more hot water.

After that, there was nothing to do but lie in the bath, keep reading the thermometers and adding more hot water until everything reached 98.4° Fahrenheit or whatever I was supposed to be in Celsius.

It turned out that I was on the Murchison oil rig. The helicopter did not have enough fuel to take me back to Lerwick, but the rig kept a stock for emergencies, so as soon as I was warmed up and had something to eat, I could be on my way. The kitchen had stayed open for me. Curry, the young man thought.

We talked about where he lived and how I came to be up there in the middle of nowhere – small talk, which I'm afraid I can't remember at all. Then he declared himself satisfied with my core body temperature and handed me a big, rough towel. Then, a pile of clothes kept on oil rigs for shipwrecked mariners.

If ever you should be shipwrecked, prepare yourself for this: The clothes must fit anybody and must be as cheap as possible. What is not necessary is that anybody needs to pick them out as being just what they were looking for.

This is how I discovered that somebody still makes Y-Fronts and matt black rubber-soled shoes. A pair of wide black trousers (large), a black T-shirt (ditto) and a black sweatshirt with some unidentifiable orange logo on the front completed the ensemble. In my hand, I carried a bright orange padded nylon jacket.

Fortunately, the sickbay did not boast a full-length mirror.

My friend, the medic, took me to the canteen, where a motherly lady in a paper hat warmed up the last helping of curry and rice. Then I had apple pie and custard. And hot, sweet tea. Hot, sweet tea is *de rigeur* for shipwrecked mariners. I wondered whether there might be a tot of rum, but apparently not.

"Would you like to make a phone call?" someone asked.

"I can make a phone call?"

"Of course."

The Daily Telegraph newsdesk answered with the bored, heard-it-all-before enthusiasm of newsdesks the world over. I explained that I had filed a piece for Saturday's Weekend section about skipping up the East coast of Scotland, but would now need to file again because I had turned the boat over.

"Hold on," he said.

After a couple of minutes, during which I wondered how much a satellite call cost the oil company, a voice I vaguely recognised said: "John, is that you?"

It was Caroline Davies. We used to sit opposite each other in the old days at the Evening Standard. She asked me what I was doing, and I told her. After a minute or two, I realised I was being interviewed. Hold on a minute, I was supposed to be writing this.

No, she said. There wasn't time. They were holding the page for the first edition.

And so, it all came tumbling out.

I can't remember quite what I said. But of course, Caroline wrote it all down in her impeccable shorthand. I still have the cutting:

"I stood there, and I looked at the sky, and I thought: I began to think of my family, very hard indeed, and I said, 'I am coming home. I am going to hold on, and I am coming home. And I had to hold on for a long time. I think I was in the water for between two and three hours. I was absolutely soaked, and there was a 45-knot wind blowing and gigantic waves breaking over me. And I held on to the keel and shouted at the sky . . ." he said, his voice trembling with emotion.

"And I shouted, 'I'm not going to die. I am not going to die' . . ." His voice trailed off as he fought to suppress tears. "Sorry, I am having a bit of a reaction. So, I just kept shouting it and shouting it. I was getting colder and colder and shaking convulsively, but I was still shouting because I believed it. I had to believe it.

"Then suddenly, I heard this noise behind me. And there was a helicopter in the sky. The helicopter took forever to come down. The waves were so high. But they were terrific. Those guys were just fabulous. They winched me up and put me in the helicopter, and I just started shaking and shaking.

"I am very sorry not to have got round for the record. But that does not really matter. I am sorry I lost the boat. But none of it really matters, does it?"

* * *

Afterwards, my minder came back and asked: "Did you get through to your family?"

Well, no. I hadn't thought about my family. I supposed I should call Tamsin too.

Over the past few hours, Tamsin had experienced the whole drama from the opposite perspective. First, there had been a call from Falmouth Coastguard, asking if she knew where I was. They had received a distress signal – the single "ping". They had treated that as a false alarm.

Now aware that the North of Scotland was experiencing storm-force winds but knowing only that I was somewhere up there, she went through the boys' tea in a haze of anxiety.

Then, an hour later, the coastguard rang again. Now, they were receiving repeated distress signals. They had initiated a Search and Rescue operation. The Lerwick Lifeboat had been launched - and a Nimrod from RAF Kinloss. Two fishing boats were on their way to the scene.

It just so happened that a friend called at the door - we never discovered whether she knew about the conditions I was facing and had gone round just in case or whether this was some sort of divine intervention. But she took over bathing the boys and getting them into bed.

Because, in no time at all, the calls started coming in from the press - in particular from our old friends at the Evening Standard - tentatively, of course, because they didn't know how much Tamsin knew. For all anybody could tell, this might be a "death knock".

In fact, there had been quite some discussion about who was going to make the call. In the end, Philip Evans pulled rank. After all, he was the one who had given me the job at the Standard in the first place - rescuing me when the Mail refused to let me go off racing across the Atlantic. Philip had been so enthusiastic that he had turned up in Plymouth bearing an enormous joint of dried beef – what the South Africans call biltong. If I didn't eat it, at least I could write about it. Philip understood.

He needn't have worried. By this time, Tamsin knew as much as anyone else - which, admittedly, was not much.

Later, the coastguard reported that the Nimrod had found Lottie Warren upside down but with no sign of life. A helicopter had been sent to investigate.

Then, the news came through that the helicopter had picked me up and was taking me to the oil rig.

So, when I telephoned, it was really quite a matter-of-fact call – more to do with how I was going to get home than any great outpouring of emotion – maybe I didn't have any left after dumping it all on poor Caroline.

By this time, they had refuelled the helicopter, and off we went to Lerwick. The press were there at the airport, and I gave them a wave which appeared in the next morning's papers. It was odd being the object of breaking news rather than chasing it. The medics ushered me briskly into an ambulance and shunted me off to hospital. I didn't think there was anything wrong with me, but all the same, I spent the night wired up to a battery of monitors, chatting to a young man in green scrubs who told me all about his new teeth. Apparently, everyone in the Shetlands ate so many sweets that they all had false teeth – even in their 20s.

After breakfast, the hospital staged a press conference.

What did I think about while I waited for rescue? I thought of my family.

Would I do it again? No, this was a one-off, and now I'd lost the boat, so, no (which got reported as "I'll never set foot on a boat again.")

Then they put me in the back of an ambulance and drove me to the airport to catch a plane for Aberdeen and Heathrow. All I had was the clothes I stood up in (which weren't even mine but the black-and-orange uniform of the fashionable shipwrecked mariner). All I had from the boat was a black binliner with the sodden clothes I had been wearing when they picked me up.

This meant that I had no money to buy a ticket. With extraordinary generosity, the local TV correspondent lent me a fistful of notes. Then, while I waited for the flight, it occurred to me to check in with the Telegraph - who promptly announced that they wanted a thousand words. Since, by now, I was the local celebrity, the airport manager put an office at my disposal and logged me into the computer.

The only trouble was that he was the only one who seemed to think my peace and quiet was important. First, I was pushed outside to have my photograph taken with the helicopter crew and no sooner had I returned to wrestle with the first paragraph than the Daily Mail came on - one of their usual stable of persuasive young women. She wanted "just a few bare bones to add to the agency copy". I was an ex-Mail man, after all...

That was why I knew exactly what was going on: "Look," I said – all understanding and patience – "I know how it works. I say something to you, and that makes it an "Exclusive Interview". You cobble it together with whatever you can get from the agency copy and a bit of colour from the local correspondent, and the next thing you know, the Mail will be making more of it than The Telegraph – who, come to think of it, won't be making anything of it at all if I don't get a move on..."

Which was just when Colin Adamson, the Evening Standard's barely tame Scotsman appeared, having flown from London. He wanted a piece for the late extra edition.

I had my own edition to worry about: "Look, Colin, honestly; I've got to file... You know what to say..."

Quick as a flash, he said: "I'll busk it, then."

"Yeah, OK."

Which was how I came to be quoted in the Standard as saying:

"My hands were like steel claws..."

By this time, we were past the luxury of the Airport Manager's office and his computer. I stood at the payphone, dictating off the top of my head. It had been six years since I had done that – but it turns out it's like riding the proverbial bicycle. After 20 minutes, the copytaker said: "Weekend section wants a word."

Weekend Section said: "Great stuff. We're going to splash on it. Can you give us 3,000 words?"

I think they got about 4,500. I went into some kind of a trance – pacing one step this way, one step that way – which was as far as the phone cord would stretch and, yes, I was right: Standing on the bottom of my upturned boat, shouting: "I will not die" as the storm raged about me did indeed make bloody good copy.

Chapter 19

Money

The Daily Telegraph paid me double for the front page of the Weekend section. I must say it did look good – I was astonished to see an enormous picture of me and Peter Mesney, the helicopter winchman, dangling on the end of the wire while, far below us, waves broke over the upturned *Lottie Warren* – and, my word, it did look rough.

There was only a picture because that particular helicopter was fresh from a training mission. It wouldn't have had a camera otherwise. But then they might not have found me at all if the Americans hadn't decided that very week, to unscramble the GPS signal and take the risk of the Russians using it to fly a cruise missile through the White House bedroom window.

Sarah Sands, the Telegraph's deputy editor and another former Standard hack, sent me a hero-gram and said that now she understood why our old editor had loved me so much. I suppose if you have a reporter who gets rescued from certain death and then rings his newsdesk before he rings his wife, it probably is true love (of newspapers). Or maybe I was just being **insensitive, irresponsible and uncaring.**

The big cheque from The Telegraph lasted a while, and there were some spin-offs for overseas publications and a bit of telly.

The insurance cheque arrived, and I bought a 19-foot Cornish Shrimper for pottering about on the river. We spent the rest on ripping up the carpets and putting down a hardwood floor.

Of course, we could have invested that money. That would have been the sensible thing to do. We could have bought a "buy-to-let" or just put it into an ISA. There is no shortage of sensible things you can do with unexpected money.

Or you can buy a new floor, a new boat and go out to lunch - no contest, really...

But then, I knew something that the sensible people didn't know: Something would turn up. I had brought my enormous desk from the flat in London. I had the gigantic computer - I set it up at right angles to the sliding doors opening onto the terrace so that all I needed to do was turn my head, and I could see the river. This way, I imagined I wouldn't get distracted.

The two little boys scampered in and out. The new baby was indeed a little girl - and, of course, we called her Lottie (I understand there are some people who call their boats after their children rather than their children after their boats.)

I started to do some freelance work for the Daily Mail's weekend section and made the discovery that every jobbing freelance journalist must stumble across in due course: That freelancing is the most miserable existence. My commissioning editor (I'm sure he had a much grander title) was a young man, apparently fresh out of university. He was too serious to understand jokes. He didn't like three-part lists either (I never knew they were called that). He didn't like me putting myself in the story – or talking directly to the reader. There was so much that he didn't like that eventually, I suggested he should correct it himself. After that, he didn't ask me to write anything else.

Never mind, something did turn up. Deborah, the friend who had found us the unseen rented house, was going back to work as a supply teacher. Her youngest child was nearly three. Would we look after Elisa for three days a week?

Well, of course, we would - she seemed to be around most of the time anyway. Besides, we were growing a houseful of our own children. What was another? Deborah insisted she would pay us.

We weren't about to turn down some extra money, but if she was paying us, that would open up all sorts of complications. What would happen if Elisa were to fall down the steps and suffer some awful life-changing injury?

But, as Tamsin said, her parents were friends. They wouldn't sue us.

But they might not have a choice. What if Elisa needed a lifetime of 24-hour care? They would have to do what was best…

In that case, we would need insurance - in which case we would have to be registered childminders. We would have to apply to the County Council – get registered with OFSTED.

I'm sure all this was a good thing: The house had to be inspected. *We* had to be inspected. We had to rip up the foxgloves in the garden because they're poisonous. Every ground-floor window and all internal glass had to be protected with an anti-shatter film. Tamsin was required to go on a first aid course - she was a registered paediatric nurse, for heaven's sake (the council relented on that one in the end).

Naturally, it wasn't worth going through all this just for one little girl. Before we knew where we were, we had five toddlers running about the place. It was something new. It was **exciting** (that again). It was fun.

I had an idea - a weekly column about childminding. It would be one of those harmless, heart-warming pieces that becomes a part of people's lives. It could go on for years.

I wrote to the Daily Mail - but this time by-passed the young man who didn't like jokes and sent the letter straight to the editor, Paul Dacre, who was becoming as much a legend as David English - and liked me just as much.

Of course, Paul was the editor everyone else loved to hate - overbearing, foul-mouthed, a workaholic and, if only he had maintained a chaotic domestic life, he would have been the epitome of all that was best and worst about Fleet Street. Still, he had always given me my head. This might just turn out to be another silk purse. He passed my letter to the Deputy Editor.

From there, the idea made its way round a succession of the famously terrifying open-plan offices on the third floor of the new Northcliffe House in Kensington. Eventually, it came back to me transformed ever so slightly: "Award-winning war correspondent John Passmore reports from the Home Front". The "Home Front" title was mocked up to look like a telex full of bullet holes.

As always, The Mail launched its new column with a fanfare of newsprint: A feature writer came to spend the day with us and wrote me up as a lovable buffoon - a cross between Colonel Blimp and the BFG. There was the usual exhaustive Daily Mail photo session - the photographer knew better than to go back to the office without a shot of me in every conceivable situation.

And finally, I settled down to write my first column.

This was easy because somewhere in the process, somebody had asked me – almost as an afterthought: "How much do you want to be paid?"

If ever there was a time to think big, this was it. We were so far down the road now that the roller coaster could not be stopped. Anyway, it had been approved by the editor. It was as good as an "Editor's Must".

I swallowed soundlessly and said: "£1 a word?"

I hoped the question mark, also, was silent.

The voice on the other end said: "OK."

Punching the air when you're on the phone is silent anyway.

A pound a word is celebrity money. You can live on a pound a word - particularly when they want 1,400 words a week. The best part is that every time you write "and" or "the" or "but", you can hear the change clinking into your pocket.

You see, I told you something would turn up. To celebrate, we booked a holiday and had the sofas recovered.

All I had to do was write my first joke.

Here it is: "Little Johnny tightened his grip on the tricycle and gave me a look I had last seen at the other end of a Kalashnikov AK47 at a midnight checkpoint in Sarajevo."

In the following week's column, we had the second joke: "Suzy was serving tea in the playhouse. From the dolls' blue plastic teapot, she poured – with the greatest concentration – a concoction which might have been orange squash, washing up liquid and pond water. I've tasted worse – I was once served mint tea in a fly-blown shack beside the Basra road during an Iranian bomb strike."

It soon became clear that this was a one-joke column. If we had gone with the original "heartwarming tales of little children," it might still be running, and the whole of the rest of this book might go off in a different, happier direction. But no: After about six weeks, the 1,400 words were cut down to 1,000… then, 600…

And finally, inexplicably, one Saturday morning, I opened the paper, and there was nothing there. In disbelieving panic, I flipped backwards and then forwards - through Health and Travel and Money. I reached the Gardening section. Had they moved it to gardening?

Finally, there came a point when it was clear that The Home Front was never going to appear again. Not that I stopped writing it, of course – and certainly I didn't stop sending in the regular monthly invoices for £5,600 (£7,000 in months with five Saturdays!)

It took the Daily Mail several weeks to realise what was happening and formally bury the dinosaur. In all, the column's lifespan had been just seven months – but it kept us going for more than a year.

So, what next? Tamsin and I sat down and reviewed our assets. One of them was the enormous attic room. When we moved in, the floor had been covered with layer upon layer of carpet offcuts and the wind whistling through the holes in the wood panelling. In places, you could see where daylight crept through the tiles. With a bit of smartening up, some insulation, a new carpet, we were ready to take in a lodger.

Mark was a nice lad but socially awkward. For two years, we couldn't have spaghetti for dinner. It wasn't that Mark didn't like spaghetti. Mark would eat anything – but we drew the line at watching Mark eat spaghetti.

From Mark the lodger and his spaghetti, we progressed to Bed and Breakfast with designer scrambled eggs. By this time, we had chickens, and many of the guests enthused in the visitors' book about my wonderful scrambled eggs (the secret is grass-fed hens and lots of butter). These went down particularly well when I would announce theatrically: "Oh dear, we're out of eggs. Just a minute… Owen, would go and fetch some more eggs, please?"

And Owen, aged five or six, would take the tiny wicker basket and trot off down the garden – to return a few minutes later saying: "I'm sorry it took so long, but I had to wait for the hen to finish laying the last one."

It was OK, we kept body and soul together – well, actually, we had some nice holidays and bought a new car but, always at the back of my mind were Mr Micawber's words, "Annual income twenty pounds…"

But, of course, it was also Mr Micawber who said "Something will turn up" – and which do you suppose I adopted as my mantra? Which would be **riskier?** Which would be more **exciting**?

What turned up was some junk mail addressed to the previous owner of the house.

Now, if you don't have a job to go to – or indeed one that you can do at home anymore. If indeed, you retired at 45 and are beginning to realise this might have been a tad impulsive (and still have no idea why you didn't realise it at the time), you tend to open junk mail – especially if it has The Fleet Street Letter written all over it.

Please understand that this had nothing to do with Fleet Street as in newspapers. Instead, the Fleet Street Letter was an investment tip sheet that I remember my father reading along with the Financial Times and the Investor's Chronicle. He was a very successful investor. In the years after the war when the economy was picking itself up off the floor and returning servicemen were starting up companies left and right, Father was a "stag" – that is Stock Market speak for someone who invests in a new company just coming to the stock market.

The best bit about being a stag was that you could apply for the shares but didn't have to pay for them until the end of the three-week Stock Market account. Of course, if the shares were over-subscribed and started trading above their issue price, you could sell them before the end of the account and show an instant profit (even though you had never actually paid for them in the first place.)

This sounded brilliant. "What happened if the price went down instead of up?" I asked my father.

"Down?" he growled. "Down? They never went down!"

I told you this thing was hereditary.

The idea of the three-week account was long gone, but during my years as a junior reporter at the Mail, I had attempted to boost my income by subscribing to the Fleet Street Letter's " Penny Share Guide" - the idea of making a modest profit from Marks & Spencer and Unilever wasn't nearly as exciting as making a fortune from some tiny company nobody had heard of such as Apple or Microsoft. The idea that my money would have been much safer with a household name backed by a proven track record simply never occurred to me. Who wants "safer"? You can imagine how well that worked out…

However, what the Fleet Street Letter was offering now was even more exciting (that word again).

What they were offering was Commodity Trading on the Futures Market – the incredibly volatile, potentially hugely profitable speculation on gold, wheat, crude oil, pork bellies – in fact, every commodity anyone might ever want to buy. To understand just how profitable (and how ***risky***) this can be, look at it this way: Mr Kellogg makes exceedingly good cornflakes, and he needs to set a price for them. Obviously, this depends on the price of corn. Prices change depending on supply and demand (the weather, global economics), but Mr Kellogg doesn't want to keep having to change the price of his cornflakes every week, so he needs to know what the price is going to be in the future.

He can do this by buying a Futures Contract - that is a contract to buy a fixed amount of that commodity at a fixed price on a fixed date in the future. These contracts are called derivatives, and before the fixed date arrives, they can be traded. The person buying the contract doesn't have to buy the wheat or sugar itself, just the contract, which costs just a fraction of the price of the actual consignment. This is called "leverage". Of course, when the Fixed Date finally arrives, the person holding the contract has to go ahead and buy or sell whatever the contract is for – in this case, all those bushels of corn.

So, there's the risk. For a few hundred dollars, you can buy a Futures Contract for tens of thousands of dollars worth of corn. But if you get stuck with it when the Fixed Date arrives, you have to come up with the goods – which will, indeed, cost you tens of thousands of dollars … or hundreds of thousands of dollars … or millions of dollars if you got in really deep.

Of course, that was never going to happen to me. I was going to get the other side of the coin, the profit of thousands of dollars … or hundreds of thousands of dollars … or millions of dollars if

I went in really deep.

You can understand why this would grab my attention. I read the leaflet from cover to cover. The idea was that you loaded some software into your computer and tracked the price movements of a basket of commodities. The program would flash up particular movements, which could be interpreted as signals to buy or sell. There were examples of how the clever program could turn an investment of a few hundred dollars into a profit of tens of thousands.

You could send off for a free copy of the program, which would work for three months while you experimented with the pretend money.

What was there to lose?

Ah, those beautiful words: "What have you got to lose?"

Did I throw it in the bin as junk mail? Or did I grab it with both hands, recognising that this was just what I had been looking for. This was the "something" Mr Micawber had promised me would turn up?

What do you think?

Of course, I went into it properly first. I devoured books on trading. I learned about The Turtles - the famous experiment conducted by two successful traders in an attempt to end the argument about whether successful traders were simply born with what it takes - or was this something anybody could learn? These two men, sitting over their vintage bourbon whiskies in their New York club, decided to advertise for a bunch of complete beginners, give them each a pot of a million dollars and a set of rules which, if they could stick to them, should make each one another million.

They called them The Turtles because one of the "Godfathers" had visited Singapore and seen how they bred turtles out there – as a writhing mass in a barrel. The room in which the young traders would be locked for eight hours a day would be the trading equivalent of that barrel.

Well, as every trader knows. It worked. One dropped out, but over four years, the other 23 made $174 million between them.

I could live with that.

Sure enough, practising with my play money, I made $10,000 on the US dollar in six weeks. This was the answer. This was the "something" that I knew would turn up. Had all those poor dead soldiers taken a hand in it? I liked to think so – because the one thing a trader needs is courage. You have to risk everything. Kipling would have loved it: "If you can risk it all on a turn of pitch and toss…"

I could do that. The more I thought about it, the more it seemed to be the answer to everything. I took to sitting up all night staring at the computer, running scenarios, refining my "rules".

Now, of course, I know what this is called. It's called "hyperfocus":

While people with ADHD are often easily distracted, they may also have something called hyperfocus. A person with ADHD can get so engrossed in something that they can become unaware of anything else around them. This kind of focus makes it easier to lose track of time and ignore those around you. This can lead to relationship misunderstandings.

Doing it for real involved a man called Patrick in Nevada. He would place the trades for me with a brokerage firm in Chicago. The brokerage firm sent through dozens of pages of contract which I had to read and sign, initialling every page and, in some cases, copying out particularly terrifying clauses in my own hand.

They didn't terrify me, though. I was happy to agree that if things went wrong, the men from Chicago could come and take my house, all my money, all my possessions – down to my last cufflink. Nothing was going to go wrong, was it?

And it didn't. I started small and began to make more money than I had earned from writing for newspapers – even at £1 a word.

Except I didn't take the money out. No, I used it to place bigger and bigger trades - and then I put more money in - and the figures went up and up. It was like magic. It seemed I could do no wrong. I was into corn and wheat and pork bellies and cocoa and coffee and crude oil and gold and the US dollar and the British pound… The screen kept flashing up its signals, drawing graphs that spelled more and more money.

I bought a laptop so I could take it on holiday with me - every day, either late at night after the markets closed in Chicago or in the morning before they opened, I would put in my hour in front of the screen. It was so easy, once you knew how - and as long as you stuck to the rules, kept emotion out it, became an automaton responding to the commands of the little green and red symbols, the blue and yellow lines intersecting…

I went from trading a single lot to two, to four, to six. The more lots I had in play, the more money I made. For instance, one lot of gold was a kilo. Imagine how much that's worth? Now imagine making a 20% profit on it in three weeks. Imagine doing the same with six lots.

Of course, I didn't make money with every trade, but what I might lose one day on gold or pork bellies, I would more than make up on Cocoa or Wheat. I would be riding ten trades at a time with anything up to five or six lots in each trade, the emails flying backwards and forwards to Nevada.

And Patrick was delighted. Every time he placed a trade, buy or sell, he charged $17.50 for each lot so, by the time I had closed the position on five lots of a commodity, I had paid out $700 - just for having someone place the orders online for me. Come to think of it, why did I need someone to place the orders for me? I could do that. Indeed, I could do it for $4.50 per lot if I went directly to the broker.

So, I did, I opened an account with a London broker and sent an email to Patrick telling him to close all the positions and send me the money. He wrote back saying: "Done. But what's happened?"

What could I do? I told him. I told him that now (it must have been about 18 months since I started) I thought I could stand on my own feet. I promised to be very, very careful (there were countless stories of so-called "fat-finger" disasters when people had typed "100" when they meant "10").

He responded by saying that he would get back to me in 24 hours.

His email arrived the next morning. It was one of those moments that make you feel ten feet tall. Here was this lifetime trader, someone whose job it was to help hopefuls take their first steps, and he was telling me I was exceptional. He said very few people had been able to do what I had done - that is to set emotion to one side and stick to the rules come what may.

Then he said how depressing it was for him to spend all that time and effort nurturing a new trader with one lot here, one lot there, only to have them spread their wings and fly the nest just at the point when it was all starting to bear fruit.

I could see his point, but this was my money he was earning. Then he went on: "I have a proposition for you…"

What he was proposing was that we should go into business together and trade other people's money: He would find the investors. I would pick the trades. The profits, we would split 50:50.

Wow! Suddenly my imagination went into overdrive: Patrick would be telling all his wealthy contacts how he had found this genius trader who had made $180,000 in 18 months and now they had a chance to hang onto his coat-tails as he headed for the financial stratosphere…

For a week or so we flipped emails back and forth across the Atlantic sorting out the details. Then he happened to mention something that was so blindingly obvious to him that he had never thought to raise it before: I would have to go to America and get myself registered with the various financial services regulatory bodies. I would have to pass exams. The exams weren't hard, Patrick assured me. (He didn't know about my school record.) Besides, I didn't want to go and live in America.

That was the point when the whole idea collapsed. It had been great to dream about it for a while – make plans for all the money that would come pouring in – a new kitchen, a second home, new cars and holidays… all that stuff that you can buy if you don't have to worry about the future because you know it's gold-plated.

Also, it was a great boost to my confidence. So, there was no problem with the four-hour recorded call to the British broker, during which I was required to repeat word for word the extent of my liability should anything go wrong. Nothing could possibly go wrong … not when I was a "genius trader".

Immediately I piled in with five lots of crude oil and all kinds of contracts for gold and the US dollar and whatnot.

And the money started rolling in.

Well, when I say, rolling in, I put most of it into new and bigger trades - after all, when you're making $14,000 in a single day, you don't have to take much out, do you.

And this went on for the best part of the year. During that summer, I remember standing in someone's garden holding a bottle of beer and talking to a man who appeared to be most interested in what I did. After all, it's the standard question when meeting someone for the first time at a barbecue: "…and what do you do?" But this man had a lot of specific questions and of course, I kept talking which is par for the course.

Finally, he revealed why he had been so interested. He worked for a bank - in the currency trading department. He wondered whether I would be interested in sharing my rules - he was sure the bank would pay me handsomely.

My ego took another step up. Best of all, I was able to reply, airily that I would never reveal my secret. It was, after all, too valuable…

Instead, the conversation spurred me on as new and bigger trades flashed up on the screen and I piled more and more into the market - and kept on winning.

Then came the day when I received a call from the young man who was my contact at the brokerage. I think his name was Julian (it would be). I imagined him as one of those flash public schoolboys who inhabit the City in the same way that tigers roam the jungle. He rang and said he had been reviewing my account and wanted to check something.

Oh yes?

Yes. I seemed to be trading seven lots of crude oil and six lots of heating oil in the same direction at the same time. Was I aware how volatile these markets could be?

What he was saying was that although I had my stops in place - orders placed to exit the trades if the price should go against me – those orders might not get filled if the market was moving really fast.

Just to give you an idea, a contract for one lot of crude oil represents 1,000 barrels. If everything were to go absolutely, disastrously, wrong - if I suddenly had to come up with the goods, I would have to pay for 5,000 barrels. So, if crude oil was $60 a barrel…

But, of course, I didn't need to worry about that. Everything would be fine. Julian had his job to do. I thanked him for his call and carried on. Onwards and upwards…

Remember the day I made $14,000? Wasn't that great?

I discovered it wasn't so great to lose $14,000 in a single day - and I was lucky it wasn't more; my orders got filled just before the market dropped like a stone. If I had been caught in that, I would have lost much more. The words "a fortune" came to mind. An awful, sick feeling began to establish itself in the pit of my stomach.

This was exactly why Julian had phoned – it might be no skin off his nose if the brokerage debt recovery department had to come and sell the house over my head and cart off my CD collection and those cufflinks – but obviously they could do without that kind of hassle. Maybe I was accepting too much risk.

This was the point at which the successful gambler walks away from the table, cashes in his chips and strolls out into the night with a smile.

But not me – I couldn't stop. Not because I was addicted to the thrill of it – but because I didn't have anything else. I took a pause, sat up late at night re-writing my rules, building in more safeguards. Maybe the profits wouldn't be so spectacular in future but now I had a bigger pot than when I started, it would even out… most importantly, I would never again experience that awful jolt of a big loss.

In fact, what happened was … nothing. There were no big profits and no big losses. But there were still the trading costs. My account began to drift inexorably downwards. Nothing dramatic - I had experienced the occasional losing month before - but never two in a row… certainly not three… surely it must turn round in month four…

What the market was demonstrating was the same message that had been drummed into me by all the trading books I read before I started: That fortune favours the brave. To win big, you have to accept big risks – go all-in where the cautious trader hesitates. Those were the rules that the banker at the barbecue had wanted – that was what Patrick had been prepared to pay 50% for. Suddenly I just didn't have the stomach for it anymore. If things went on like this, I was going to lose all my profits.

But instead, I held – firmly believing that something would turn up – constantly **taking risks.**

Until, one day when the account had drifted down by another few hundred dollars and I was back where I started and beginning to actually lose money overall, that it occurred to me there was an essential truth in all this – one that had been conveniently omitted from all the books by all the experts which I had sat up reading late into the night. It was that in order for those experts to win – to make all their millions – there had to be thousands and thousands of little people who had to lose. It just never dawned of me that I might be one of them.

I called a halt. It was a whim - there was no setting a limit, no waiting for a line to be crossed. I'd had enough. I closed my account and called for the money that was left.

Then I and looked round for something else – for the next thing that was going to turn up.

Chapter 20
Desperation

I don't think you can claim the dole if you own a five-bedroomed house with an acre of garden and no mortgage or if you take bed & breakfast guests in one of the bedrooms. Or, come to that, you have enough savings to live on.

There were many people in deeper trouble than me. But when you have convinced yourself that all your money worries are over – and suddenly you find that you were completely wrong, it can unsettle the soundest mind.

With a mind that constantly bounces off the walls, this spells trouble.

I turned to the Situations Vacant section of the local paper. I was ready to apply for anything. I filled in application forms. All of the employers asked for "date of birth". I never heard from any of them again – it didn't take much arithmetic to work out that I was 54 years old.

The council wanted someone to clean public conveniences. You got your own van and worked to your own schedule with no one looking over your shoulder. It sounded just up my street. I would be quite happy cleaning toilets (well, given the choice, I'd rather not - but it appeared I didn't have much choice.)

Tamsin looked across the kitchen table: "I am not having you coming back into the house after spending the day cleaning public toilets," was what she said.

So, I didn't apply for that one (actually, I was secretly relieved). However, what about this: An organisation for promoting home composting was looking for someone to make their case to gardening clubs and the crowds at county shows. It would be mostly evening and weekend work which wasn't ideal, but that was reflected in the pay - £22,000 a year, which sounded quite good compared to the bog job. Besides, I was sure I could stand up in front of a bunch of gardeners and talk about compost – or at least, I was sure I could just as soon as I found out how to make the stuff.

Best of all, we had a really impressive compost heap of our own. Our gardener had built it, but I didn't need to tell anybody that. It had three bays, proper wooden sides and removable slats at the front for throwing in the potato peelings. This was composting to a gold standard. Tamsin took a picture of me in my wellies, leaning on my fork with the children in wholesome poses on top of the decomposing humus.

For good measure, I got out my water colours and painted flowers in the margins of my application. There was no way I was going to be turned down for an interview for this one.

Sure enough, I was summoned to Hatfield. Maybe they just wanted to look at someone who would paint flowers on his application. I didn't get the job. I did get a speeding fine on the way there.

So, it was going to be down to me. I sat and thought: "What do I want to do?"

I wanted to work from home - in my lovely office with the sliding doors opening onto the terrace with the grapevine behind the hammock overlooking the river. I wanted to work when I pleased with nobody telling me what to do and cutting out all my jokes.

Now there was a thought. If I produced nothing but jokes,

nobody could very well cut them out. Years ago, when I freelanced for Yachting Monthly, I had drawn simple cartoons to illustrate the articles. Yachting Monthly published them. They paid me for them, too.

I pulled a sheet of paper out of the printer and picked up a pen.

Years and years ago, I had taken a correspondence course in cartoon drawing. I could think of nothing nicer than earning a living from making people laugh. Also, I remembered a time, late at night, when the Evening Standard's cartoonist Bristow had come into the newsroom in a state of joyous inebriation and started drawing hilarious and very rude cartoons. He just churned them out, one after another, taking only a minute or so over each one. I expect you can find them in downstairs loos in Notting Hill and Barnes today. Certainly, the night staff kept grabbing them out of the wastepaper basket. The thing I remember most was how easy he made it look.

I inspected my effort. It didn't look easy. It looked laboured and amateurish. But that was only a first attempt. I tried again… and again…

I made a lightbox - a device to make tracing easier so I could keep the good parts and add to them. I sat up late at night, I got up early in the morning. I devoured Private Eye.

Of course, what had happened was that I had gone into **hyperfocus** again. Just as trading commodities was going to be the answer – going to get us out of all our troubles – so, cartoons was the most brilliant idea. It never occurred to me that I might not be any good at it. Instead, I started wondering whether you could get a portable scanner. That way, even when we went on holidays to exotic places, I would be able to keep up the daily output to my national newspaper - whichever one it was that would shortly be offering me a contract.

After a couple of weeks, with a huge file of gradually

improving samples, I submitted the best half dozen to Private Eye. Two days later, I had heard nothing. What had happened? I couldn't afford to wait around while they dragged their heels.

I sent the next one to the Daily Mail. I didn't hear from them either.

Then I struck on a brilliant wheeze. Every day, I would draw a topical cartoon, and by lunchtime, I would fax it to all the national dailies. I would do this every day. I got hold of the numbers for all the newsdesk fax machines and discovered that the computer could fire off the same drawing to all of them at one push of the button. If I did this every day, it was inevitable that on each newsdesk, someone would get used to seeing them… and, in time, would start looking forward to seeing them… and show them to their colleagues… more colleagues and more senior colleagues… until one day, a particularly good cartoon would reach someone with the clout to say: "This is great. Who is this guy? What, the same John Passmore who used to write those wonderful pieces for the Mail and the Standard? He's a cartoonist now? He's brilliant. Get him in here. I don't care what he costs…"

On the strength of this, I set to with a will. Every morning I listened to the news on the radio and then stood in the shower and tried to exercise some lateral thinking. My hero was Matt, the Daily Telegraph's pocket cartoonist. Already I had several books of his drawings, given to me over successive Christmases. They lived in the downstairs loo, and I knew them all by heart. Matt's secret was simple: Take two events from the news and find a humorous way to link them together: Delays at Heathrow and Brexit? "The plane is departing now, but there will be a three-hour transitional period before it actually leaves."

Unseasonably bad weather and American politics? "The dog doesn't mind thunder, but he's terrified of the Trump presidency…"

There was a knack to it. Apparently, Matt would wander round the Telegraph newsroom with a faraway look on his face. I stood in the shower with the windows open to let the steam out and so that I could see the view. By the time the water went cold, and before my skin shrivelled up and fell off, I would have an idea.

Then I would go downstairs and take my coffee cup and breakfast bowl to my desk and start sketching. I had the lightbox. Paper was cheap. I was completely absorbed, and every day, the morning seemed to fly past in an instant. This was great. This was my vocation. Sometimes, I would draw two cartoons - just to show how easy I found it. Every day, the fax machine would squirt them down the wire. Quite a long time went past before I began to wonder why nothing ever came back.

Oh well, just keep at it. What else was I supposed to do?

At this point, somebody suggested Tamsin might like to sell greeting cards. Tamsin likes greeting cards. She sends them to her friends. Her friends send them to her. Why do women do that? Anyway, these were very nice greetings cards. The deal was that you bought them at half price and then sold them at full price. You could set up a stall at craft fairs and the like. Besides, if one of your customers wanted to do the same, you got an override on what they sold as well. It sounded a rather clever idea. It would bring in some money while we waited for Fleet Street to jump on the cartoons. Besides – although I didn't realise it at the time – very soon we would have a lifetime supply of greeting cards.

And, in its own small way, this was one of those moments which you don't recognise at the time as being hugely significant.

One Saturday in the early spring of 2005, Tamsin was running her greeting card stall at our local community hall, and at the end of the day, I went down to help her pack up. There were stalls and table displays all over the hall - people selling homemade jewellery; several antique dealers had brought china and cutlery and the sort of Edwardian seaside souvenirs your grandmother said would come to you in her will but actually ended up in the junk shop.

In the middle of it all was Tamsin packing cards into boxes. I went to help, but she gestured to the stall next door: "The man there says he's got a way of making money."

Well, I didn't need to be asked twice.

"I understand you've got a way of making money," I said.

The man on the other side of the table looked startled. He was immensely tall with a long face and side whiskers. His hand, when he shook mine, was enormous. Yes, he did have a way of making money. It was just that he wasn't very good at explaining how. Maybe he didn't know how. Never mind, I was in the market for money. I took his leaflet. There was a sticker on the back with his name and phone number: Fred & Lena Moreton.

Now, it just so happened that the very next day, the Sunday, we were going on holiday. In those days, Tamsin belonged to the National Childbirth Trust, and they had a register of families wanting to do house swaps. We would stay in their house. They would stay in ours. It was brilliant – much better than the soulless holiday let and, best of all, it cost nothing. This one was in a village in Yorkshire. It was delightful - there was a stream running through the garden. You could hear running water as you lay in bed.

By this time, we knew what was involved and always spent the first day settling in. This was necessary because the children would want to play with all the toys belonging to the other family. You cannot imagine what a delight it is for four children under the age of ten to be introduced to a completely strange playroom.

Similarly, Tamsin was either delighted - or possibly horrified - to be cooking in another woman's kitchen.

Me, I was thrilled to find the other husband had left instructions for using the computer. I had something I wanted to look up.

Fred Moreton's leaflet had indeed piqued my interest: It described a company which supplied household utility services to homes and businesses throughout the UK - gas, electricity, home phone, mobile and broadband. However, the reason I had never heard of them was that they didn't spend millions on advertising. Instead, they relied on word of mouth: 200,000 happy customers telling their friends.

Some of these happy customers took it a stage further. For £199, they could become "distributors" and earn an override on the profits the company made out of the friend who had recommended them. It was like Tamsin's greetings cards – with a difference: People don't send greetings cards every day. Even if they do, when they come back to buy another one, it's not exactly expensive. The seller's cut is measured in pennies.

But when people have to pay their utility bills every month, it's a direct debit for hundreds of pounds. There was real money in this. There were stories of policemen and building workers, single mothers and students who were now rich beyond their wildest dreams – and all they had done was tell a few people and some of those people had gone on to tell a few more people… and the next thing you know, there were hundreds of people… and then thousands of people…

Like ripples radiating out across a pond, the word spread – and here was the clever thing: As each person joined, the over-ride was not just paid to the one who told them – but also to the one who told *them* … and so on and so on up the chain - ad infinitum.

Of course, this was when the alarm bells started to ring. It was like a chain letter - one of those pyramid schemes you hear about. Obviously, there has to be a limit; after all, the day must come when everybody in the country is in the chain. There will be no one new to tell – no new money coming in. The whole thing must collapse. People warn you about this sort of thing…

Ah, but here was the clever bit: not *everyone* got paid; only the ones who kept bringing in more customers – at least until they had introduced 50. After 50, you got paid forever – even if you never did anything ever again. That way, it would work.

And guess what: The first 50 were the difficult ones. If someone got to 50, they weren't going to stop there – and, of course, these weren't greeting cards selling for 50p each. These were the major expenses going out of every home and business in the country – and the customers were billed automatically every month (even if nobody knocked on the door and said: "Please would you buy some more electricity, I want to get paid again…)

I could see how this might work.

So, as the children squealed with excitement in the new playroom and Tamsin experimented with a Chinese puzzle disguised as a food processor, I started looking up the company on the internet. At this point, it would make sense for me to tell you the name of this company. But if I did that, I would have to submit this book to the company's marketing department for approval. It would be like fighting to get my copy past the newspaper's lawyer. I'm done with all that. If you're interested, contact me through the blog – https://oldmansailing.com/money.

Meanwhile, I can tell you that I discovered the company was real. It had a proper Stock Market listing. It was regulated by the government watchdogs Ofcom and Ofgem. In fact, now I looked at its website, there was something familiar about it.

It took me a while to work out what it was – but yes, I was sure that a friend had mentioned this to me ages ago, before I started trading, when I was still complaining about running out of money. I had taken a look at the website, but it seemed all rather complicated with all the different services and so on. Besides, saving money is boring. Making money, on the other hand – now making money. That's ***exciting***.

But when I had looked at it before, I didn't remember seeing anything about making money – no flashing button saying: "Click here to solve all your money worries" or "Click here to achieve financial security for life." If I had, I assure you, I would have been in there faster than the council's HR chief meeting someone with their own loo brush.

In fact, now I looked again, as the children raced around the house with the new toys and Tamsin abandoned the food processor and wondered how to turn on the extractor fan, I still couldn't see anything about making money until … ah yes: a small button hidden among a lot of others labelled in tiny letters: "Earn with Us"

I crawled all over that website. I looked up reviews and comments (they were mixed, as reviews and comments always are). But I decided that I had a better chance with this than I did with selling cartoons.

For one thing, once I had been paid for a cartoon (if I ever did get paid for a cartoon), the only way I could get paid again would be to draw another one. I might be able to put them in a book of cartoons and sell that – but even then, people would only buy it once.

Not only was this latest idea something new (which, of course, had its own appeal), but once I introduced someone to the company, I would get paid every time they paid their bill. Or, to put it the way the leaflet explained it: Every time someone switched on a light, made a phone call, used the internet…every time their central heating kicked in. Every time they used any of the services, I would get paid. Imagine that!

As soon as we arrived home from the week in Yorkshire, I called the number on the back of the leaflet. A couple of hours later, Fred and Lena turned up. Lena was as small as Fred was tall – but with the same easy, friendly manner… although on this occasion, both of them seemed desperately nervous. They didn't mention it at the time but, it soon became clear: They were as new to this as I was.

Fred set up a huge leather (imitation leather) folder on my desk. Awkwardly, he began to turn the pages, carefully reading them to me as if I wasn't capable of doing it for myself. After the first couple of pages, it dawned on me that this was his sales presentation.

"I've seen all that," I said. "I've seen it all online. Just show me where to sign."

I went up to London to the head office – one half of a tiny industrial estate somewhere in Edgware with nowhere to park. In a cramped conference room, with a lot of role-play and use of flip charts, a couple of dozen newbies like me learned to present the company to our friends and relations.

It went like this:

>Me: "Hi Jim. How's it going?"
>Jim: "Great. You?"
>Me: "Fine. Say, Jim, there's something I need to ask you."
>Jim: "What's that?"
>Me: "How much is your phone bill?"
>Jim: "Oh, I dunno. About £40 a month."
>Me: "D'you like paying that much?"

At that point, Jim was supposed to say "No," and I would say that I had discovered this brilliant discount club that saved you money on your phone bill and a lot else besides. If he liked, I could come and show him how it worked. Which would be best for him, Tuesday at six or Thursday at eight?

Apparently, this would work. I went home and tried it on my father-in-law. He knew exactly how much he paid for his phone bill. He sat through my presentation (what else could he do?)

Reaching the end, I said, as I had been taught to say: "So, would you like to give it a go?"

According to the script, this was his cue to say: "Yes."

Instead, he said: "**We'll** see how you get on with it."

Clearly, this wasn't as simple as it sounded.

I called Fred.

"That happens sometimes," said Fred. "Tell you what: a bunch of us are getting together for a stand at the Flower Show on Saturday. It's a big event - the Suffolk Showground – lots of people. Since they won't know you, they won't know you've just got started. They can't very well say they'll wait to see how you get on, can they? Why don't you come along?"

Fred didn't know it, but this was exactly the right thing to say. It came naturally to him (because exactly the same thing had happened to him). I paid £5 to help with the cost of the stand and went along.

There were six of us. We had a folding picnic table with a bottle of champagne and a big plastic jar of piggy-shaped sweets (the company logo was a piggy bank). All that people had to do to win the champagne was guess the number of piggies in the jar. We had forms where we wrote down their guess – and then their name and address (so we could contact them if they won).

Actually, the man who had set up the stand, an enormous crane driver from Felixstowe docks, already knew how many piggies there were in the jar. He had counted them as he put them in. But as he explained: "By the end of the day, the ones at the bottom will have melted into a great big sticky lump. You can't get them out, let alone count them."

The real reason for the forms was the list of questions underneath the contestant's name and address: "How much is your phone bill? Do you like paying that much…"

The six of us stood in a row behind the stand and pinned on winning smiles while the crowds walked past and smiled back – and walked on.

I could see that we would be standing there all day. Someone was going to have to take the initiative. I stepped out in front of the stand – into the middle of the slowly-strolling crowd.

"Here you are, you can win a bottle of champagne," I said to anyone who looked at me, wondering what I was doing there. "Just guess the number of piggies in the jar…"

Within five minutes, I had my first appointment. Her name was Mrs Susan Perrett (you never forget your first).

On the Tuesday evening, I drove into Ipswich to see Mrs Perrett. I opened my big leather folder (imitation leather - and it was called a "presenter" not a folder). I read carefully through all the pages, showed her what it was about. If she wanted a free quotation, all she had to do was sign the form and write a cheque for £10.

Why did she have to hand over a cheque?

Oh, that's to prove you've got some money. If you didn't have any money and we start supplying you with gas and electricity, the other customers will have to pay your bill for you, and that wouldn't be fair … although, of course, that's what happens with all the other companies…

It was years before I discovered this was a classic sales technique: The prospect is always going to have an objection. The trick is to prompt them to raise an objection which you can turn into a benefit.

Just as Mrs Perrett was handing over the cheque, her daughter arrived home from work. It turned out that the daughter still lived at home – and she had her own telephone line in her bedroom for her computer (dial-up in those days). But she had a question: If she switched as well, would she still be able to access the AOL chatrooms? She wouldn't want to lose touch with all her online friends…

I had not the faintest idea. But Fred had said I could call him at any time if I needed help. I called Fred. Could members get into the AOL chatrooms?

Fred had no idea.

But he said he would see if he could find out.

Two minutes later, my phone rang. A man I had never heard

of introduced himself as Richard. He was calling from somewhere in Surrey and said the answer was Yes, members could still access the AOL chatrooms. He cut through my protestations of thanks: "That's the way the network operates," he told me. "You keep on going up the line until you find someone who knows. Tonight, it was me." I had the impression he was going back to his dinner.

Me, I signed up the daughter as well.

I could see this working.

Chapter 21
Luck

I had a customer called Peter - a somewhat terrifying character who lived just around the corner. I had been given his name by somebody or other as a very canny retired businessman who was very careful with his pennies. He might have been careful with them but that didn't stop him spending them. As we sat outside over coffee, the sun came out and, with an unexpected whirring noise, automatic sunshades began winding themselves out of the wall. Meanwhile, I had reached the last page of my presentation and he said: "I understand how it all works but I should tell you now that if anything goes wrong, I will be on the telephone to your chairman."

I could believe it. He was the sort of person who would know everyone.

Much later, he rang me and said there was something wrong with his latest bill. I couldn't see anything the matter with it, but he insisted he had been overcharged by £15.41 or something. Anyway, I took the view that the customer is always right. I apologised for the mistake and wrote him a cheque from our joint account for £15.41. He took it, checked it - and handed it back.

"I don't want your money," he said. "I just wanted someone to admit they were wrong – and your apology is appreciated."

I have always believed that if you do the right thing, it will come back to you as a welcome surprise.

Out of the blue, my phone rang with a call from Christiane, the French-born widow of the local doctor. Apparently, she had been to dinner with Peter, and he had asked how she was coping after Ian's death.

She had come to terms with that – after all, it was no surprise; he had been ill for a long time. But coping with all the bills – that was a nightmare she had not expected. Suddenly she had to deal with the gas and the electricity and the phone company and every time she rang them, she had to wait on the line for heaven knows how long...

So, Peter said: 'You should talk to John Passmore. He'll sort you out."

A couple of days later, I went round to see Christiane and went through the bills with her. Then, as I had been taught in the cramped little room on the industrial estate in north London with the flip charts and the role play, I said: "As I say, the company operates entirely by word of mouth, which is why Peter suggested you – and now you have joined it means that you get to recommend the next person. So, who would that be?"

"Well, there's the woman next door - young Mum, Jo..."

So, I went to see Jo. I opened my imitation leather presenter. I showed her how she could save money on the things she was buying already.

But I was only halfway through when she interrupted me – not with the usual questions about whether she would have to have her house rewired or change her phone number or objections like "You know where you are with British Gas". Instead, she said: "What do you get out of this?"

So, I said: "Shall I show you how the money works?"

Five minutes later, she said: "I could do that."

It turned out that – even though I had never met Jo before –

I had just recruited the perfect Network Marketer. Jo was bright and chatty with lots of friends. Everybody liked Jo. More to the point, although she now had two daughters at primary school, she had worked ever since she had left school herself. Her father had a toy business; in a little factory on the riverbank, he turned out toy sailing boats – that actually sailed. The secret was that, unlike my toy boat that sank on the Round Pond, these were solid so they couldn't leak. Also, they were made from a wood that was almost as light as balsa but hard enough to endure years of being knocked about the playroom. They were a big success, Skipper Yachts – if you've got a model yacht in the attic, it's probably a Skipper Yacht – and a lot of that is down to Jo.

Jo was the sales manager and every month she had to sell enough little boats, or somebody didn't get paid. The trouble was that the boats were so well made that not only did they sail (and not sink), but they survived the toybox and lasted from one child to the next – sometimes going down through the generations for years. In other words, once a family owned one, they would never need to buy another. While this was good for the company's reputation, it was not so good for Jo's sales figures. What she needed was a way of generating repeat sales.

Then, one morning she turned up at the factory and asked them to make a bath-toy sailing boat. It had to be small enough to fit in the soap rack, and yet, the idea was that if you blew on the sails, it would scoot all the way down to the tap end. When it was finished (and had completed sailing trials in Jo's bath), she took it to one of the top London hotels – it may have been the Ritz or the Savoy or somewhere like that. How would they like to put one of those in each of their guests' bathrooms?

Well, it turned out they would like that very much.

And how many hotel guests are at a loss over what to give their grandchildren when they get home? At £10 each, the little boats were ideal – and would hardly be noticeable on a Ritz Hotel bill.

That was, of course, if they paid for it. But even if they slipped it into their suitcase on the quiet, the hotel would still have to order another one. To put it another way, Jo had her repeat business. She moved on to the next luxury hotel...

But when I went to see her, all that was coming to an end. Her father was not well and had been advised by his doctor that he should retire. At the same time, a German toy conglomerate wanted to buy the business. The deal was irresistible - best of all, Jo and her father would be retained for two years as "consultants". Essentially Jo didn't have to do anything for the next two years, although she would continue to be paid every month.

But anybody who knew Jo would tell you that she wasn't going to sit around doing nothing for two years.

Sure enough, Jo spotted a gap in another market - the wedding market. Churches were banning confetti - they saw it as litter. But flower petals would be OK - particularly the tiny, delicate bougainvillea leaves that grew in profusion all over East Africa... where Jo's sister happened to live. In no time, Jo had arranged the import, the packaging, the pricing...

There was only one problem: Repeat business. If marriage was supposed to be for life, there wouldn't be any.

But with gas and electricity, with telephone and internet bills - if she could get paid every time someone switched on a light...

And so overnight, Jo ditched the bougainvillea leaf business and got started with utilities. I went with her to sign up her parents, and after that, she was off on her own and flying. Everything that I had found hard, she found easy.

So far, so good. But that is not the end of the story of Jo.

Up the line from me (up the line from Fred and Lena and Richard with his answer to the AOL chatrooms question) was a young man called Mark.

Mark had left school at 14 with no qualifications. He started work on building sites - but even with no education, he was not short of ambition. Pretty soon, he had graduated from building sites to buying run-down flats and doing them up. Then he moved on to houses. He built up his own property portfolio. Like a lot of landlords, he realised that a utility business was the perfect add-on – after all, his tenants had to get their services from somewhere. Why not from him?

But instead of going out and looking for other landlords to join him, Mark had a much better idea.

He went to see a man who ran property training workshops. As a way of making money, this was almost as clever as the discount club: People paid £3,000 to join, and that entitled them to attend a workshop once a month. On top of that, they had access to all sorts of online resources and a hotline to the organisation's tame solicitors and financial advisors (who, of course, were happy to pay the workshop for this endless stream of clients). Whether any of the trainees went on to make their fortune out of property, I never knew – but there were certainly plenty of them who wanted to try.

The only problem for the man who ran the show was finding people to stand up and talk at the workshops. This was where Mark came in. He offered to get up and do a monthly 20-minute slot about the discount club. Then he planned to sit at the back and answer questions – and, of course, sign up the trainees as discount club distributors. In doing so, he would build an entire business underneath the man who owned the workshop, thus adding yet another income stream to the whole conglomerate.

It was brilliant.

There was only one fly in the ointment: How on earth was Mark going to find the time to look after all the dozens of new distributors he was about to recruit? He would need somebody else to do that – someone keen, someone hungry – but also someone efficient, bright and chatty who could motivate all kinds of people. Someone like – no, not me – someone like … Jo.

So, on one Saturday a month, Jo would drive up to Kettering and sit at the back of the property seminar and sign up a dozen or more new distributors. Then she would spend the rest of the month helping them get started. Some of them were good. Some of them were hopeless. But as they say in Network marketing: It's not how good you are that counts, or what you know. It's *who* you know - and how good *they* are that counts. Or, in other words: "Every dud knows a stud".

One of the duds knew a man who had such a big property portfolio that he employed someone else to source likely rental units for him. This was big business: It meant keeping up to speed with building projects and planning applications all over the country. It was worth doing. There were a lot of investors who needed that information. One of them was a former NHS doctor, originally from Bangladesh, who had left the health service because he couldn't stand the bureaucracy. Instead, he set up a finance company specialising in the transfer of money between the UK and Bangladesh - and doing it cheaper than the banks or Western Union. In no time, he was channelling hundreds of thousands of pounds a month from East London to Dhakar - and he invested the profits in property ... which he was then able to let to the clients of his money-transfer business.

Of course, as a landlord, it wasn't long before someone told him how he could add an extra income stream to his business by becoming a distributor with the utility company. However, the person who told him about it was clearly not wealthy, himself – which suggested that maybe this opportunity was not so great either...

But when the doctor heard about it a second time from his highly respected associate with the property-sourcing company, he thought that maybe he should look into it after all.

Being scrupulously fair, his only honourable course was to go back to the person who had told him about it first and ask him to come round and deliver his presentation.

If that's what had happened, he might never have joined Jo's business - or, come to that, mine. But this is where luck plays a part.

That night, it snowed.

No, that's not right. It didn't just snow; this was a blizzard – what the Daily Mail once described in a memorable front-page headline as *White Hell*.

When the doctor rang the first distributor to say that he was now interested and could spare an hour at 8.00 p.m. the poor man looked out of his window at the chaos on the roads and said: "But it's snowing."

The doctor – ever polite – said: "Oh well, never mind..."

And rang the second distributor.

Although this person was very successful and confident in his property-sourcing business – and even willing to come out in a snowstorm – he was very new to the utility business. Truth to tell, he didn't really know much about it at all. But what he did know was that if he could sign up someone who was a major influencer in a large immigrant community – someone like The Doctor with his East London Bangladeshi following, then he would be made. So, as the company recommended, when someone found themselves out of their depth, he called his sponsor. That would be Mark, the builder's labourer made good.

Mark said: "But it's snowing."

"I know, but this guy is a really big shot in his community, and he just rang me and said he could give me an hour at eight o'clock. Honestly, if I turn him down, I doubt I'll get another chance – and he's the sort of person who will expect all the answers…"

So Mark, bless him, got into his car and drove from Northampton to East London in a blizzard.

And the doctor joined.

What happened next became a legend among the many stories told about the history of network marketing. While most people suggested being ready for openings in everyday conversation when you could casually mention saving money or the part-time earnings opportunity (awkwardly – in most cases) and then sign up maybe one customer a week, The Doctor went at it on an industrial scale.

By the time I realised what was going on, he was holding his own meetings in his living room – with 80 people at a time. This was something of an eye-opener. For a start, this being a Muslim community, there would be 80 pairs of shoes piled up in the porch, and, although The Doctor must have had the biggest house in the neighbourhood, the audience was packed in so tightly on their folding IKEA chairs that nobody could get out (which might have been the whole idea). At half-time, 80 polystyrene boxes of chicken and chips were delivered from the local takeaway and passed down the rows (the Doctor explained that nobody would come if he didn't feed them).

In due course, the company took over the East London Opportunity Presentation and hired a hotel conference room. But even then, after I wrapped up the evening, The Doctor would stand up and gather his prospects around him (a couple of dozen, usually) addressing them in one of his six Asian languages. Heaven knows what he told them, but they all signed up.

Later, he stepped it up a gear and bought lists of mobile phone numbers, which he hooked into a computer program and fired off endless text messages promising the earth.

After that came the "Ramadan Blitz": During the Moslem festival of Ramadan, the faithful will go to the mosque to pray five times a day. As a result, every mosque in east London was heaving all day and all night. The Doctor recruited teams of teenagers to stand outside handing out envelopes containing a brochure, an application form and a stamped, addressed envelope.

Back at the house, his wife and four children checked the

application forms and faxed them to head office – and then got on with stuffing more forms, brochures and letters into more envelopes for tomorrow. The customers rolled in.

It wasn't quite the way the business was supposed to work – but work it most definitely did. The numbers went up, the money went up. I kept a graph, and that went up like a jet fighter on afterburners.

The thing about graphs is that it is the easiest thing in the world to take a pencil and project the upward curve as far as you like into the future.

The mistake is to believe it.

Then two things happened over which I had no control. One was that although the company was delighted with The Doctor's energy and enthusiasm (he seemed to work all day and all night and once gave a PowerPoint presentation showing his bed next to his desk) they were not so pleased with the sort of people he was signing up. Quite a few of them didn't pay their bills. Part of the distributor's role was meeting the new members personally and making sure that at least they looked as if they might be able to pay the bills. The Doctor was in far too much of a hurry to bother with things like that.

Secondly, there were some uncomfortable statistics regarding tenants: On average, tenants move house every six months. That means that every six months, their utility company has to get involved in a lot of paperwork and expense transferring the supply to the new people. Also, some tenants skip without paying the final bill.

Homeowners, on the other hand, stay put for an average of 14 years – and almost always pay their bills.

There was only one thing for it: Make it more profitable to sign up homeowners than tenants. The Doctor was furious. This was a classic case of moving the goalposts. He said so to me. He said so to his teenage son, Ridwan.

This lad was about 12 when I first met him – a studious boy with three bossy older sisters. But if The Doctor was a clever man, the boy was a genius – particularly when it came to computers. He ran all the technical side of his father's presentations.

By the time he was 14, he built an amazingly sophisticated website for the business. I asked if I could have one too. I didn't expect it for nothing. I said I would be happy to contribute some pocket money…

I received an invoice for £100 from "The Ridz Corporation".

What did I expect? The IT teacher at his school had given up trying to teach him anything. Instead, the poor man just turned the class over to his prodigy. When Ridwan reached 16, and the head was getting excited at the prospect of the sixth form and the school's first Oxbridge scholarship, the Doctor decided this would benefit the school more than it did the student. The following year, Ridwan left school and set up an online business showing Amazon traders where to invest – and was soon making more money than his father. After that, the whole family sold up in East London and decamped to Dubai where there's no tax at all and, I understand, the son's business keeps them all in some style. You can look him up: Ridwan Mahmood, internet entrepreneur.

Meanwhile, I still have hundreds of customers in East London, still paying me every time they switch on a light…

Chapter 22

Excitement

Flashing lights, pounding music, the audience on their feet, all screaming in unison…

But this was no pop concert. This was the company's annual convention. Every Network marketing company in the world stages a day of wild razzmatazz to get everybody worked up – because network marketing runs on excitement like a spaceship runs on rocket fuel.

There's a good reason: If people have a job, they go to work because they know that if they don't, they'll get the sack. But a Network marketing business isn't a job – there's no boss. Nobody can sack you if you decide you'd rather crawl back under the duvet on a Monday morning. So, Network Marketers have to be motivated – and the best way to motivate people is to surround them with other people who are so excited they can hardly contain themselves. **Excitement** is contagious.

Are you beginning to realise why I took to it like a duck to water? I sat there somewhere towards the back with my first two team members and watched as, one after another, perfectly ordinary people walked onto the stage and said that all you had to do was keep going.

And then, right at the end, Stephan Longworth took to the stage. Everyone knew Stephan. He used to be one of those people at Manchester airport waving ping-pong bats at the aeroplanes (apparently, he once lost a jumbo jet in the fog). But he hadn't done that for a long time. Now he drove a Jaguar and wore sharp suits, and actually got onto the planes to fly where he wanted, when he wanted (turning left inside the door for First Class instead of right to Coach). His secret was that he didn't quit. Even when his friends laughed at him, he didn't quit.

He caught one particular friend reflected in a window when the guy thought Steph couldn't see him – he was standing behind Steph's back, making pyramid gestures.

Steph invited all his friends round to his house so he could show them his new business. He bought beer and wine. He had snacks.

Eight o'clock came - eight o'clock went. Nine o'clock came and went... Ten o'clock...

"That night, I went to bed fat and drunk," said Steph.

But he didn't quit. That would have been deemed a serious error of judgement, he told us.

"Don't quit," he said. "Just don't quit. Whatever you do, don't quit. Quitting would be a mistake. Just don't quit."

And because he didn't quit, eventually somebody said "Yes".

So, what was the lesson from Stephan's story? It was that one day - years later - he pulled up at a set of traffic lights in Salford. He was in his pale blue Jaguar XKR. In the next lane, a ten-year-old hatchback pulled up beside him. In the hatchback was an old colleague called Larry. Larry had been the one with the pyramid gestures. "Larry the Dreamstealer" Stephan called him when he told the story.

"Nice car," Larry mouthed through the window.

Stephan just smiled. Then he floored the accelerator.

"Don't quit." He said it again. "Just don't quit."

Sitting at the back, eyes shining, the **excitement** washing over me, I vowed then and there that I would not quit – not until I reached the top. Not even then.

So, I didn't stop, and one day, a few years later, it was me standing up there on the stage – me taking a bow and telling people not to quit – with the standing ovation swirling around me…

Actually, I had been counting on this. I had rehearsed and rehearsed, honed every word – prepared every pause for applause…

I told them how much I needed this – pictures of Tamsin and me on the boat – and then with all those children (things were so hard, I even had to sell my hair!)

I explained how my father-in-law hadn't wanted to know. But I told them about Jo and The Doctor. I showed them how my business had grown through no effort of mine. If you looked at it closely, all I had done right was to start … and once I had started, not to stop.

But isn't that all that really matters?

And then I hit them with this:

> Everything we have learned so far has been based on the Law of Averages. As Jim Rohn said: "If you do something enough times, a ratio will appear".
>
> And the Law of Averages is a natural law – it cannot be refuted. Nobody would dream of arguing with the Law of Averages anymore than they would argue with the Law of Gravity. It is a Law of Nature.
>
> But there is also the Law of Human Nature – and this states that there are two kinds of people in the world – the special people and the ordinary people.
>
> And there will always be more ordinary people than there are special people – which is the way it is supposed to be because the special people are going to need a lot of ordinary people to do the ordinary things they don't want to do.

They need ordinary people to service their cars, wait on their tables, design and build their houses, look after their teeth and their health, mind their money…

Let me explain: The special people have big dreams, and they achieve them because they control their own lives.

The ordinary people allow others to dictate how their lives will turn out. This is not natural for human beings. The cavemen didn't allow other people to decide what happened to them. They went out and determined their own destiny. So why is it that so many people today are content to put their future in the hands of others?

Because that's what most people do when they go to work for someone else. This is because nobody has told them what a job means.

With a job, it's the boss who decides whether you can have the job in the first place – the boss who decides how long you can keep it and how much you're going to get paid… and a boss will always pay you less than you're worth, otherwise they don't make any profit out of you.

With a business, it's different. With a business, you invest in yourself. That is to say, you pay out money up front because you believe in yourself. Then you decide how much work you're prepared to do – and you will always get paid exactly what you're worth… which may be more or less than you thought.

So why is it that so many people are content to have jobs – especially when you consider that what they tend to be doing in them is servicing the lifestyles of the special people?

After all, deep down, they know this, and normally they would resent it – but for the fact that they have something the special people can never have. Something the cavemen didn't have: Something noble, something virtuous. It is this: *A fair day's work for a fair day's pay*.

If you go into a school in the middle of the summer term, you will find the 15-year-olds being taught about the world of work; practising their interview techniques… being shown how to write a CV. Being prepared, in other words, for the world of employment. A world in which the greatest achievement they can hope for is to find someone to give them a job where they can put in a fair day's work for a fair day's pay.

Now, I don't know about you, but I'm not interested in a fair day's work for a fair day's pay. I want sensational pay for part-time work!

So how did we end up with this situation? I'll tell you: History – because you can explain anything if you know enough history.

So here is a potted history of employment:

It started with the dawn of civilization – in the days of ancient Rome. This was employment law ancient Roman style: You had the citizen of Rome, and you had the slave – and the slave did all the work. And the citizen of Rome would pay the slave in food – just enough food to ensure that the slave was able to get up and work again the next day. And, of course, the slave had no choice.

That was employment law ancient Roman-style.

But civilization moved on, and eventually, we came to the Middle Ages. Now in the Middle Ages, England was at the cutting edge of employment legislation with the system of the Lord of the Manor and the Serf.

The way this worked was that the Lord of the Manor owned the land, and he allowed the serf to work upon a strip of that land – and the serf could keep all the produce he grew there to feed to his family… on one condition….

The condition was that on certain days of the year (as designated by the lord), the serf would work on the Lord's land instead. And he did get a choice.

On one day of his life, he had a choice – either on the day he came of age or the day his father died. On that day, he could choose: Either he could take his chances in the world as a free man, or he could choose a life of serfdom.

But if he chose serfdom, he could never change his mind. If he grew tired of working on the land and sought to leave it, men-at-arms would be sent to hunt him down and bring him back with an iron collar around his neck – and, according to the whim of his lord, he might be required to wear that collar around his neck for the rest of his life. And on the collar would be stamped the words: "This man is the property of…" and the name of the lord…

That was employment law, medieval-style.

But civilization moved on again, and in the 1800's we had the Victorians. Now, the thing about the Victorians was that they were great philanthropists. They recognised that every man was created equal in the eyes of God and that it was the right of every man to choose his own destiny – and that necessitated the free movement of labour: Also, it was necessary to adopt the concept of A Fair Day's Work for A Fair Day's Pay.

…for every man, that is. Not for every woman. A woman didn't get equal pay – and any property she owned belonged to her husband. We didn't get that sorted out until the 1960s.

But now we're in the 21st century, and civilization is ready to move on once more – and do you know what is causing it to move on? Celebrity magazines!

I bet you didn't know that celebrity magazines were responsible for the progress of civilization!

But they are - because for the first time, the ordinary people are invited into the "beautiful homes" of the special people – to "share in the joy" of their expensive cars and luxurious world travel… living lives of abundance.

And A Fair Day's Work for a Fair Day's Pay is no longer the panacea it used to be. So now the ordinary people need to have a whole new series of mantras:

This person was born with a silver spoon in their mouth…

That person was in the right place at the right time…

…knew the right people.

This shows the ordinary people that their predicament is not of their making. The way their life turned out is not their fault. Or, as they say: "Some people have all the luck."

But logic dictates that this cannot be true. Luck – or, to give it its proper name – "opportunity" is not presented to a select few. Opportunity is available to all.

What makes the difference is how a person reacts when that opportunity presents itself.

And this is where the population gets divided. You see, the ordinary people will look at the opportunity and say: "These things never work. Besides, I couldn't do that – not in the place where I live, not with the people I know. Anyway, I don't have the time."

And here's a good one: "If something looks too good to be true, it usually is…"

Do you think Richard Branson ever said that? No. If Richard Branson sees something that looks too good to be true, he says: "I'm going to grab that before somebody else does."

But, you see, Richard Branson is a special person. And when a special person is presented with their opportunity, they will always say: "This is just what I've been looking for. This I can do – or I can learn to do… I know the right people… or I can find the right people…

Oh, they may make a mistake sometimes, Richard Branson made plenty of mistakes – but does anyone remember them? No, when the special person makes a mistake, they pick themselves up and press on.

Now, it is true that there are some ordinary people who will pretend to be special people. They will "talk the talk and walk the walk", but when they stumble, will they pick themselves up? Or will they stay on the ground? Because you see, what they were really doing all along, was trying to prove that these things never work – because that's what would fit with their version of reality.

So, here's what they will say as they lie on the ground: "Ah well, at least I gave it a try."

What was it Yoda said? "There is do, and there is not do. There is no try."

Meanwhile, the special people who think only of success find exactly that. It's the law of nature.

Now, I don't know who, hearing these words today, are the special people. Nobody knows – and we won't find out until the end… by which I mean the end of life.

But what I can promise you is this: If these ideas have quickened your pulse. If you feel yourself to be one inch taller, and your breath is coming faster – then that is a clue.

Because that means you have something inside you that sets you apart from the ordinary people. No matter what anybody may have said to you in the past or where your personal history may have placed you in the world today; if you now have that certainty – that total conviction that you and you alone determine your destiny,,,

… and you can seize your opportunity and act on it with certainty and vigour.

If you can persist in doing that, picking yourself up when you stumble, always keeping your eyes fixed on your goal...

If you can go out and get 10,000 "No's", then you will know you are special!

And you will hold in your hand the golden prize.

And everything your heart desires will be yours.

* * *

Putting something like that in a book like this which will be read by a majority of people who rely entirely on their jobs is, of course, deeply offensive – after all, it is as if I am denigrating them as "ordinary". But please remember there is more than one way to become "special". If you have a job and you are happy in it, but you would still like to join the 1% who become financially independent – that is to say, they have no need to work. Instead, they can spend their time doing whatever they like with whomever they like whenever they like and wherever they like, then I have a solution for those people too. It is even more simple:

Get used to living on 90% of your income.

Every month, without fail, from the very first day you receive any kind of wage or payment, put 10% of it aside into a savings account.

When there is enough to invest, invest it.

Whatever the temptation, never spend that capital and always re-invest the income.

When the income from your capital is more than the income from your job, then you can afford to retire. It should happen when you are around the age of 50.

I gave this advice to all my children. Most of them didn't take it. But then, nor did I when my father gave it to me. But now, every month, I pay myself before I pay anyone else.

Looking out at the audience as they listened to the Law of Human Nature, it was clear that many of them were already past retirement age, and without a pension, they could afford to live on. Some of them were clearly just scraping by. For them, the only hope of becoming "special" was Network marketing: Just learn to do it and then keep on doing it – the same thing over and over again ... and then do it some more..."

It sounded simple. It was simple.

But once all the excited, pumped-up people streamed out of the doors to "take their businesses to the next level", once the music stopped and the lights went out, some of those people found that doing the same thing over and over again wasn't exciting at all.

For instance, remember how I got started with the Win-a-Bottle-of-Champagne competition? The company realised this was a great idea and so they took it over and ramped it up with a brand new BMW Mini as a prize. As the years went by, I must have organised scores of these Win-a-Mini events at school fetes and county shows – at supermarkets and garden centres – anywhere you could find a crowd.

The trouble was that a Win-a-Mini event had to be organised. I had to pay for the venue, buy a collapsible stand and cart it around in the back of the car. I had to find other distributors to man the stall - collect their contribution towards the cost (and then find a replacement when they cried off). Certainly, it provided lots of new people to talk to, but you had to give up the time, pay the money and – if you stripped away all the fake excitement we threw at it, underneath it was the same thing over and over again. I'd been doing it for years. In other words, the **excitement** had worn off.

And then, one day, I was walking down my local high street thinking about this. I had booked a three-month contract at the garden centre and very soon discovered that garden centres get a lot of repeat business – the same people coming back week after week to replace their broken trowel or buy their bedding plants. In other words, after the first few weeks, we weren't meeting new people at all.

I looked around at all the people in the high street - there must have been hundreds of them, young Mums with toddlers in pushchairs, old ladies with shopping baskets on wheels, career people in business clothes, tradespeople – an entire, representative cross section of the British population streaming past. If only there was a way of persuading them to come to the garden centre and our Win-a-Mini stand ... or, to put it another way, if the Win-a-Mini stand could be brought to them...

But I couldn't just set up in the High Street. I'd be causing an obstruction. I'd need a licence...

But think about it: Did I really need the stand? After all, it was the form for the free prize draw that was the important part – and I had a stack of those on me. What if I just turned to the nearest person – a completely random person and – just to see what would happen, asked them: "Would you like to win a Mini?"

So, I did.

"I beg your pardon?"

"I've got a Prize Draw here. You can win a brand new Mini. It's free. Do you want to have a go?"

And this total stranger – who I had never spoken to before – who was about to walk past me without ever discovering that he could save money or make money, said: "OK."

It was the beginning of a phenomenon. Best of all, it was something new – something **exciting.**

After that, every morning, I walked down to town to do half an hour of my pop-up Win-a-Mini. I found a favourite spot – just where people had to walk between the car park and the shops. I stopped asking a question that people could answer with a simple "No". Instead, I got their attention with: "Here you are... you can win a car!"

There was another unexpected benefit, too: Remember how my nearest and dearest had said: "We'll see how you get on with it?" They did join in the end – although my father-in-law took five months, my two sisters four and five months, respectively. Tamsin's brother thought about it for two years – and her sister (who was clearly trying to make some sort of obscure point), took four-and-a-half years! But I saw them regularly and once the company had given me my own Mini covered in pink pigs and purple stripes, they could hardly avoid asking: "I see you're still doing that utility thing. How's it going?"

"It's going great."

"D'you think we should join?"

But there were a lot of other people who had said they would get back to me but never did. Now, when they found me by the car park with my Win-a-Mini forms, their curiosity would get the better of them – they couldn't help it: "Hello, it's John isn't it? What have you got there?"

Of course, as we know, **I had no idea who they were.** But that didn't matter. I just handed them the form and they wrote their names down for me.

Pretty soon I gave up organised events altogether. Instead, I just carried my little satchel of Win-a-Mini forms everywhere I went. After all, you never knew when you were going to get a chance to bring them out...

For instance, my laptop packed up. The repair shop said to bring it in. The man behind the counter reckoned he could fix it while I waited. Now, I could have spent that time waiting. Maybe I could read the labels on all the dreadful video games. Instead, I went out onto the pavement and opened my little satchel. In those 15 minutes, I got five forms filled in. Three of those people made appointments. One was cancelled, another asked me to call him back in six months - and the third signed up (I've just looked him up and see that he joined on November 22nd 2011 (and, I just looked, he's still a member today, using all the services.)

Suddenly it wasn't difficult to get my four new members a month. The company holiday became a foregone conclusion – Las Vegas… six star cruises. The share options piled up…

One by one, members of my team began to ask how I did it and I took them out into their local High Streets and showed them. Then, I took them two at a time. After that, I booked a conference room and put 20 people in it.

Word began to spread. People from other teams – people I didn't know – came up to me at company events and asked for my "Top Tips". Naturally, I revelled in all the attention – what was this but gratifying my **desire for approval** – and of course, all the time I was refining the system, tweaking it and changing the wording. Every day it was new all over again – never **boring**. How great was this?

Pretty soon, I booked a room for 120 people and called it *The Cold Market Academy*. It sold out. After that, I was doing an event every month. The company was delighted. I was offering something that could help all those people who said: "But I don't know anyone… I don't have the time…"

More to the point, they quite understood that I couldn't be expected to do it for nothing. Actually, I wasn't doing badly out of it at all. I was like those brash American Network marketing gurus who swoop down on the UK with their £120-a-seat weekend events. I still have shelves full of the notes that I never read – after all, how many times do you need to hear someone recite: "If-it-is-to-be-it-is-up-to-me" and repeating endlessly "Just do it!" – and if "Just do it" doesn't do it for you, look up the YouTube video of Art Williams repeating "Just do it".

I bought the CDs and played them in the car on the way home. There was always a CD – invariably ending with an invitation to sign up for the online coaching course or a link to buy the book. There would be a website advertising the next seven-day residential "Boot Camp" in Hawaii…

I should have a CD to sell...

I hired a sound man to record me telling my stories at the Academy, designed a cover, called it *Believe and Succeed!* I had a thousand run off and sold them at £5 each - sitting at the front of the hall with somebody dragooned out of the audience to sit beside me and take the money while I signed each disc with a personal message in gold pen. I cringe to think about it now. I've still got a box in the attic somewhere... In fact, why don't I put them online as a podcast (have a look, I've probably done it by the time you read this).

The Cold Market Academy lasted 18 months. Just under a thousand people came through the doors, and at £20 a head (plus the CDs), it was a respectable little earner. But once it was up and running, it became a routine. In other words, the **excitement** wore off. The trouble was that, just as somebody with a job might go to bed on a Sunday night, groaning at the prospect of having to get up for another week's work in the morning, so I grew to dread packing the car, checking everything twice (I couldn't afford to forget anything) – the night in the hotel next to the conference centre (I couldn't afford to be late) – the early morning walk to rehearse The Law of Human Nature finale...

I was like an actor stuck in the cast of The Mousetrap. I couldn't afford to give it up.

Fortunately, the company gave it up for me. The Network Director decided that this was a conflict of interest – I was a company trainer, after all – and they wanted to keep the emphasis on "friends and family". I was telling people that they'd be much better off with total strangers: Total strangers don't know you've just started. Total strangers won't try and avoid you at the office party in case you try and sell them something. Anyway, you don't care what total strangers think of you – you'll never see them again…

And so, the Cold Market Academy closed its doors. The company was happy. I was quietly relieved. It had become a job – paying a linear income (if I didn't work, I didn't get paid – which was not at all what I was supposed to be advocating). But the distributors who had heard about it from their friends and now wanted to buy tickets felt that they had been left out.

A conundrum.

But what do the *special people* know? In every setback, there is an opportunity. Every cloud has a silver lining...

What if I put the Cold Market Academy online? I had videos of myself standing in the street with my forms, people stopping to talk to me (the local wedding-video company had filmed me with a long lens and a hidden microphone like Candid Camera.) Instead of screening them in conference rooms to demonstrate that it worked, I could put them online.

Better still, once I set it up, it would sell itself. It would be global. I could be on people's screens in the middle of the night, showing them how to make a success of their business while I was fast asleep. The idea was the very definition of a residual income.

Moreover, the internet is a different world. Normal rules do not apply. People don't buy a book in Waterstones for £20. But hit them with it at three o'clock in the morning, when the house is quiet; when their spouse who would tell them not to be so stupid is sleeping peacefully upstairs. Tell them this is the answer to all their problems and that for this one-night-only it's not $899 for the course, it's not $399 ... and they're going to get *Free Material* worth $760 if they hit that button *now!*

I knew all about this because it had worked on me: I pitched the *New* Cold Market Academy at $67 and dispensed with the "free materials" and the NOW! NOW! NOW! I was British, after all...

The best thing about it was that, once I had set it up, the whole thing ran by itself. People made their PayPal payments. All I had to do was send them the link to the download page. In other words, it was a Residual Income - the very thing you get from network marketing which you don't get from a job.

It lasted for a couple of years. Then somebody hacked it and started diverting the money to their PayPal account instead of mine. Now, of course, there are ways around this (I expect there were then, if I could have been bothered to find them). But it was no longer new. I had lost interest - I couldn't be bothered. I took down the videos, and I suspect that was the end of it.

Note: Out of interest, I just searched for The Cold Market Academy – and it's still there (and I still have hair!)

Of course, if I had put all of this time and effort into what I was supposed to be doing - signing up new customers and new partners for the utility company, I would have done a good deal better in the long run. This was something I knew only too well. In fact, I delighted in telling the story of being taken to dinner by the top distributor only six months after I started. There must have been 20 people round the table and at the end of the meal he apologised for it taking so long because he had to earn enough to pay for it. *He'd just learned that he was earning £1 a minute day and night, year in, year out.*

And that was in 2005 – and I've just worked it out on my phone: It's £525,600 a year. If you're wondering what he's on now, I can save you the trouble: Eventually, the company realised this was going to get obscene and not good for their image, so they introduced a £1million-a-year cap and diverted the extra money to the people just getting started. The Top Man doesn't complain.

But no matter how good the money is, you have to be a certain type of person to keep on doing the same thing day in and day out.

The other type of person is **continually scanning the environment for more stimulation... starting new tasks before finishing old ones...**

Chapter 23
Health

Ask most people how they are, and they'll say: "Not so bad," or "Mustn't grumble." Ask a Network Marketer how they are, and it's all "Great! Amazing! Kerpow!"

What's that all about? Actually, it's an integral part of every Network marketing business. Whether you're promoting face cream or diet pills or, come to that, utility services, how are you going to get anybody wound up about it if you're full of negativity, yourself? So how are you again?

Fantastic!

That's better. Year after year, I was relentlessly Fantastic! Everything was perennially Great!!

Until it wasn't. An unexpected anomaly in the energy market meant that suddenly dozens of little companies started popping up and undercutting the big boys and we – despite the no advertising, word-of-mouth model – were representing one of the big boys. Suddenly, when we sat down with potential customers, our gas and electricity turned out to be more expensive than they were paying already – or certainly more expensive than they were being offered on the comparison websites.

The message from the top of the network was that we just had to keep up the momentum. Things would be back to normal in a year or two - just keep doing the do...

A year or two?

By this time, I had been a company trainer for five years. That might sound like a long time to be doing the same thing, but in fact, the courses changed every year as the offering changed or we found better ways to present it. But then a new training director arrived, and he had some very radical ideas.

Where we used to stand up at the front and present our Powerpoint slides and – in my case – tell our stories (get me to tell you about the Airport Cat sometime), now it was all going to be "interactive": People would be on their feet role-playing and absorbing "kinetic learning". More to the point, both trainers would be busy all the time - one "facilitating the module" while the other "interacted" with the trainees (an arm around their shoulders, would you believe...)

No, no. This was not my thing. Couldn't I just stand up at the front and tell stories?

Obviously not. Now it was all about "connecting".

I drove home from the trainer training (sorry, the "facilitator facilitating") with a feeling that the world had overtaken me. I stopped halfway and slept in the driving seat for an hour – I had taken to doing this on longer runs. Come to that, I didn't fancy all that time on my feet. My feet hurt if I didn't get to sit down while my co-trainer did their bit. I was 66, after all...

Actually, my age was beginning to show itself in other ways too. I kept getting infections: Every winter – a couple of times every winter – I would find myself coughing ... and then cough up green phlegm. The doctor would diagnose a chest infection and put me on a course of antibiotics (we don't want you getting pneumonia). In the summer, insect bites became infected (another course of antibiotics) The crunch arrived when I banged my elbow while sailing my Laser on the river (and coming last as usual). The insignificant bump grew into an enormous and vividly colourful bruise. But, instead of fading over the next few days as bruises usually did, this one turned an alarming purple colour and started throbbing.

The doctor diagnosed yet another infection. To give him credit, he wasn't at all happy about giving me more antibiotics – but, as he said, what else could he do? And, as he had suspected, they didn't work. I ended up in hospital hooked up to a drip. I remember sitting there with industrial-strength antibiotics going straight into my bloodstream and thought: "I'm in hospital because I banged my elbow - surely that's the sort of thing that happens to old people. I'm only 66 for heaven's sake…"

When I came out, I went to see the doctor again. This time I asked: "What's wrong with me? I seem to be in here every few weeks for something or other – and I feel tired all the time. If I sit down, I go straight to sleep (Passmore nodding off was the universal joke at company events). I fell asleep at the wheel half a mile from home and wrote off my brand-new Mini. What was going on here?

The doctor said: "Well, you are getting on..."

Oh great. I was 66 and I was being dismissed as an "old person".

I looked at the doctor and it was on the tip of my tongue to say something very rude. I didn't, of course, but I did go home with a burning determination to do something about it.

Quite what I was going to do about it, I had absolutely no idea.

Then, once the elbow had cleared up, I went out in the Laser again and, pulling it up the slipway, I slipped (why do you think they call it a slipway). I ended up flat on my back.

People came running. They didn't laugh. There was real alarm in their voices: "Are you all right?" and "He's had a fall!"

"Having a fall" is something that happens to old people. Young people just fall over and get up again. "Having a fall" calls for "Don't try and move" and "Someone call an ambulance!"

I was only 66, for heaven's sake!

They do say that it's when you're looking for something that opportunities present themselves. And there are some advantages to ADHD – opportunities don't just present themselves, they arrive with sirens and flashing lights, screaming: **"This is new! This is exciting! Go for this! Do this now!"**

Which must have been a bit startling for the friend who walked into my room a few days later and found me massaging my knuckles. I wasn't even aware I was doing it, but I had been typing, and after 15 minutes of typing, I would get pains in my hands.

He said: "I know what you've got. You've got arthritis."

"Oh God, I hope not," I said. "I'm only 66."

He laughed at that – and then he told me a story (if you want anybody's attention, tell them a story – it's an old Network Marketer's trick).

This friend of mine told me about a friend of his who was a really good amateur golfer. He used to go in for those big weekend competitions: 18 holes on a Saturday morning – then another 18 in the afternoon. A third 18 on the Sunday morning, then lunch and the prize-giving before everybody sets off home to beat the rush hour.

Except, this friend found that after 36 holes on the Saturday, his knees couldn't cope with another 18 on the Sunday – and, of course, without that, he couldn't go in for the competition at all. It was too much of a step down to go back to the one-round Stableford at his local club, so he was sitting at home feeling sorry for himself ... when another friend recommended a natural mineral supplement...

Well, within a few weeks, the golfer was back on the circuit – and winning again...

If it could do that for his knees, could it do the same for my hands? My friend didn't see why not. He left me with a website address.

With the same kind of focus I recognised from looking into

the utility company – and before that, the trading system, I researched the supplement - the company behind it – the man behind the company...

It turned out to be quite a story:

His name was Peter Willoughby, and as a teenager, he had been involved in a very serious motorcycle accident. A drunk driver behind the wheel of a lorry ran into him – and then panicked and ran right over him ... and then panicked once more, slammed the lorry into reverse and backed over him a second time, breaking some of the bones he missed the first time. Then, would you believe it, he put the lorry into first and drove over the poor lad a third time.

When they scraped him off the road, the only bones that weren't broken were his spine, his skull and his left arm.

Surviving against all the odds, Peter Willoughby refused to accept the doctors' prognosis – which was that if he ever did manage to get out of his wheelchair, he would be back in it by the time he was 30 because arthritis would start in all his broken bones.

The young man didn't go for this at all. He had been a bodybuilder. He knew what you could do with exercise and determination. Also, he knew about nutritional supplements. He found one in America, said to have achieved remarkable results with a wide range of conditions. He imported it by the case and drank it by the bottle. It tasted disgusting, but in due course, he got out of his wheelchair. He walked. He astounded the doctors...

Then he went and got a job with a merchant bank in the City of London and made a fortune. After that, he joined the utility company that I joined. He was one of its very its first distributors (and made another fortune).

As you might imagine, he was a bit of a character – before long, he was falling out with the management and looking for somewhere else to invest his money and his enthusiasm.

The magical supplement might be a good opportunity. He

contacted the company with a view to importing the stuff into Europe. In the course of the negotiations, he somehow ended up buying one their subsidiaries.

So, what exactly was this stuff? That side of the story begins in Utah in the 1800's. When the native Americans and the settlers stopped fighting and started talking to each other, one of the bits of knowledge the locals were able to pass along was that if anyone got sick, they should drink from a particular mountain stream. It had healing properties, so the native Americans said.

Fast forward to the 1980s and the local community was a model of good health. Sure enough, these people who believed in the folklore and drank from the magic stream did indeed have lower rates of heart disease, arthritis, cancer, stroke... you name it. They lived longer than the national average. The whole town was happy and healthy – the epitome of the American dream.

So, what was in this water? A team of researchers analysed it and found an astonishingly high concentration of minerals and trace elements – far higher than the normal water supply. So, they started to dig down at the head of the stream. The first thing their excavation exposed was a layer of limestone – which is, of course, porous. Underneath this was what appeared to be petrified compost. The conclusion was that this must be plant matter from a forest which grew there millions of years ago - before a flood swamped the land. In the course of more millions of years, generations of fish and crustaceans died and sank to the bottom of the lake and their bones turned into limestone (remember this from your school geography lessons?)

Next, along came the ice age and compressed all the forests and turned them into coal – but this one was protected by its limestone cap and so remained as vegetate – which meant that all the nutrients left behind from the prehistoric forest remained in a vegetable form - instead of being converted by the pressure of the ice into a metallic state and becoming coal (which accounts for the old-wives' tale about pregnant women sucking lumps of coal because they crave the minerals).

More to the point, if this vegetate was soaked in purified water, the minerals and trace elements would leach out into the water – 75 of them could be identified: From Aluminum to Zirconium – and everything in between like Molybdenum and even Arsenic (yes, you do need a little of that - just not too much!).

In other words, everything the body needs to heal itself – and more to the point, everything that is lacking in modern farmland.

As I continued to research this, I learned that the World Health Organisation, the British Ministry of Agriculture and all sorts of other respectable organisations such as Save the Children had been monitoring the gradual deterioration of soils around the world. In Europe, the average farm had seen its nutrients depleted by 70% over the past hundred years. In North America, the figure is over 80% and some farmland no longer contains any nutrients at all.

So, you might wonder how the farmers manage to grow anything in such poor soil.

Well, of course, they use fertilizers. The most popular fertilizer is called NPK - which stands for the chemical symbols for Nitrogen, Potassium and Phosphorus. This particular combination produces a bumper crop. The farmer gets a tonnage per acre that his great-grandfather would not have believed - and fortunately, he gets paid by the tonne.

If he got paid by the nutrient, it might be a different story.

And there, by the way, is your obesity crisis in a nutshell – and why it is worse in the USA than anywhere else. Look at it this way: You're hungry; you pick up the phone and order pizza. Your stomach starts digesting the pizza – after all, the brain had pressed the "hunger" button – pizza should fix it. But no sooner is the pizza digested than the stomach reports: "That was no good, all we got was carbohydrate. We need some Iron and Molybdenum - and what about that little bit of Arsenic?"

So, the brain sends another message: "Quick, order another pizza..."

Result: Obesity - also, the lack of nutrients hampers the body's natural ability to heal itself resulting in increasing rates of heart disease, arthritis, cancer - particularly in the USA.

The doctors, having been trained in medical schools funded by the pharmaceutical industry, are adept at treating these ailments with (you guessed it) pharmaceutical products.

Even the "Health Food" shops are full of pharmaceutical products made from clay taken from river beds and by-products of the oil industry. The glucosamine I had been taking for my hands had been made from seashells. Everybody knows you can't digest seashells (which was why I had been taking higher and higher doses – and, of course, spending more and more). In fact, I discovered that glucosamine was a compound I was supposed to be making inside my own body from the nutrients in my diet...

The more I read, the more it all made sense. Even the very expensive organic produce from the farmers' market was hardly better - because the organic farmland had been under cultivation for years - and every harvest left fewer and fewer nutrients in the soil, no matter what organic fertilizer the farmer might spread on top.

What I needed were nutrients from plants which grew before anyone had invented farming.

Fortunately, the disgusting liquid which had helped young Willoughby after his motorbike accident, had since been replaced by an effervescent tablet in a choice of pleasant fruit flavours – yet it still contained the 75 minerals and trace elements from the original preparation. I started taking one every morning.

Nothing happened. I still fell asleep every time I sat down. My hands still hurt – but I had been warned not to expect instant results. After all, if I had a headache, I would take Paracetamol and the headache would be gone in half an hour. It was the same with antibiotics – within 24 hours, you could tell that an infection was beginning to subside. But those were pharmaceutical products designed to force the body to mask the symptoms while chemicals dealt with the cause.

With this stuff, nothing happened because it wasn't masking the symptom like paracetamol or introducing foreign pathogens with antibiotics. This stuff was providing the body with the nutrients it needed to fulfil its designed purpose of maintaining good health.

"Look at it this way," said my friend: "If you had been living on junk food and fizzy drinks for 20 years and suddenly switched to a healthy diet, could you run a marathon the next day? Have patience – but be alert for some changes."

So, I agreed to give it three months.

In fact, things started happening in three weeks.

I had a patch of skin on my nose that would bleed if I spent too long under the shower. This was embarrassing – I had to come downstairs with a piece of toilet paper stuck to my nose. It was nothing to worry about – the doctor had looked at it with a magnifying glass and said it was not malignant – just a lesion that could be fixed with laser surgery if I wanted to pay for it. I didn't. I just tried to remember to take shorter showers.

But now, it suddenly dawned on me that I had stayed in the shower for ten minutes and I didn't need to stick toilet paper on my nose. I inspected myself in the mirror. There was no sign of any lesion.

A few weeks later, I was walking in the woods when I stepped on a tangle of rusty barbed wire. I was wearing shorts. The barbs tore all the way up my shin. There was blood everywhere. All I had was a scrap of tissue in my pocket. It took 20 minutes to get back to the car and even then, I had no water to wash the wound – just some ancient sticking plaster in the glove compartment left over from when the children were toddlers. I did the best I could with that and arrived home, where Tamsin took one look and said: "My God, what happened to you?"

She dressed my wounds, but whatever muck there had been on the barbed wire must surely be well into my system by now. I readied myself for the inevitable infection - after all, if that's what I got from an insect bite, with this I'd be lucky to keep the leg...

Yet there was no red swelling – no pain. Within 24 hours, it was obvious the scars were well on the way to healing. After a week, the new skin was growing. There was hardly anything to see at all.

It took three or four months for the pain in my hands to go. This wasn't something I noticed as it happened, but one day, when I was playing the clarinet – playing along to a Spotify trad jazz station – I discovered I had been going for the best part of an hour. Typing was the same – no pain at all.

After that, I began to keep a log of what was happening to me. One of the most surprising and the most welcome changes was that, after three years on the supplement, the optician reported "Significant improvement over the past year in the distance vision of both eyes." Already I no longer needed glasses for reading. Now I could prove that I didn't need them for driving.

As you might have guessed by now, this was another Network marketing company – after all, the man behind it had made his money in the industry with the utility company. Besides, if he put his product into health food shops, it would be indistinguishable from all the other stuff on the shelves. This was something unique.

Of course, I signed up for it. Here was something I really believed in - something I was passionate about. I wouldn't need books and CDs to pump me up to talk about this – you wouldn't be able to stop me telling everyone about it!

Actually, that didn't always work out so well. I was invited to stay with some friends. They invited another sailor to make up a foursome. It was a very convivial evening – probably too convivial on my part, but what could I do, they kept filling my glass and I kept talking – as in **talking over people**.

And what did I talk about? Why, my wonderful new supplement, of course – along with all the prejudices I had learned about the pharmaceutical industry.

"Take cancer, for instance," I announced, waving my glass for emphasis. "People have chemotherapy – which, incidentally is poison. They say they're cured – they've beaten the big C. But more than 90% of cancer patients die from cancer in the end. Oh, they might get another few years, but they're not being cured. They're just putting off the inevitable."

The next morning, my hostess found it necessary to leave the house before eight o'clock in the morning. Her husband didn't give me breakfast – just a cup of coffee (standing up).

At the time, I thought this slightly odd (was I being **insensitive**?) It was only later that I learned both of them had been through cancer treatment.

Even now I curl up with embarrassment at the memory of it. All I can find in my defence is that, at that time, I knew nothing of ADHD – and certainly, I didn't know I had it.

Now that I do know I have it, I wonder why the minerals didn't fix it. It seems they're only good for physical conditions…

Meanwhile, my colleagues in the utility business were equally upset with me. By joining another network marketing company, I had placed myself beyond the pale. I was one of the top bananas, for heaven's sake – in the top 0.2% of the entire company. I had been one of the elite band of trainers (and one of the conditions of that position was that I must not be involved with any other Network marketing operation). As I used to tell the trainees: "If you try and chase two rabbits, you end up with no dinner."

But by now I had given up the training – and besides, I wasn't getting any dinner anyway. Time after time, I would sit with people to show them how much money they could save – only to find that I might be able to save them a few pounds a year if they went shopping in the right stores (which they might not want to do). Was it worth it? I had to admit they had a point. A colleague in the wilds of Norfolk calculated how much he was spending on fuel driving all over the county to his appointments and worked out that, actually, he was losing money. Quite sensibly, he decided to stop until things improved.

Things did improve in a couple of years – but, by that time, he'd forgotten how to do it – and anyway, he was out of the habit.

What was it Stephan had said: "Don't quit. Whatever happens, don't quit…"

Meanwhile, I had switched my attention to the health supplement. It was easy enough to do - I just changed from Win-a-Mini to a Win-a-Hamper: "Here you are, you could win a hamper or £20. It's a free prize draw, we just put your name in a hat..."

It turned out that people didn't care what they won. They just liked something for nothing. I had my questions about their health and energy, told them a bit about the supplement and made an appointment to go round so they could try it at home.

It was so much easier than calculating how much they would save on their utility services: I just played them a video, gave them a sample to taste and filled in the order form. This was great. More to the point, this was new. This was **exciting**. By the time the company's first national event came along, I was on stage, being applauded as a superstar.

But no matter how good I thought it might be, the supplement business had two big drawbacks. The first was that people expected instant results – after all, that's what they got from an aspirin. No matter how much I warned them this was not a "quick fix", when they didn't feel better immediately, they stopped taking it – and then, after a few more weeks, they cancelled their order. Worse still, they could now tell their friends: "Oh, I tried that stuff.

It didn't work."

Secondly, they would insist on asking their doctor for a second opinion – and doctors have a very, very low opinion of everything that doesn't come from a reputable pharmaceutical company and hasn't undergone years of double-blind testing and so on...

The next thing you know, another order had been cancelled.

But then things got even worse: A woman who had been suffering from psoriasis for fifteen years and was being treated by her doctor with steroids (with all the associated side effects) started to take the supplement. Within a few weeks, her skin cleared up completely.

With great excitement, she showed her doctor what she had been taking. He was furious that she hadn't consulted him first and confiscated the tablets because, he insisted, they must contain some illegal growth hormone, since that was the only explanation for such a recovery.

However, the report from the National Health Service laboratory showed no sign of any illegal human growth hormone – although it did say that the concentration of certain minerals was higher than the recommended daily allowance...

So, the company received a visit from the local council's Trading Standards Officer. Peter Willoughby argued that these were minerals in a vegetable rather than a metallic state. Taking them was really no different from eating a very large plateful of cabbage.

The Trading Standards Officer remained adamant: The regulations did not differentiate between types of minerals. Either the company would have to reduce the amount per serving or stop selling the product altogether.

In the view of many of the distributors, what the company did next was somewhere up there on the stupidity scale along with Icarus and his wings – no more sensible than Chairman Mao declaring war on sparrows. First of all, they reduced the amount of the mineral complex from 600mg per serving down to 100mg. Then they made up the deficit with extra magnesium, potassium and phosphorus – which *were* allowed. Finally - and most inexplicably – they decided not to tell anyone what they'd done.

Instead, they said: "How wonderful is this! We have given you extra Magnesium, Potassium and Phosphorus for the same price!"

It took about six months, but gradually the complaints started to come in. First, it was the Multiple Sclerosis sufferers who reported their "fatigue crashes" had returned. Then the blood pressure people said their readings were off the scale. I could feel the pain in my hands coming back...

If the company was being naïve, it was nothing compared to the distributors. Why didn't we think to look on the label? Because there it was, as plain as day: "Mineral Trace Elements: 100mg."

However, all was not lost: If you switched from the effervescent tablets to the capsules you would still get the original formula - which resulted in a frantic scramble to get back to all the customers, explain what had happened and advise them to change their order.

But then the company changed the formula of the capsules as well! That left only the powder which came in a little plastic tub with a scoop and instructions: "Sprinkle on food".

In between tearing my hair out, I went back to the few loyal customers I had left and explained once again... until the label on the tub changed to: "Serving suggestion: One scoop a day" and "**DO NOT EXCEED DAILY DOSAGE**".

I was taking two heaped scoops a day - six if I thought I might be getting an infection. One level scoop a day wasn't going to do any good at all - besides, at that rate, a tub would last four months. How could people be expected to sign up a monthly delivery if it was only going to pile up in their kitchen cupboard?

Again and again, I emailed the company asking what was going on and how we could rescue the situation. After all, this stuff really worked - as long as you took enough of it...

But I never received a reply. Meanwhile, the company website now contained virtually no information at all – not even a list of ingredients. Presumably, with a naturally-occurring product, not every sample is going to contain the exact same ingredients in the exact same proportions – which means they couldn't publish any ingredients at all.

In the end, I think the only thing that was keeping them going was the fact that Peter Willoughby – the man who owed his life to these minerals – had to get them from somewhere, even if only for his own use. Fortunately, it appeared he was making enough money from his other ventures to keep the company afloat.

I'm still taking them. I still think they're wonderful and have a page of my blog devoted to them. Most days, I get an email from someone asking where they can order the stuff.

It's a steady little income, but the excitement has gone out of it – for one thing, once the profits dropped, the company switched from the Network marketing model to an "Affiliate" compensation plan. With this, the customers could still get paid for recommending it to friends – but there would be nothing for the people that those friends recommended. No "and so on ad infinitum…"

It wasn't nearly as exciting - and you know what that means. Still, I can plug it on the blog: If you're feeling older than you think you should, have a look at https://oldmansailing.com/good-health.

Chapter 24

Rich

There is always a great deal of astonishment when someone with a high profile in commerce or industry – or come to that fashion, politics, the arts, you name it... is suddenly revealed in the Sunday papers to have a drug habit.

Everyone says they had no idea.

Well, of course they had no idea: As long as a junkie gets their fix, they can function perfectly normally. Apart from being a bit more dramatic - more than ever the life and soul of the party… Apart from that, there would be nothing to tell them apart from any other member of the population.

As long as they get their fix.

Excitement is the drug of choice in the ADHD world.

Looking back now, it all makes sense: It is easy to see how getting married and buying a house was **exciting** – so was having babies and starting each new business. Even learning to sail a Laser on the river was **exciting** – to begin with...

But novelty wears off. Here we were in 2017. I was 68 years old. The near miss with old age had been a frightening experience. At a time like that, even a "normal" person might start to take stock. Someone who is completely self-absorbed is likely to be stopped in their tracks, asking: "Is that all there is?".

The savings were all but gone. The never-ending succession of things that "turned up" had not, in the main, proved to be a permanent solution- the only one with any lasting benefit was the utility business. At least that kept going with its flood of upbeat vibes and the whoop-whoop, rah-rah events. For a day, I would feel "fantastic" and "amazing".

But the rest of the time, it seemed that I had screwed up. We were doing all right: The utility business continued to pay me more than most people earned from their 40 hours a week in a job. I had my newspaper pension – and the bit from the state that everybody gets. There was the Bed and Breakfast (now in the converted garage), Tamsin worked part-time with vulnerable teenagers at the local college.

But it was all a long way from where I had always imagined I would be at this stage. I found myself buying Lottery tickets – not in daft amounts. Just one or two a week…after all, why not me…

So, as had been the case so many times before, I was looking…

…and, as usual, the opportunity presented itself: John Breadstill had found something. John and I had been "Success Buddies" in UW ever since his phone had beeped one day in an attic where he was doing a rewire and thinking he was too old to be an electrician (he was a year older than me). That was in the mass-texting days.

Now the situation was reversed and he was asking me if I would like to look at something new and (that word) **"exciting"**.

I got back to him in ten minutes: "Looks like a scam to me. Typical Ponzi scheme. Probably a money-circulating operation."

John said: "Did you look at the videos?"

No, I hadn't. The website had been enough: You put your money in, and you made money without risk and without having to do anything for it. In other words, a typical trap for the gullible and the greedy. Besides, this involved Bitcoin – and Bitcoin was the currency of choice for arms dealers and drug smugglers and people traffickers, wasn't it? In other words, it looked too good to be true.

"Did you watch the videos?"

Oh, alright then, I would watch the videos – he was a friend, after all. I owed him that.

And this was where something clicked. The video showed an interview with one of the founders of the company – a surprisingly subdued German who explained that he had been trading currency futures for many years, but the days of the individual trader were over as the big banks and hedge funds automated their trades. By the time the little guy in front of his computer in his back bedroom had spotted a trend, the bank's machine had placed its orders in a nano-second.

Worse still, those people who had bought into a trading system weren't just the little fish in the pond, they had entered the food chain: The banks' computers now looked for unexplained market movements – unexplained, that is, unless the reason for them was that a trading system had flagged a trend and hundreds of little people had jumped in.

What happened next was that the bank would dump a few million dollars into a counter-trade. This was big enough to move the market in the opposite direction. The price steamrollered through all the little people's stop losses, wiping them out in an instant and adding more fuel to the price movement.

When the bank judged that things were slowing down, it reversed its position – and cleaned up all over again as the market returned to where it had been in the first place. Millions more for the bank. Back to the day job for the now-chastened small-time traders.

But the clever chap on YouTube explained that they didn't play that game. They had a computer program of their own that jumped in and out looking for a point here, a point there, profiting from movements that were so small and so quick that nobody could track what it was doing.

The trouble was that it took huge sums of money to make this work profitably. That was where I came in – me and thousands of other little people around the world. Together we were big enough to take on the banks.

This was starting to make sense. After my own foray into the futures markets, I could relate to this. In particular, it explained how my system had worked so brilliantly for a while and then suddenly stopped: Just as the man at the barbecue had wanted to buy my rules, so a hedge fund manager in a bunker somewhere had been tracking the movements in the oil market and instructed his computer to take me out – me and all the other people using the same software.

And Bitcoin? I knew nothing about Bitcoin, but it quickly became clear that this company could never hope to comply with the financial regulations in every country of the world, so in order to attract the numbers of people they would need, they had to operate outside the regulations … and Bitcoin was an unregulated currency. The fact that it was going up (like a rocket) only added to the attraction.

I was in.

After all, Richard Branson never said: "If something looks too good to be true..." If Richard Branson sees something that looks spectacular, he turns to his people and says: "Hey, check this out. If it's as good as it looks, I want a piece of it before anyone else gets in."

In this scenario, you understand, I was Richard Branson. Here was the deal: You put in your money and you made a 40% return in 140 working days. That's about seven months. That's amazing. Not having "people" to check it out, I checked it out myself – sitting up late into the night, trawling through the internet, deep in **hyperfocus**.

The company was called USI Tech – United Software Intelligence Technology. The public face of the company was an

American of tremendous energy and charisma who had worked his way to the top of one Network marketing company after another, only to have them collapse under him as the owners pulled the plug and ran off with the money.

Thoroughly disillusioned, he went back to his home in Mallorca to lick his wounds – and there he had a friend, a German who had made his money trading the currency markets – a lot of money, it appeared. So, the American asked the German to teach him to do the same. It certainly looked a better bet than network marketing.

Day after day, the American would turn up at the German's house, and together they would sit in front of the screens and analyse the graphs and the "candlesticks" and the lines of resistance and what-have-you.

After a couple of days of this, the network marketer was climbing up the walls: He was a people person. He was used to standing in front of packed conference rooms, getting people whooped up by the sheer force of his personality. He couldn't sit in a darkened room with a geek staring at screens.

And yet, what he saw on those screens did get him excited: An automated and apparently fool-proof system for making money by trading currency pairs – that is, for instance, buying US dollars at the same time as selling Japanese Yen. If the dollar goes up against the yen, you make money. If it goes down, you lose.

When and what to buy and sell was dictated by a computer program invented by a Portuguese trader. This man had a long and successful history of building these programs for banks and hedge funds. Now he had started working with a few "high net worth" individuals like the German.

Day-dreaming while he should have been concentrating on the latest trade, the American thought to himself: "If the clever stuff was done by the computer program, then why did it have to be restricted to a handful of rich people? Surely, it would be just as easy to have thousands and thousands of small accounts – thousands and thousands of little people.

And if anyone knew how to get thousands and thousands of people…

So, as the story went, the German trader got in touch with the Portuguese programmer and said: "Could you build an automated system to trade huge sums of money remotely for hundreds of thousands of people?"

A few weeks later, the call came back from Portugal: "It's ready."

The minimum stake was 50Euros – so in seven months, your 50Euros would have grown to 70Euros - or, 500Euros would be, amazingly, 700Euros!

And, of course, since this was network marketing, if you introduced someone else (as my friend proposed to introduce me), then they would be given free 50Euro "packs" as a thank-you for building the network. People were making enormous sums this way.

After all, this was the spring of 2017. Ordinary people had only just heard about Bitcoin. But suddenly it was dominating the news with its meteoric rise and stories of teenage millionaires and how the first pizza bought with Bitcoin would now be worth millions (let's hope it came with lots of toppings!)

In other words, while your 50Euros turned into 70Euros in 7 months – by that time, the price rise of Bitcoin could well have doubled it! Was this **exciting** or what?

It was at this point that the excitement overruled common sense (as it would do). Being diligent, I investigated all three of these people. I found that the guy in Portugal had been banned from taking part in any financial activity. The German had been involved in various Network marketing opportunities, all of which had collapsed in suspicious circumstances. The American had had his account suspended by the juice company Monavie which folded owing $182million.

At this point, anybody with any sense would have walked away. But if these people really were crooks, would they be all over YouTube showing their faces and using their real names? Surely, they'd get caught.

Then they brought in a Swiss businessman - ostensibly because they needed someone with experience in running a big international company – and certainly, this guy knew all about that. I looked him up. There was nothing dodgy about him at all. In fact, he had been running a huge airport security firm. Now, why would someone like that get mixed up with something dodgy?

Besides, everybody else seemed to be piling into this. It was all over the USA, of course – and in Guam, the tiny South Pacific US territory, the local Senator was promoting it so successfully that people were cashing in their pensions and re-mortgaging their homes.

How could I not get involved? Sure, there were financial authorities all over the world issuing warnings – but that was just because the authorities didn't like anything they couldn't control. Besides, didn't Bitcoin threaten the whole "Global Politico-Financial Status Quo", which everyone knew was "rotten to the core"?

We USI Techies were like revolutionaries – like Robin Hood - helping the little people get a slice of the billionaires' pie.

Little by little, I began to put my reservations in their proper place. So maybe, some of these people had been involved in Network marketing operations which had turned out to be no good. Was that their fault? Hadn't they been looking all along for a good one... like this...

I bought a 50Euro pack. It was only 50 euros after all - less than a tank of petrol. The next day I made 50cents. Hey, this thing worked. I couldn't get at the money, of course. I would have to wait until it had reached 140%. But when it reached 100%, I would be able to buy another pack while the first kept growing – and all the time, the value of Bitcoin was going up, so you wouldn't want to get out anyway. This was great. Maybe I had better put some more in...

The excitement was contagious: This was better than sitting at people's kitchen tables and going through their bills or having them cancel their supplement order because they still had a pain the next day. The company staged an International Convention in a hotel at Heathrow – hundreds of people from all over the world: Some of them had invested their life savings. The more they had invested, the more the crowd cheered.

Best of all, now we were getting into Bitcoin mining - opening a huge facility in Iceland and here was our new partner, an American tech wizard who had invented a revolutionary gadget to harness the heat from the mining machines to create electricity at a fraction of the normal cost. That would give us even bigger profits!

Nobody thought to ask how it was that this unknown inventor had achieved what the civilised world had been searching for ever since the days of Faraday and Edison. Well, there was an easy answer to that: He had been working on it in secret, of course.

During the lunch interval, the company owners came down and mingled with the crowd. "Ask us anything," they said. "We have nothing to hide." This was a legitimate business – the best-ever opportunity for ordinary people to achieve the financial freedom they deserved...

I waited patiently to come face to face with the German. Why, I asked him, had they registered the company in Dubai – or, more to the point, in Ras al Khaimah, which was famous for its secretive business registration facilities?

He looked at me in all honesty and said: "Why should we submit to regulation when we don't have to?"

Actually, it made sense. The whole point of Bitcoin was that it was beyond regulation – in fact since it was based entirely in cyberspace, Bitcoin was impossible to regulate.

Meanwhile, the afternoon continued with further exciting announcements. We soon forgot all about questioning the legitimacy of the company – or even the astonishing concept of free electricity from the world's first perpetual motion machine. That was dull stuff by comparison. Now there was going to be Techcoin – a completely new crypto-currency, better, faster, shinier than any other – and USI-Tech members would be able to buy it before anyone else could rush in and push up the price. This would be like getting into Bitcoin at one cent (it was about $15 at the time). Half the audience pulled out their mobile phones and started buying it there and then.

I wasn't that daft. I didn't make snap decisions to spend thousands of pounds on something that consisted of no more than a few microwatts of electricity running through a bit of silicone just because the video looked fantastic and everyone else was doing it. I'm not stupid.

I bought mine in the car on the way home.

Looking back on it all with hindsight, it's astonishing to see how the whole world was caught up in this. Meanwhile, wise and steady friends in the utility business shook their heads and worked steadily through their difficult patch – with lots of references to the seasons and the way farmers don't leave the land and get a job in the city just because winter has come.

We didn't have time to listen. We were too busy counting our money.

And we did count it: By this time, we had little plastic cards to put in the side of the bank and draw out the maximum £245 every day (actually, it became a bit of a chore. I kept having to drop everything and rush down to Barclays before the stroke of midnight. I seemed to have turned into Cinderella).

Then the cards stopped working – something to do with Visa

feeling threatened – after all, the banks hated Bitcoin, didn't they?

Next, the Texas State Securities Board issued USI with a "Cease and Desist" order, saying the company was offering an unregistered financial product – more evidence of the Establishment trying to keep The People in their place. We just punched the air and bought more.

The following month, the company announced that certain distributors in the USA and Canada had manipulated the system and stolen millions of dollars. In order to protect the company and the honest distributors, it was necessary to shut down the operation in North America. No money would be repaid until the situation had been stabilised.

For some reason, the situation never was stabilised.

Facebook groups lit up with urgent discussions about whether we had all been scammed. Alternatively, could Americans open new accounts with a VPN? Should they relocate outside the US to Mexico or the Caribbean? The financial authorities in Spain issued a warning about the company. New Zealand followed suit, saying USI had all the hallmarks of a Ponzi scheme...

The company owners – once all over YouTube - were now strangely absent. The Facebook groups abounded with rumours; the tone becoming more despondent - or more angry.

Then suddenly, a new announcement: The lengthy accounting operation had been completed, and the situation was much more serious than first thought: Many more millions of dollars had disappeared. It was necessary to follow the US shutdown with a global shutdown. This would be temporary while further investigations were carried out. In the meantime, no more packs would be issued – and no more payments made...

Meanwhile, Bitcoin peaked at nearly $20 and was in the process of crashing as fast as it had risen. Suddenly, the massive USI mining farm in Iceland wasn't so profitable after all. People began asking why we had gone into it at all when the currency trading had been so successful and why couldn't the company go back to that. Others posted pictures of the supposed USI mining farm in Iceland ... which looked suspiciously like one owned by a completely different company ... which issued a statement saying they had nothing to do with USI. Had there been any USI mining farm at all?

It was all very worrying. The collapse was following a familiar pattern – at least, familiar to those who had been through this sort of thing before: The top distributors – the ones who had the biggest teams and therefore the most to lose – were the last to admit that anything was wrong. "Keep Faith" they kept saying. Obviously, the owners were too busy to make YouTube videos - they were trying to sort out the mess caused by those unscrupulous distributors who had stolen from the rest of us. People who disputed this were dismissed as "haters".

Then, after several more weeks, another "update": With the fall in the value of Bitcoin, the mining operation would be put on hold. Curiously, there was no mention of the economies from the "perpetual motion" generators – nothing about a return to currency trading…

Meanwhile, don't worry. Everyone was going to get their money back – there was a complicated explanation of how this would work. People who struggled through the Byzantine calculations worked out that it would take 50 years. Others predicted that it would be more like 700.

It was all over. The excitement had lasted just under two years. Even now, nobody can guess at how much money was poured into it - nobody, that is, apart from the company owners who, presumably ran off with the pot. Of course, there was no trace of them – just a lot of speculation about plastic surgery and new identities. Considering the anger on the Facebook groups and the number of Americans filming themselves with their assault rifles, that's probably quite likely.

As for me, I just felt foolish — after all, it was on the strength of all this that I had announced my retirement. Now what was I going to do?

Chapter 25

Samsara

The Laser is a small, light and very fast sailing dinghy - just under 14ft long and with one enormous sail. There are more than 200,000 of them in every part of the world, and the great attraction of the Laser is that to race one successfully, you have to think of yourself as part of the boat - shifting your weight just an inch or two can make all the difference between getting round the buoy ahead of the next boat – or missing the mark altogether and dropping all the way down the fleet.

That's what makes it **exciting** – and that was why I was so bad at it.

Joining the Laser class at Waldringfield had been Tamsin's idea. She realised that I had never really thrown myself into the life of Woodbridge. I had one or two friends but did not see them regularly. I belonged to no clubs or teams – and, of course, I still couldn't remember the names of people who said hello to me in the street. Joining the sailing club and having a commitment to race every Saturday from March through to October would be good for me.

Yes, of course it would; if I saw the same people every Saturday, surely I would remember their names. Besides, it was sailing again. I threw myself into the Laser class with enthusiasm. I bought a boat. I bought a book on how to sail it.

And every Saturday, for years and years, relentlessly, I came last.

No, that's not quite true. In the second year, a new sailor joined. He knew even less than I did, and – to my enormous satisfaction – I beat him. However, by the end of the first month, he was beating me. This happened every year as new people joined and progressed. To sail a Laser successfully, you have to concentrate all the time – and concentrate very hard on getting the best out of the boat and the wind and the tide and the other skippers' mistakes...

But I kept finding my mind wandering to other things.

Also, when the wind pipes up, you have to be ready to move about the boat really fast. You have to be agile to sail a Laser. I wasn't agile. I noticed that the people at the front of the fleet had been sailing Lasers all their lives. I didn't expect to be at the front of the fleet, but I did keep turning up every Saturday – and turning over while everyone else sailed past.

And then, one day after years of this, while walking the dog along the river, I ran into one of the sailors whose name I did remember. Well, I should do – for a while, she had been a keen distributor for the utility company. Her son was our son Hugo's best friend, she went running with Tamsin...

We got to talking about the Lasers and, out of nowhere, I said: "The problem is that it's not really my idea of sailing."

"Well, what is your idea of sailing?" she asked me.

Of course, I knew the answer to that. I just blurted it out: "A proper boat - something around 35 or 40ft and crossing oceans on my own."

And she said: "Well, why don't you?"

Just like that.

It was something I hadn't really thought about. Not for 20 years, anyway. I'd put all that behind me, got my head down, lived in a house, chauffeured children to cubs and brownies, stood on windy touchlines, learned to get excited about Network marketing.

What had happened to crossing oceans? What had become of The Dream?

And now, as if I had opened some sort of Pandora's box, it was out there again. I couldn't leave it alone – and the more I thought about it, the more I became preoccupied with the sense of life having passed me by. I mean, think about it: When Tamsin and I had first met that day on Hampstead Heath, imagine she had said to me: "Oh, and by the way, all this business about giving up everything and running away to sea? That's not going to last. In five years, you're going to be living in a house in a small market town in Suffolk and going to Wine Club every two months."

If she had said that, I would have said: "No, no absolutely not..."

Don't get me wrong; there's nothing wrong with living in Woodbridge – everyone else there will tell you it's a wonderful place. Did I mention that it features in that "Best Places to Live" list in the Daily Telegraph? And, besides, we'd just finishing building one of those enormous kitchen/living-room extensions with full-width patio doors opening onto the terrace overlooking the river. What was not to like?

Well, everything, really. Now I started to think about it, it seemed that underneath – buried by the need to get my head down and make a success of family life – carefully pushed aside by the "fantastic" and "amazing" personal development which drove me on to ever more dizzy heights in the utility business – was a very, very, disappointed man.

Also, a very bored one.

When all this started, I had been a rock star newspaper reporter living in London (when I wasn't jetting around the world or sailing Largo singlehanded across the Atlantic.)

Anyway, not boring.

The man Tamsin had fallen in love with had disappeared. His place taken by this dull, obsessed substitute busy pretending to be "fantastic".

Of course, I didn't notice anything wrong. It happened gradually – and gradually, we grew further and further apart. Tamsin had no interest in network marketing – and certainly none in personal development or "Self Help", as she called it. We stopped sleeping together. Oh, there was a good reason for it: I had signed up for a marketing course which involved online coaching from the USA – at three o'clock in the morning. It made sense for me to spend the night downstairs. Somehow, I never managed to move back up again.

The things we used to do together, we didn't seem to want to do anymore. Even the weekly ballroom dancing classes followed by a bottle of pink fizz in the pub fell by the wayside. Going out to lunch on a whim? Forget it.

I can't remember when it was that we stopped saying goodnight. And when was the last kiss? You should notice a thing like your last kiss – you certainly remember your first.

This is the reality of growing apart. Nobody thinks it's going to happen to them. Everybody is special in the beginning. Everybody is ordinary at the end.

Ordinary is boring, and although I didn't know it at the time. I just don't do boring.

By pure chance, this happened just as the money was pouring in from USI. Everything was going to be great. I would never have to worry about money again. Besides, the utility company had given me a stack of share options and the price had gone up and up. I could cash in and buy a "proper" boat.

Why not? If not now, then when? I was 67, after all...

Tamsin was surprisingly keen on the idea. I say "surprisingly" because there is a popular notion that wives can always think of better ways of spending money than buying boats. Maybe she recognised that, with the first child away at University, the second about to start, and the other two well on the way to following them, maybe this should be "my time".

Maybe she just thought it was a good way to get me out of the kitchen.

Once again, I had something to get **excited** about.

And, of course, I went at it with the same compulsion as I did everything else. The first decision was a budget. The utility company shares were worth £60,000, so that was the budget - nice and simple.

That would get me a good sea boat of around 34-36 feet, maybe ten or fifteen years old. Largo had been a Rival 32 - a good, tough boat capable of taking me anywhere. However, she did have one serious disadvantage: The designer had tried to cram in too many berths. This meant she and all her sister ships had a dinette arrangement offset on one side. The idea was that the table could be lowered to make a double berth (and in Largo, in my 30s and 40s, this had been very useful). However, if you didn't put the table down, the two settee berths were impossibly narrow. The only way to get comfortable in harbour was to empty all the clobber out of the fore-cabin, pile it into the cockpit and sleep up at the front end. I didn't want to go through all that again – so a 36 it had to be.

But then, searching through the Rival 36s on the second hand boat sites, I came across a photograph which didn't seem to belong there. This was like no cabin layout I had ever seen on a Rival, no matter what size. There were two good-sized settees and no table at all - although there was mention of one in the inventory. I checked, and sure enough, this was a Rival 32 - one of the earliest. In fact, she was more than 40 years old; a classic – and unique.

As far as I could discover, what had happened was that in the 1980s, a Cornish doctor and his wife had owned her and cruised extensively, making at least four Atlantic crossings – and they had come to the same conclusion as me: That this was really a two-man boat. There were just too many berths – in fact, the dinette was a particularly pointless arrangement.

Maybe they did what I did on *Largo*: During the second Azores and Back race, I was becalmed for three days somewhere west of Lisbon and settled down to amuse myself by writing down all the things that were wrong with the boat – all the things that I would change if I had the money or the expertise.

I would install a hatch in the deck to relieve the sometimes dark and stuffy cabin. I would change the rigging to give me an extra sail.

I would ditch the permanent table. There is nothing more useless at sea than a table (even if you can make a double berth out of it). This would make room for decent-width settee berths.

Ah, here was the problem: To do this, you would have to gut the whole cabin, move the mast-compression post (in which case the mast would punch its way down through the deck). You might as well buy a new boat.

Which, of course, was why I wasn't looking at Rival 32s as my dream boat.

Except that it appeared the doctor and his wife had already done all this.

I took a train from Woodbridge on the coast of East Anglia to Conwy on the coast of North Wales. This is about as great a distance as you can travel in the UK without falling into the sea. I checked into what turned out to be the worst B&B in Conwy (the whole house smelled of stale milk). I took a walk in the fresh air down to the marina to find out what I had come all this way to see.

It was not an encouraging excursion. *Samsara* was nearly 50 years old – and she was showing her age. The hull was covered in scrapes and dents – the worst of them, repaired haphazardly with patches that didn't match. Around the bow, it was clear that the anchor – a monstrous, rusty artifact – had been allowed to crash against the hull. The paint on the bottom was as thick as a navvy's sandwich – pitted and pockmarked all over.

I borrowed a ladder and found the decks thick with bird

droppings – and not just any bird droppings: It seemed the adjacent tree bore deep red berries of some kind – which went straight through the avian digestive system.

Underneath this putrid goo, the decks had been painted – and the paint was lifting in places. The rail was covered in black plastic, and this had shrunk, leaving three inches of aluminum showing at each end like the bare leg between sock and trouser.

Feeling that this was a wasted journey, I went out for dinner and ordered a bottle of wine (and No, I told the waitress, I did not want to keep the cork).

The next morning, the vendor was there well before our agreed time – hurriedly trying to tidy the cabin. And that was where *Samsara* began to show what she'd got: Sure enough, the settee berths were a full two-feet wide. One of them had a backrest which swung through 180° to stop you falling out when rolling down the trades.

There was an extra hatch – and the table… why, the table was the cleverest of all: It slotted into two tubes bonded into the keel. It was even angled slightly to give just enough room to slide around to get to the loo between courses.

Later on, I discovered you could still have a double bed. Although I presumed the doctor and his wife had reached an age when such refinements were superfluous (years later, I was to discover this was nonsense – they used the fore-cabin while their three children crammed into the saloon. But by then, I had met the next owner. He was a retired policeman and we ran into each other by pure chance in Torquay, where he had brought his next boat to sell, now that he considered he was too old for all this nonsense – sailing as well as double berths.

But he did take great delight in reliving for me his middle age when he had devised a system for fixing a double berth athwartships (that is to say, across-ways). It meant temporarily demolishing the rest of the cabin, but I don't imagine I shall be needing it. Anyway, I've removed the supports.

Samsara had many other clever touches – a lot of them becoming apparent only later as I began to get to know the boat... worked out the reefing system, learned to appreciate the sense of space you get if you have storage in open racks instead of having to look at a row of locker doors... wrestled with the vagaries of the charcoal stove...

Because, yes, I bought her, of course - paying just £14,500, which was exactly what I had paid for *Largo*. This meant that allowing for inflation, I had a very cheap boat indeed and could now begin to blow the rest of the budget on restoration and a wish list as long as your arm.

The horrible black plastic rail went – to be replaced with beautiful teak to match the new cockpit locker lids. The surveyor insisted on a purpose-built gas locker – and got it. There was new and expensive copper anti-fouling (which fell off – but that wasn't the fault of the paint). Never mind, I was very pleased with the shiny new folding propeller for the price of a small second-hand car, and I spent hours watching YouTube videos of underwater anchor tests before splashing out £450 on a new one (and then, five years later, swapping it for another costing £750). Anchors are important.

When the money from the shares ran out, I got myself a credit card interest-free for 30 months. Repaying it wouldn't be a problem – the USI money would pay it off long before the deadline. Bring on a rope-cutter on the propeller shaft and a new bearing - new this, new that. I was beginning to wonder whether I might have been better off buying a new boat.

But the thing about having an old boat is that it's like having an old car. Imagine having an old MG? Think of the admiring glances you would attract in Sainsburys car park? It's like that with a boat – only better.

All through that summer, I drove back and forth across the

country from Suffolk to North Wales – and gradually, as the work progressed, I began to spend longer and longer periods living aboard high and dry in the marina car park.

And then, one day, the man who had been engaged to polish the hull pushed up his goggles and said: "Hang on, this has been painted."

You can't polish a painted hull – and obviously you can't trust a surveyor to notice it's been painted, even though something like that should knock thousands off the price. It would cost thousands to have it sprayed again – and, more to the point, the process would take weeks (already we were into September). Besides, by now the first cracks were beginning to show in the glittering edifice that was USI-Tech. I went out and bought a tin of yacht enamel and a paintbrush. I've since found there's a lot to be said for yacht enamel – nobody notices you haven't had an expensive paint job and it's the easiest thing in the world to touch up any scuffs.

So, at the end of the sailing season of 2017, *Samsara* was lifted into the water. That was about the time I discovered that she had not been named after her first owners (Sam and Sara, as I supposed) but in fact, "Samsara" is a word in Sanskrit meaning both the journey and the world. The word is generally taken to mean a journey through the world in search of Truth and Enlightenment. Once the Samsara has been completed, the traveller will achieve the state of Nirvana – the all-knowing oneness with all things.

I couldn't think of a better name for a boat. I set off for Woodbridge.

Tamsin had asked that, for her peace of mind, I should not undertake any long singlehanded passages – after all, there were plenty of harbours around the coast. I could make short hops.

However, after crossing Cardigan Bay, I was faced with making a 60-mile detour to overnight in Milford Haven – or I could carry the fair wind across the Bristol Channel and round

Land's End.

Which do you think I chose?

It was my first 48-hour passage in the boat. She behaved beautifully and I slept like a babe.

Chapter 26
Poor

So, I had the boat. What I did not have - thanks to the Bitcoin fiasco - was the limitless income to go with it. Worse than that, I had an old boat and no matter how much the antifouling had cost (and the teak rail and the new propeller), she was still an old boat worth pretty much what I had paid for her.

But this was the dream. Was I going to give up on the dream? OK, so I had kissed goodbye to plan A when I fell in love with Tamsin and resigned from the Evening Standard fifteen years early. That was long gone, so there was no use crying over the "ultimate boat" and plenty of money to keep her to Lloyd's A1 specification. Even the idea of writing for yachting magazines now seemed to be a non-starter. I went and looked at Yachting Monthly in the newsagent. I hardly recognised it.

People who were interested in sailing, didn't buy magazines anymore. They went online and spent hours in front of the sailing "vlogs". Why pay £4.99 for a few pictures of life in the Tuamotus when you can click on *Sailing La Vagabonde* for nothing and watch Elayna Carausu and Riley Whitelum cavorting in high definition. The fact that these two young Australians are very attractive people and, living in the tropics, never seem to wear many clothes, probably doesn't do much harm to their audience figures either.

There are lots of stories like theirs, but the *Vagabondes* are, without doubt, the most successful. Riley used to work on oil rigs but had a lucky escape when something blew up. He decided to get out of the oil business and go travelling while he still had all his limbs. In Italy he found four guys arguing over an old 40footer and solved their problem by buying it cheap. The fact that he didn't know one end of a boat from the other didn't stop him getting to Greece where he met Elayna who was working as a singer for a tour company. A few weeks later, she agreed to join him. As she said: "I would rather say Yes to everything in life than No - and then spend my time wondering what might have happened if I had taken the chance."

She was 22. That was 2014.

Five years later, their YouTube channel was getting more than 10million views a month, with people making $50 Patreon payments to help them on their way. Meanwhile, the French Catamaran company Outremer realised this was the kind of exposure that was a marketing executive's dream. So, they asked whether the couple might like to sail one of their boats instead. In the end, Outremer gave the Vagabonde's a 45footer costing somewhere north of a half a million Euros - and just as well because pretty soon they had a baby… and then another…

So, they built an even bigger boat.

Admittedly their videos are very professional with drone footage and whatnot. I wouldn't want to do that. Besides, I don't think anyone would want to see me in my Speedos.

But I could write – and there are still some people who like to read. So, I started a blog. To set it apart from the hundreds of others which catalogue the weather and the course, and every sail change and which crew joined the ship and which left. Mine set out to be a celebration of my life-long dream. It would consider the astonishing usefulness of the humble clothes peg, catalog the recalcitrance of the charcoal stove. There would be lyrical descriptions of that magical moment when an ocean calm gives way to the first breath of a new breeze, and the boat slides over the surface as if drawn by magic…

And sunsets - lots of sunsets.

Apart from anything else, I enjoyed writing it. No, there was more to it than that: as soon as I started, I knew that this was what I had been waiting to do all along – waited for 57 years, as it turned out. Hadn't I told me parents: "I want to live on a boat and sail the world and write about my adventures."

However, I didn't like the idea of trying to get people to pay to read it. There are all sorts of devices to encourage people to sign up for "special content" or to get the posts "exclusively". To me, that seemed like begging – or at the very least it would be like having deadlines again. What I wanted to do was just put the stuff out there when I felt like it – and if people liked to read it, that would be a bonus.

All the same time, if there was something on the site that I was happy to promote and they were happy to buy…

The obvious product was my unpublished book - the "novel in the attic". Every old hack has a novel in the attic.

Mine was a thriller written in the 1980s. The Daily Mail had sent me to Greenham Common where the US Air Force kept its nuclear cruise missiles. People of a certain age will remember the protests this generated – in particular, the Women's Peace Camp. This was a constantly changing group of hundreds of women in woolly hats and wellies living in tents and makeshift shelters, singing protest songs and refusing to be discouraged by the squalid conditions. On the occasion I went to meet them, they were attempting to "Embrace the Base" by having thousands more women come from all over the country (all over the world) to join hands around the perimeter, which was enormous.

In a decade noted for its violent protests (remember the miners' strike?) this one was remarkable for its peacefulness – and also for the fact that it rained all day, turning the Berkshire countryside into something reminiscent of Passchendaele. I remember writing "Peace is Hell".

However, the Daily Mail newsdesk was not at all happy with my sympathetic treatment of what was, after all, civil disobedience, not to mention blatant defiance of Margaret Thatcher's Conservative government. The Mail, like all good newspapers, understood its readers' prejudices and catered to them in spades. It knew what the readers would think of these "so-called peace women" with their "woolly hats and woolly minds".

I rewrote. Of course I did. If I didn't like it, I should go and work for the Guardian and accept their meagre salary. That night, the press corps gathered in the hotel dining room and I regaled everyone with what the newsdesk had said. What I didn't know at the time was that one of our number was from Private Eye and shopped me.

And of course, once you're in the cuttings, as Julia Roberts says in *Notting Hill*: "Newspapers live forever". Sure enough, I ended up in a book on the disarmament movement. I believe it's out of print.

But it did start me wondering: There were an awful lot of those women – and they were so ordinary; typical mothers and grandmothers you would find in any branch of Tesco or behind the tea urn at the church fete. Most of them had never been on a protest before.

But what would happen if the Women's Peace Movement grew?

What would happen if it became just The Peace Movement - something so large it could not be ignored?

What would happen, I wondered, driving back to London, if The Peace Movement became a political party and contested the General Election?

Now there was a thought: What would happen if The Peace Movement won the General Election?

When I reached my flat in Chiswick, I went straight to the little Brother typewriter – the same one that I had bought from the Sloane Square branch of WH Smith when I was 19. I wound in a fresh sheet of paper and started typing.

I typed pretty much all through the night. In fact, I kept on typing every night for the next year. The reason it took so long was because, not knowing how much of a doorstep a bestselling novel should be, I counted the words in Ken Follett *Eye of the Needle* and based my target on that. The total was 108,000. I hit the number almost exactly and sent it off to the Laurence Pollinger Agency (they had managed once to get me into print with a children's book.) Gerald Pollinger wrote back kindly. He said it was a shame I hadn't asked him first because 108,000 words was far too long for a first novel. Would I cut it to 60,000?

I hate cutting. If the book had 108,000 words, it was because it needed them – every one of them. Otherwise, they wouldn't be there in the first place, would they?

A few months later, I returned a new manuscript - rewritten from start to finish with 60,000 words.

In the weeks that followed, I waited as anxiously as any new author for the phone call. I knew that was how it was done because I had interviewed Ken Follett about exactly that.

The reason I was such a fan of his was because, like me, he had been a newspaper reporter – he was on the Evening News and sat up late at night writing his first book. Of course, now he was a bestselling author and worth millions.

When the Daily Mail ran a promotion promising to make some random reader a millionaire, they sent me to find out from people who were already millionaires what it was like when they first discovered they had joined the club.

Follett didn't do interviews at home, but he was prepared to meet me for lunch at his local restaurant. First, he explained that he would be paying. Then he ordered a bottle of Dom Perignon.

This was followed by a bottle of claret that would have wiped out my expense account for a month. He was enjoying himself. He had been a hack once.

As for the moment he first realised he was a millionaire: *Eye of the Needle* had found its way into the hands of the wife of the legendary American literary agent Al Zuckerman. She was reading it in bed. She was keeping her husband awake.

"Put the light out, honey," said Al.

But Mrs Zuckerman wouldn't. She kept on reading way into the small hours.

Within the week Follett had joined the Zuckerman stable of authors. But that wasn't the moment he realised he was a millionaire. That came later.

"It was 1978, I was walking down Bond Street," he told me. "In a shop window, I saw a nice-looking jacket so, on a whim, I went in and asked to try it on. I had never felt fabric like it – it was just so soft, you wanted to stroke it. I thought: 'I must have this. I asked the price and the salesman didn't bat an eye when he said: "This jacket is £500, sir."

"I tell you, I couldn't get it off fast enough. £500 for a jacket! Nobody pays £500 for a jacket! I walked straight out of the shop, took ten paces down the pavement and stopped dead. 'Fuck me,' I said. 'I'm a fucking millionaire!'

"I went back in and bought it - and I haven't thought twice about buying anything since."

It was a great story. I had to clean up the language, of course, but I looked forward to experiencing that moment myself when my book earned me the big contract. Already I had celebrated being signed by the Pollinger Agency – with champagne at the Savoy. The rest, I assumed, was a foregone conclusion.

Instead, I received six rejection letters one after another. Each arrived with a sympathetic note from Gerald explaining that he was disappointed but expected a better reaction from the next house on his list.

The thing about these letters was that they were all very encouraging. They described the book in terms such as "workmanlike" and "promising". In fact, they gave the distinct impression that the publisher would really like to accept the book, but their list was full. Certainly, they would like to see anything else from this author.

After a while, I began to see through this nonsense. Why didn't they just say: "No thank you." I think the most absurd of all was the one which said the book was "too good" for their general list but not quite good enough to justify the promotional budget required for a lead title. In that case, why didn't they just publish it on the general list and raise the quality of that?

In the end, I shut the manuscript away in a bottom drawer and there it stayed until we moved aboard *Lottie Warren* when it went into Tamsin's parents' attic along with all the photographs and sentimental items which survived the big clear-out. When we bought our own attic, it made its way into that – quietly forgotten.

Until, one day, I woke up to hear on the news that Jeremy Corbyn, the leader of the Labour Party had appeared on the Pyramid Stage at Glastonbury Festival and been cheered like a rock star. That night, he stayed with the organiser, Richard Eavis and, over breakfast, mentioned that when he became Prime Minister, he would abolish Britain's fleet of Trident nuclear missile submarines just as soon as he could.

I thought: "Hang on, I've got a book about that somewhere."

I climbed up into the attic and, after an increasingly frantic hour or two, finally found the manuscript in a tin box with my grandfather's birth certificate and a lot of photographs of stern-looking Victorians. I dusted it off and started reading.

It was fantastic. I hadn't read it in something like 40 years. I had forgotten how good it was. More to the point it had a Russian president meddling in other countries' elections and an isolationist in the White House, yelling "America First" or some such. Does any of this sound familiar?

I called the local printer: I had a typewritten manuscript – on paper. In fact, this was typed on quarto paper, not even A4. If I brought it round, could he scan it into a digital file for me? He did - although the scanner couldn't tell the difference between the ancient Brother's full stops and commas. Also, I had forgotten that in the pre-history of typescript, we used to leave two spaces after a full stop. I went through it again, bringing the style up to date a bit and getting rid of some passages which you just wouldn't expect to read today ("homosexuals on street corners", for heaven's sake!)

My son Owen had just graduated from the University of East Anglia's prestigious Creative Writing course. He read it. He was supposed to be proofreading but had to apologise that he found the underwater battle so exciting that he might have missed some split infinitives.

If ever a book was ahead of its time, this was it! I found a cover designer on the Internet and battled with Amazon's Kindle Direct Publishing tool. This would teach all those publishers with their condescending rejection letters! Who needs a publisher now? Come to that, I founded my own publishing house. If you look inside, you will find that "Trident" is published by "Samsara Press".

I sent two copies to Paul Dacre, the long-standing and fearsome editor of the Daily Mail. He sent a kind letter back saying he would read it on holiday. He didn't say what he would do with the other copy, nor did he mention my suggestion that he might like to pass it on to the books editor.

Months passed with supportive family and friends buying a copy here, a copy there. Once in a while, some total stranger who had stumbled across it on the blog might buy a copy. Then, without warning, I saw that 135 copies had sold in a single day – a Friday.

Eventually, it dawned on me that Friday was the day the Daily Mail published its book reviews – and there it was: "Trident by John Passmore" reviewed by Geoffrey Wansell. I read Wansell's review and, in a state of shock, looked him up. Who was this man?

"Geoffrey Wansell is a London-based author and freelance journalist, who now works principally for the Daily Mail," said his website. "He has published twelve books, including biographies of the movie star Cary Grant, the business tycoon Sir James Goldsmith, and the playwright Sir Terence Rattigan, a book which was short-listed for the Whitbread Prize as Book of the Year."

This was big-league stuff. Also, I knew how the Mail worked. If Paul had passed the second copy on to the books editor, they would feel compelled to get it reviewed – but not necessarily to publish that review. If Wansell had declared it to be rubbish, his review would have been quietly spiked.

In fact, he had written: "Former Daily Mail reporter Passmore first wrote this novel in 1983, when it was dismissed by publishers as 'a little far-fetched'. How wrong they were. Featuring a new Left-wing British Prime Minister committed to scrapping the Trident missile fleet, a Russian President meddling in foreign elections and a U.S. President determined to put his country first, it feels astonishingly contemporary. The plot revolves around a Trident submarine captain and his Admiral father intent on ensuring Britain keeps its nuclear options open, a newspaper reporter and a secretary in the Defence office who falls into a honeytrap set by Russian intelligence.

"Fast-moving and immensely prescient, there are echoes of the early works of Ken Follett and Frederick Forsyth – and that is no faint praise. The tragedy is that it remained hidden in the author's attic for 34 years. Let us hope he has time to write many more."

I was ecstatic. "Echoes of the early works of Ken Follett!" *The*

Eye of the Needle had been among the early works of Ken Follett!

Every day I checked the sales figures – but after that Friday, and a few more on the Saturday, the graph dropped to the floor again. But "Trident" is still on the Amazon list – and I suppose it will stay there forever now, selling a handful every month.

Meanwhile, how to "monetise" the blog? I couldn't use it to promote the utility business – at least not without getting every post cleared by the marketing department. Besides, if someone was interested, I could hardly go and sit at their kitchen table and go through their bills if I was in mid-Atlantic or sitting in a beach bar in Bequia.

I did have the health supplement but that business had gone into a decline after the debacle of reducing the mineral content without telling anyone. The stuff still worked, but you had to take enough it, and the label said not to.

If only there was some way I could sit down with every prospect and explain it.

And that's when I came up with the idea of automating the whole process. Think about it: If you are a man of a certain age and you tick the "male" box when you sign up to Facebook and fill in your date of birth, then pretty soon Mr Zuckerberg's microchips are going to bombard you with adverts for prostate cures.

I could do that. I sat in the cockpit as *Samsara* ate up the miles on the way to The Azores. I held my phone in front of my face and recorded the story of my health scare and how I did not intend to see a doctor again as long as I live (unless I get run over by a bus).

I explained how most people's ill-health is down to their bodies failing to do what they were supposed to do and heal themselves.

As the towed generator rotated hypnotically in the background and the wake trailed out astern, I talked into my phone about food in the shops lacking the proper nutrients, the depleted farmland - I talked about my good friend who had been diagnosed with cancer of the spine and saw it off with herbal tea. I urged people to educate themselves about this - after all, it is no small thing to decide to ignore your doctor's advice.

I created a "Good Health" page on the blog and posted the video there – along with a list of the improvements in my own health. This list grew with periodic updates - dozens of them as first the liver spots disappeared from my hands, the optician said I didn't need glasses to drive anymore – there was the dentist poking around and saying, "all clear, come back in six months" (I hadn't been to see him for nearly three years).

Now, as I explained so proudly in the video, I did not carry any pharmaceutical products on the boat at all - not even an aspirin.

I did what I advised other people to do: If had an infection, I tripled my daily intake of the supplement. It worked on the way back from the Azores when a bruise went bad. I had trapped my arm between spinnaker sheet and shroud. Pretty soon, the whole bicep was a sort of purple colour but after a few days the infection stopped spreading and began to retreat. By the time I arrived back in the Solent, there was nothing to see.

But then the body is supposed to heal itself. Look what happened to Robin Knox-Johnston: In 1968, on his way to becoming the first person to sail non-stop around the world, he suffered agonising stomach pains. He tried to summon help from passing ships (which, to his horror as a British merchant navy officer, completely ignored him).

Of course, if he had been rescued, he might have slipped back into obscurity instead of becoming probably the most celebrated yachtsmen of all time. But, in fact, the pain subsided and he completed the voyage and earned his place in the history books. A year later he had his appendix removed before his next long voyage. The surgeon told him it had already burst – and healed itself.

So, although I still remember how worried I had been by my comparatively insignificant infected bruise, I still do not carry any antibiotics on *Samsara*.

I repeated the story on the Good Health page of oldmansailing.com but it must have been the most cumbersome sales funnel in the history of marketing: I was still not allowed to mention the name of this wonderful supplement, nor the website where people could buy it. The regulations for health products expressly forbid any advertising which includes unverified testimonials or other claims as to benefits or efficacy…etc…etc.

What this meant was that, if people visited the company website, there was hardly any information at all - not even what was in the stuff.

We were supposed to spread the good news by word of mouth – and there was only one problem with that: I could go for weeks without speaking to anyone at all.

But lots of people were reading the blog. If they watched the video and read my story, they could email me for information. Then I could send them a private email – and I would be able to say what I liked in that.

It was brilliant! It was the answer!

Sure enough, as Mr Micawber promised, something had turned up.

Chapter 27
Fame

There was a time when children asked their parents "What did you do in the war?" One day, they will ask: "What did you do in Lockdown?"

When COVID-19 struck in 2020, and everyone had to stay at home and isolate, an enormous number of people took the opportunity to do all the things they had never got around to doing because they were so busy going to work and meeting friends and going on holiday and all the things that weren't allowed anymore (unless they worked in Downing Street).

Suddenly, everybody had their Big Chance – at least they did if they chose to see it that way instead of complaining that they were going to be stuck at home all the time.

There was more gardening done that summer than in the whole of the history of horticulture. The Do-It-Yourself stores were overrun with people installing new bathrooms. Dog-breeders ran out of puppies, Amazon had a run on artist's supplies and exercise bikes. Whatever you wanted to do but had never found the time for, now was your chance.

I was in Lowestoft, monitoring the Ocean Cruising Club's Facebook page as COVID went round the world, shutting it down country by country. French Polynesia was "closed". Visiting yachts had been told to leave Florida's Key West. Marinas in France and

Spain were in lockdown. Panama was still open, but crews coming from the Caribbean were not allowed ashore. Someone who had hauled out for maintenance on the Costa Blanca could not get their boat back into the water because the boatyard staff had all been sent home. Now they had to cope with three children under the age of eight who could not be allowed on deck because it was a three-metre drop to the ground.

I could see that I had nothing to complain about – at least, not compared with the crew of a Norwegian boat which had just arrived off Curacao, only to be told that the authorities would use force to remove the vessel from their waters. Where were they supposed to go?

But wait, what was this? France had banned all forms of pleasure boating entirely. Any recreational vessel found navigating French territorial waters would be arrested, said the communiqué. Marinas were refusing to open lock gates. Bridges remained closed.

Bridges? There was a bridge in Lowestoft – and I was on the wrong side of it. What if the Lowestoft harbourmaster followed the lead of his French counterparts and refused to open it?

I was gone within the hour. Taking deep breaths in the Royal Norfolk and Suffolk Yacht Club marina on the other side of the bridge, I considered my options. I couldn't stay there. It would cost a fortune – and anyway, the north-easterly wind blows straight into the Royal Norfolk and Suffolk marina. What I needed was a secluded bay somewhere to anchor. There were plenty of secluded bays up in the Orkneys – no, that was no good; just as I thought of it, the local authority issued a plea for owners of caravans and second homes to stay away. It didn't need much imagination to see they were including people on boats.

Regulations and officialdom blocked me at every turn. So much for the freedom of the seas. I sailed round to Walton Backwaters to consider my options.

Then it dawned on me: What I needed to do was go to sea –

properly. There were no regulations outside territorial waters. All I had to do was get myself beyond the twelve-mile limit, and nobody would be able to touch me.

That was it: I would sail off into the sunset and come back when it was all over. I started to stock the boat with food – 250,000 calories of food. Tamsin and Theo, who was studying medicine by this time, advised on pasta, mayonnaise – and Nutella. Nutella is 57% sugar. Nutella would keep me from starvation.

I made a cursory inspection of the boat, crossed off a couple of the most urgent items from the maintenance list and set off (before dawn, and carefully avoiding the radar station that monitors the approaches to Felixstowe Docks).

In fact, I was so paranoid that I avoided the Dover Strait as well. Everyone knows there are only 22 miles separating France and England – which means that half of it is in French territorial waters (where they would arrest me) and the other half is British – where the ever-vigilant Border Force would tow me into Dover's Granville Dock, there to serve out my Lockdown as if in prison.

So, that meant turning left, going over the top of the Shetlands (there isn't a 25-mile gap anywhere in the northern isles) and down into the Atlantic.

Once I was out, a wonderful feeling of freedom descended on me – freedom and isolation. I went and looked at Rockall, which is very good for promoting feelings of isolation. This is the desolate lump of granite some 250 miles off the west coast of Scotland. More people have landed on the moon than have landed on Rockall – and coming upon it just as a threatening yellow dawn lit up a boiling sky only added to the sense of solitude.

I had some notion of sailing down to the Azores. I'd done it before – three times, in fact: twice in the Azores and Back race in *Largo* and then in 2018 when the family came to join me for a week in an Airbnb in Ponta Delgada. That was 1,200 miles – although, that's only if you measure it from Falmouth. I was starting from the Muckle Flugga. That would be 1,700 miles – or 2,300, if you added the trip up the North Sea.

In the event, I got there remarkably quickly thanks to a series of gales while everyone back home was enjoying week after week of perfect beach weather (although, of course, they weren't allowed to go to the beach).

I was just considering using up a bit more time by doing a figure-eight round the Canaries as well when I woke up to find the mainsail in tatters – not just ripped so that I might have to take it off and spend a day sewing it back together – but actually destroyed.

Instead of turning left for the Canaries, I bobbed around off the island of Graciosa for two days, tapping into their mobile phone signal and organising a replacement sail. The obvious thing would be to have it posted to Horta (where I could update *Samsara's* painting on the harbour wall at the same time) but I've had packages sent to islands before and it rarely goes smoothly. Anyway, there would be all kinds of COVID complications. But I could get it sent to the harbourmaster in Falmouth on a 24-hour delivery.

So, I turned around and headed for Land's End. We had some fun on the way – there was a gas leak. There was a water leak. I arrived home eating cold food and with just five litres of fresh water to my name.

But lots of beer. The beer saved me! It made a good blog post. My 80 subscribers seemed to like it.

And that was that – just 80 people, and they got it for nothing. With any luck, they would linger on the site long enough to click on the "Good Health" page. If I was really lucky, they would have a look at the book – maybe click on the "Money" tab and ask how to get a residual income so that I could tell them about the utility business. But 80 people reading a blog post didn't pay the £35 a night at Pendennis Marina.

That was when my sister Georgie suggested Yachting Monthly might like to publish something. There was a time when I would have sent in anything without a second thought. But not now. On the other hand, maybe Georgie had a point: Somebody might want to read about my trashed mainsail and potential gas explosion and nearly dying of thirst (a bit of hyperbole never goes amiss when pitching to commissioning editors). I would call the Daily Telegraph. Surely they would remember me.

This is the sort of mistake you make when you're 71 years old and the last two decades have slipped by more or less unnoticed. You can't ring the Daily Telegraph switchboard anymore. As a member of the public, you can't ask to be put through to the newsdesk like I did from the oil rig. Now you need a direct line, which means you need a name – and all my old journalism contacts had long since retired. Now they pontificated on Facebook – the ones that hadn't died from the effects of a lifetime of over-indulgence. In the end, an old friend gave me a name at The Guardian. They never rang back.

It was in this atmosphere of despondency that I had my head under the sink trying to find out why the galley pump was squirting water all over the dustpan and brush, when Jeremy Vine came on the radio wanting to know what everyone would miss about Lockdown, now that it was coming to an end.

Well, of course, I'd missed Lockdown, hadn't I? I told him so – from under the sink. Then I had to extricate myself and ring up the Jeremy Vine Show to make it count. At least Jeremy read out a number to call.

He never read out my comment, though.

But it had seemed like a good idea. Any publicity is good publicity, right?

So, a few days later, when he was on about it again (you can never have too much of a good phone-in topic), I sent an email. I never got to hear whether that one got onto the air because somebody rang me wanting a piece of the utility business and I couldn't bring myself to tell them to piss off.

Anyway, apparently Jeremy did read it out my email because, the next morning, I was tipped out of bed by a call from Radio 2: Would I like to do a ten-minute interview with Jeremy at 1.30?

Well, I supposed I could…

Quick: Make a list of topics to cover… should I measure the distance to Rockall from the mainland or the Outer Hebrides? Don't forget the Nutella salad - that's good for a laugh. Remember to mention the blog…

I didn't forget; and Jeremy – bless him – repeated the address at the end. By midnight the oldmansailing blog had received 45,000 hits. At one point, the WordPress site crashed under the onslaught.

The BBC rang to say how pleased they were. Then they rang back to say a literary agent had called asking for my number and was it OK to give it out? Did I want my number given to a literary agent? Don't be so bloody stupid. How much can I pay you to give my number to a literary agent?

And this was not just any literary agent. This was Jeremy Vine's own literary agent (he's written a novel). I said that yes, I thought I could write an 80,000 word book about my experiences – and yes, I could write it quickly (he was worried that if we didn't have it in Waterstone's by Christmas, everyone would have forgotten Lockdown and moved on to Brexit.)

So, I went and anchored in the Scilly Isles and for a month, I wrote from seven in the morning until seven at night with an hour for lunch and produced those 80,000 words. If I do say so myself, every one of them was a golden gem.

At least, the agent was satisfied. He sent them off to his contacts in five of London's most prestigious publishing houses. The five contacts sent them back – all with roughly the same kind and encouraging letter of rejection.

The book, they found, was interesting – even entertaining. But who was this author? Was he perhaps a Premier League footballer or a disgraced politician? A contestant on Love Island? Was he Jeremy Vine, come to that?

The agent had to admit that the author was just some old bloke who'd gone off sailing.

Ah, said the publishers, one after another. In that case, unfortunately, the book would not be commercially viable.

Now, you might consider this to be bad news – and certainly, it was a blow to the self-esteem but, in fact, it was the best thing that could have happened.

There was a time, not so long ago, when an aspiring author faced with a rejection letter like that was left with only two options: throw the manuscript into the attic and forget about it - or pay to have it "vanity-published," put it on their own bookshelf and look at it.

Now there is a third option: Anyone can publish their own book on Amazon. I'd already done it with *Trident*, which still sold the occasional copy.

I created my own cover from my own photograph of Rockall. I formatted the content using Amazon's software, I uploaded the manuscript to the Kindle Direct Publishing website. Within 72 hours, *Old Man Sailing* was available for anyone to buy - pretty much anywhere in the world. Best of all, I put a note in the foreword that if readers noticed any typographical errors or spelling mistakes, if they were the first to alert me, I would refund the cost of the book. Three people took up the challenge and cleaned up the whole manuscript better than a professional editor would have done. Only one of them accepted the refund – and of course, unlike a traditionally-published book, I could go back in and make as many changes as I liked whenever I wanted.

Also, I could set my own price – and keep on increasing it as it became clear that people really wanted to read my book.

In three years, *Old Man Sailing* has sold over ten thousand copies and consistently sells more overseas than it does in the UK. People buy it in China and Brazil and Micronesia…

Compare that to what would have happened if one of those publishers had accepted the book: They would have paid me an advance of maybe £1,500 (of which the agent would have taken 15%). The print run would have been maybe 2,000 copies in hardback with photographs and priced at £16.99. It would have sold a few dozen copies to my closest family and friends and by the following Christmas would be remaindered down to £3.99. There would, of course, have been no second printing.

Instead, no sooner were people buying the print version than I set about getting it on Audible. I did try to record it myself but that was a disaster. I spent six months wrestling with the technology, buying better microphones and a more powerful computer to run audio-enhancement software. It didn't help that I started in Walton Backwaters, where the geese kept interrupting the soundtrack with their incessant honking – and I ended up in Lossiemouth, just down the road from the RAF station, where the Eurofighter pilots honed their take-off and landing skills with endless (honestly, incessant) practice.

Eventually, I found a professional narrator to do the job for me, and although I still resent having to share the royalties, some people just don't read books at all, so this is a completely different market which would otherwise be closed to me.

Once you start down this track, there's no end to it: What about France? The French are great sailors and make a point of not learning English (OK, so the English make a point of not learning French. We're as bad as each other). Anyway, here was another untapped market.

I investigated getting *Old Man Sailing* translated: A proper, professional job would cost between £5,000 and £10,000. Someone suggested Google Translate and then a French-speaker to go through it and clean up the howlers. In the end, I looked on

UpWork and found a half-French, half-American translator in California who would do it for $2,500. He took eight months and the finished book was so bad that French speakers thought I'd given it to Google Translate in the first place. Of course, he didn't give me my money back.

But the trouble with *poor* **decision-making** is that you keep thinking that next time everything is going to turn out better. I gave the job to my sister Georgie's Paris-based stepson, Christian. It turned out that he had a degree in comparative French and English literature and had already translated two books of poetry.

Christian made a brilliant job of it. The narrator in Montreal who was doing the Audible version as the chapters came in, said it was amazing: "It's like Balzac!" he said.

I told Christian. That was another mistake. If he was that good, he said, then he deserved more money (more "biscuit" as he put it). He refused to finish the job unless I upped the price.

Just as Peter's Café in Horta now takes up the whole street with a museum, a branded clothing store, restaurant, whale watching trips… you name it… so Oldmansailing developed into complete cottage industry. I cast around for what else I could put up on the Amazon bookshelf.

On a last trip home before setting out for the Canaries, I happened to stumble on a Tesco's carrier bag full of old cuttings – years of contributions to yachting magazines and latterly, newspapers as well: bits and pieces that I had written long before Amazon was a twinkle in Jeff Bezos' eye. On a whim, I stuffed them into my bag when I returned to the boat. Then they got pushed into the bookshelf between the Atlantic Islands Pilot and Caribbean Passage Making. It wasn't until I ran out of reading material on the way to Grenada that I pulled them out.

Immediately, they emptied themselves all over the cabin floor: The mother of all gales off the Grand Banks, navigating by smell, the search for lunch in Milford Haven…

This was good stuff. I sat there for most of a day, reading bits at random. They call it **hyperfocus**, don't they: A lot of the material was from the Dogwatch column in Yachting World, which I wrote every month for a decade. Then, there was the column for the Daily Telegraph - a piece here for Practical Boat Owner – one from the Daily Mail – even Women's Weekly in Australia…

This was definitely good stuff. In fact "Good Stuff" was exactly what Andrew Bray, the editor of Yachting World, had called it when I faxed him after a couple of years thinking that my constant search for copy was leading me in some pretty odd directions (the knicker locker, the Law of Lost Hats). He faxed back: "It's good stuff. Keep it up."

So, *The Good Stuff* joined the Oldmansailing series – and if, inadvertently, I click onto another window while writing this, I find the next book just nearing completion.

Think about it: here I am, sailing the world and writing about it. Now, pause for a moment: do you know of an eleven-year-old boy who dreamed of doing just that?

OK, so he's not eleven years old anymore. He's 73, for Christ's sake – maybe even older by the time you read this – that dream seems to have taken its time in coming true.

But here's the kicker: If you don't give up on your dreams – alright, if you have ADHD and you don't give a damn what anybody else thinks of your dreams - then sure as God made little onions, those dreams will come true.

Chapter 28
?@*&!

If you have been paying attention, you will have noticed that this ADHD thing can be responsible for a lot of trouble: Impatience, lack of attention to boring details - you will be familiar with the list by now…

Usually, a healthy dose of optimism is all that is required to see the bright side (something which those closest to us can find utterly infuriating.) But it's true: If the commodity trading had not been a disaster, would I have got into network marketing? If the Bitcoin shambles hadn't happened, would I have emerged from it with my boat?

Of course, this "glass half full" philosophy does take a bit of work.

Let me give you an example:

Owen - that tiny baby who occupied whole chapters at the beginning of this book, eventually left school and, like every other young person, declared that he wanted to go travelling.

He and his friend Fabian were going to India.

India is mystical. India has wonderful food. You can't get much more foreign than India.

Owen sent off his visa application to the Indian High Commission, enclosed his passport - and set about shopping for cool clothes for a hot climate (cool, as in "student-traveller-chic", that is).

Some weeks later, some months, it might have been, the conversation turned unexpectedly to the fact that Fabian had his colourful visa in his passport - but Owen's had still not been returned.

More days passed (it might have been weeks), and the passport still did not appear. When the mild curiosity turned to nagging worry and then serious anxiety, he rang the High Commission. Days later, the reply came back. His visa had been granted and his passport returned.

What followed next is burned into my memory in a way that no amount of "forgettery" can obliterate.

The passport - being a valuable item - had been entrusted not to the Royal Mail but to a private courier company. The courier company was most meticulous. They didn't just post it through the door. They required a signature at the door.

They had a photograph (attached) of the signature.

They had a photograph of the door.

It was my door. My signature.

I should explain. I had not moved out - but I did have my own front door. I think I mentioned that we built one of those huge kitchen/living room extensions with a wall of glass which folded back to bring the garden into the living space - and this had required the demolition of my office.

And since the drive had been turned into a building site, we could hardly carry on putting up bed and breakfast guests in our converted garage (or, as we promoted it on the booking.com site, The Studio). So, I moved in there instead.

And it was the front door of The Studio which featured on the courier company's photograph - and what looked suspiciously like my hand in the act of taking delivery.

I think the phrase "Bang to Rights" comes to mind.

So, what had I done with it?

Here are some of the things I did in trying to answer that

question.

I emptied the wheelie bin all over the path and sorted through it as if I was trying to find embarrassing secrets in a celebrity's rubbish.

I sorted through all my own paperwork - and found all sorts of things I had been looking for ... and then, of course, sat there reading them and wasting time.

I looked through all my drawers and cupboards (and ended up reorganising them, starting a new filling system... sitting and reading some more... and wasting more time...)

I tried sorting through Tamsin's paperwork which she kept in a huge wobbly pile on the kitchen table. You can imagine how well this went down.

I took the dog for long walks trying to cudgel some other ideas out of my recalcitrant brain.

I leapt up in the middle of the night with brilliant ideas about where Owen's passport might be.

Only to find it wasn't.

There was only one answer - and it appeared very gradually, like a big red London bus advancing slowly through the fog.

The courier company which was charged with delivering the Indian High Commission's very important mail - by hand, as we have noted – chose to wrap it carefully in their own plastic envelope - emblazoned with their big red logo. You really couldn't miss it... just like you really can't miss half the junk mail that comes through the door. I sometimes think that the more brightly-coloured and urgent-looking, the packaging - the more likely it is to be junk mail.

So when, I noticed a pile of brightly-coloured plastic envelopes on the corner of my desk, I swept them tidily and efficiently into the wastepaper bin ... and then, for good measure, because in my flurry of efficiency, I was about to remember to take the recycling wheelie-bin down to the end of the drive, I tipped all the contents of the wastepaper bin into it first.

This is how efficient I was being.

It gave me the satisfied feeling of one who is on top of things.

Have you heard about the man who spent the early years of Bitcoin mining the stuff and then, when it didn't amount to much, threw away his computer? When his stash turned out to be worth something like $200million, he asked the council whether he might sort through their tip looking for it. He even offered them $11million if he found it.

They still said No.

But his hard drive was under nine years' of rubbish.

Owen's passport would be right on the top, surely? I could see it in my mind's eye, perched on the summit of a mountain of old hard drives…

In the end, Fabian went to India on his own and Owen and his girlfriend blew his travel money on a night in London and tickets for Book of Mormon.

Next summer, the guys went to Vietnam together.

It's all been forgotten now. Well, nobody mentions it anymore - and I brood on it only in dark moments when I'm trying to convince myself that in every misfortune there is a silver lining.

I have yet to find this one.

* * *

Then there was the time in the Canary Islands when I bought a pair of counterfeit binoculars. Well, I found out they were counterfeit afterwards. I suppose that was why the salesman was so eager to agree to discount after discount which made absolutely no sense when you came to think about it.

But then, I wasn't thinking about it, was I?

I was so excited by the idea of a cheap pair of bins that it never occurred to me to walk round the corner where I could quietly check on Tripadvisor and see what they had to say about counterfeit goods in the Canary Islands.

Worse still, I didn't notice when the salesman added the discount back on at the end and calmly tapped the new total into the credit card machine which – you guessed it – I did not look at even though it now required me to swipe my card because it was over the contactless limit.

I have no idea why I fell for that. I suppose I'm just too trusting.

Or, you could say I'm easily conned.

There is a certain type of salesman who can see me coming as soon as I walk in the door. I once bought an expensive camera in San Francisco – and when I got it back to the hotel, found I'd walked out of the shop with the cheap model. Worse still, the receipt confirmed that's what I paid for.

Who looks at receipts?

Of course, sometimes being taken for a sucker is done with such panache that you really ought to be paying for such a demonstration of artistry.

Look at what happened in Rio: I was with a Daily Mail photographer and we'd just flown in with a Soviet Spy who was being swapped for a British one – Rio at that time, being the place where such exchanges were made. Once Igor had disappeared down the diplomatic channel, and I'd filed my copy, the photographer had sent his pictures (by giving the films to a returning BA cabin crew to take back with them), our job was done. We were free for the evening.

As was the rule in those days, we had arrived with wads of cash. We had been warned that hotel safes in Rio were not "safe" at all. The best advice was not to keep too much in one place. Even so, the exchange rate for the Brazilian Real was so generous that we were hard put to it to find space under the mattress, in the cistern, stuffed down the backs of drawers…

The rest just had to go in our pockets.

Then we went out to walk along Copacabana.

The hooker saw us coming at 50 paces. Like a butterfly drawn to an over-ripe plum, she glued herself to my thigh, rubbing her crotch against me in a way that made further progress impossible. At the same time, she pulled down her top to reveal a very large brown breast.

We suckers from Fleet Street thought this was hilarious – but on the other hand: "Thank you for the offer, my dear, but really, we're just looking for a beer before dinner…"

She was surprisingly good about it, unglued herself and fell behind as we walked on.

That was when I put my hands back in my pockets. I hadn't really thought about it, but I must have removed them in an attempt to remove her. Which was when all the crotch-rubbing had covered up a slim hand diving into my trouser pocket and withdrawing a week's takings for the average Brazilian streetwalker.

When I looked back, she was crouching in an attitude of abject disappointment – one hand begging for her lost love, the other holding the money firmly between her legs. I could just imagine her pimp's reaction if I made a grab for it.

But then, as I say, it was an honour…

I always believed I would never top this story but, when you think about it, £500 of newspaper money is very small beer compared to what I've lost over the last two years. At the last count, it was £342,500.

Yes, I thought that would make you sit up and take notice. It certainly concentrated my mind on the consequences of not taking notice – or, to be more precise, not reading the contract…

I would like to tell you all about it. In fact, I have made six previous attempts at writing this chapter and every one of them I rejected as being just plain boring.

Why do you think I didn't pay attention, myself? I don't do **boring**.

There I was sitting in the lawyer's office at one end of a long conference table, turning pages, signing at the bottom, reading every word but acutely aware the "statutory provisions" and "subordinate laws" meant about as much to me as the Dead Sea Scrolls.

At the other end of the table, the lawyer who had drawn up the contract sat next to the other signatory – the one who stood to gain from what was in it, both of them watching me expectantly.

I wish I'd thought about it then. I could have gathered up the papers and announced: "You know, I think I will get my lawyer to look over this after all…"

But, of course, I didn't, did I? I just kept signing away, page after page, hardly able to wait for the wretched business to be over.

I suppose they just thought I was stupid.

But then, even I would accept that losing £342,500 at the stroke of a pen is pretty stupid. In retrospect, I'm not even sure it was clever to lose another £5,600 in legal fees trying to get it back.

Could there be anything more stupid than that?

Oh yes! How about recounting the whole convoluted story in these pages? Not only would the readers throw the book aside and cast about for something more entertaining (particularly the ADHD readers), but I'm fairly sure that anyone who can make themselves that kind of money that fast and all perfectly legally would have no qualms about going back for an extra helping with a libel suit.

Mind you, I like to think I would win a libel suit. After all, I'm not alleging anything illegal or improper – only a certain ruthlessness on the part of the other signatory. I learned about the law of libel when I was 20, doing journalism training. Later, I sat through Gillian Taylforth vs. The Sun in the High Court (agog for much of it, like the rest of the country). In my experience, a libel case is held in front of a jury – and juries act on gut instinct. Not like a judge: A judge in a civil case, when faced with two conflicting testimonies, is likely to dismiss both of them and call for the dull grey documents.

A jury might just choose to believe me instead of the other guy.

But when I sent this chapter to Carter-Ruck, the famous libel solicitors, they told me the law abandoned juries for libel cases in 2013. Now it's all down to one expert judge – so we're back where we started.

Also, while a libel case might be very **exciting** (not to mention excellent publicity for a book), The Law favours the wealthy. If someone has enough money, there is absolutely nothing to stop them filling Court 13 at the Royal Courts of Justice with a pack of lawyers each charging £600 an hour. If a humble author is going to defend himself against that, he needs to do the same.

It's OK. If you win, you'll get most of it back.

But, A: You have to fork out in the first place.

And, B: You have to be there, not in the Solomon Islands.

If I had wanted to spend any more time in Court 13, I should have stayed in newspapers.

Meanwhile, here's something else to consider now we've got on to the Solomon Islands: The case couldn't even get started without me being served with a writ. That might be fun. I imagine a beery colonial notary in a sweat-stained tropical suit being rowed across the lagoon in a commandeered canoe – and me upping anchor before he's halfway and skipping off to the next island – or perhaps the next island group which, of course, would be an entirely separate legal entity requiring reams of duplicate paperwork, more months of applications in flyblown courtrooms under creaking ceiling fans…

It could be enormous fun. Mind you, I would have to switch off the AIS transmit function and avoid writing blog posts beginning: "Anchored here in the crystal-clear waters of the island of Ta'aru…"

But it shouldn't be that difficult to hide. Apparently, the Florida Keys are thick with fugitives on boats, running from the DEA and the IRS and the FBI…

But while such a life might appear excitingly romantic; in practice, it could just turn out to be really tiresome.

And besides, it wouldn't only be my money I would be risking all over again. It would be Tamsin's, too. We're still married, after all – and while I have long contended that I can live on sunshine and coconuts, I can't expect her to.

Also, along with coconuts, I do have a penchant for cold beer and Pringles - as regular readers will have noted …. and I need to budget for paying over the odds for binoculars…

So, am I really going to roll over and let them get away with it?

When the full consequences became clear, I did entertain fantasies about shooting this other signatory who had cost me so much money – and his beastly lawyer. I had it all worked out. I googled "easiest place to buy a gun" and was offered Alaska or Alabama. I didn't fancy sailing to Alaska – not without upgrading the tiny charcoal heater (even though the holes are fixed and I no longer have to take the batteries out of the carbon monoxide alarm.)

So, Alabama it would have to be – all you need to buy a gun in Alabama is a driver's licence. Even without that, you can buy firearms privately on any number of websites. I see Troy on Armslist Classifieds is selling a Glock 17 fourth generation for only $400 (with very mild holster rash).

All I would have to do would be sail back to the UK with it tucked under the spare watermaker filters.

And what then? Actually shoot someone and spend the rest of my life in jail? That's if I really could bring myself to pull the trigger in the first place. Somehow, I can't see myself as a killer.

I could cope with prison, though. I went to an English public school. I've read Jeffrey Archer's prison diaries. I could hack that part of it.

But the novelty would wear off pretty soon, and I don't expect they'd give me Ronnie Barker for a cellmate.

And what's £342,500 anyway?

Thinking about it now and looking back over my life (looking back through this book), it does seem that I keep on having to start again after the latest financial disaster.

I started again when I got divorced in my 20s and lost the house. I went and made a career in Fleet Street.

I started again when I met Tamsin and got smitten with the idea of sailing off into the sunset, giving up our jobs and living on our wits. I wrote freelance columns for Yachting World and the Daily Telegraph.

And I started again when we came ashore with the two little boys and nobody would give me a job. I learned network marketing. It's still paying me today.

I suppose that now, at the age of 75, I should look on this as just another new start. Already, I feel I have a new lease of life as a network marketer – Facebook sailing groups introduce me to any number of people who want to emulate what I have done. Besides, the timing is perfect: The company just hooked up its millionth customer – and plans on two million in the next two to three years. If I double my customer base at the same time, that would recoup my losses all by itself.

And maybe this book will help: Think about it: Five percent of the world's population has ADHD, that's 395million people. Fifty million of them will be English-speakers. That must be worth £342,500 in Amazon royalties.

If it's not enough, I could get Christian Calliyannis to do a French translation (and agree the price up front). Maybe Spanish would be better – 485million people speak Spanish: *"Más alto, más rápido, más riesgoso, más sexy"*.

Perhaps not. Maybe it will come out better in Chinese…

Anyway, the point is that the vision that so worried me back in 1992 is once again lurking in the shadows. When Tamsin suggested we shouldn't wait until I was 55 to run away to sea (or even 50) my greatest fear was being poor. Well, I'm certainly poor now.

Not poor by most people's standards, maybe. But I've just moved out of a marina to save €25 a day, and now I'm rolling around off a beach which actually has a wrecked yacht on it to remind everyone what happens when your anchor drags and you don't have wreck-recovery insurance.

Anyway, I hate marinas – there's something about an anchor that appeals to the soul: Lying in your berth at night, seeing the moon swinging in the centre hatch, thinking about tomorrow: Go ashore and explore? Sail on somewhere new?

Or spend the day with my feet up on the opposite berth, laptop on my knees, writing about it all, and knowing there are people out there – people all around the world – who want to read my words. Ten thousand of them read Old Man Sailing at the last count. I just looked at the Amazon Direct Publishing site for this month's sales: Colombia, Finland, Czechia, Singapore...

And if I didn't have ADHD, would I have lived a life that's worth a book?

So, like most things, it's a choice.

Either you can be the type of person who doesn't do stupid things – someone who does insist their lawyer reads the contract, someone whose life does go according to plan...

Or you can be the type who loses the money, says a rather rude word and then just goes and gets it all back again.

Tell me, which of those two people is going to have more fun. Which of them is going to find life more **exciting**?

Chapter 29
Marriage

It is fully seven years since I started writing this book. That means it has become something of a diary - albeit a very sporadic one. You will have read in the very first chapter how Tamsin made the long trek down the passage from the kitchen (where she lived) to the office (my domain), and this was not something that happened every day. After 32 years, we had arrived somewhere we never intended to be. At a relationship we never wanted - never imagined. It had grown up around us imperceptibly, like ivy up a drainpipe.

So, when I went off on my boat, it was a relief to both of us. Communications were few and brief - pruned to the bare essentials.

By that, I mean there was no affectionate salutation at the beginning of emails and text messages: No "My Darling", no "Sweetheart" - not even "Hi" and certainly no "XX" at the end, let alone heart emojis. Actually, it was only the children who knew about emojis in those days. Grown-ups still went for :)

Except, we didn't.

And yet now, after my **carelessness and lack of attention to detail** cost us that eye-watering £342,500, Tamsin found it in her heart to write: "It makes me sad - and sad for you."

I had just written: "It's all my fault."

There was comfort offered on both sides. This was a couple

being kind to each other. It was the way we behaved in the early days - those days of big plans and car boot sales, mini-breaks and long lunches.

Would this have happened if we had stayed under the same roof, living separate lives at opposite ends of the corridor? Or would the air be full of angry recriminations and sullen excuses?

It was while I was mulling over this question, wondering whether our discovery was, in fact, a common phenomenon - whether, indeed, it might merit its own chapter in the book (does it?) that Facebook provided the answer - as it tends to.

There, in among the politics and the Ukraine war and the cat jumping for the sausage, was a post from The Insider.com about something called LAT.

You don't know about LAT? You haven't been following Gwyneth Paltrow? Actually, now I look it up, I find The Insider had pinched the story from Harpers Bazaar - or possibly The Independent, or NBC. Maybe it was Vogue - or, the other way round…

The point is that like everything Ms Paltrow does - from steaming her vagina to drinking moon dust - this latest wheeze had gone viral. Suddenly everyone was talking about how the former actress-turned-lifestyle-guru and her husband Brad Falchuk lived in separate homes for almost the whole of the first year of their marriage. Apparently, it helped with "preserving mystery" and also nurtured the concept that each party had their own life. It was something she was "trying to remain aware of as we merge together."

So, it appears that what Tamsin and I had done was really rather fashionable. It is possible, perhaps, that the Paltrow-Falcuks picked up the idea from us - in which case, what else can we come up with? Can we think of some unlikely anatomical destination for Goji berries?

Or maybe it's enough that we now get along better than we

have for years.

I went home to clear out my stuff (Tamsin is downsizing). I took my three suits to Oxfam but kept one tie just in case. I was making a statement that in future, my wardrobe would be confined to shorts and T-shirts.

But then, along with the clearing of the wardrobe, I volunteered to go up to Southwold to empty the beach hut before the council moved it for the winter. Tamsin loves Southwold. She has a week there every summer - a week of recreating family rituals: the walk to Walberswick (preferably in the rain). Cockles with vinegar at the harbour and hot pies from the Black Olive Café. Tamsin can spend hours browsing the charity shops which seem to have more designer stock than Knightsbridge. Would she like to come with me?

Obviously, we would both need lunch. I hadn't got as far as thinking about lunch. The idea of us having lunch together was as fantastical as a day on the moon - although lunch used to be one of our greatest delights, funded by the Treat Fund when we first lived on the little catamaran. Since then, it had dwindled away, like the goodnight kiss, like touching - I don't have to provide a list, do I?

I remember the last time I had suggested lunch. It must have been 15 years ago. We were going through another bad patch. Did I really think risotto and pinot grigio would miraculously make everything right?

Sure enough, she turned me down with an expression I can remember to this day. It might just as well have been a slap in the face. I never asked again.

But now Tamsin suggested it. She said: "I'll see if I can get a table at The Swan."

I think we both sensed the fleeting acknowledgement that something momentous had shifted.

That day, lunchtime was an hour and a half of pure delight.

Lottie said: "Whatever did you talk about?"

Lottie, you would be surprised.

But even so, you can overdo these things. After Christmas, I set off back to *Samsara* on December 27th. They do say that more marriage breakups begin at Christmas than any other time of the year.

Even so, we are lucky - well, either we are lucky, or inadvertently, we have managed things rather well. I have just heard that some very dear friends are splitting up, and it doesn't appear to be amicable. Money can get in the way, of course - and that is probably more likely if you have been struggling to maintain a relationship against all the odds instead of giving yourselves distance and time for reflection - and also time for the affection you once held for each other to stir from its long hibernation.

During the last few days, there has been a flurry of phone calls and inevitable follow-up messages - not just about the house sale but also this year's skiing holiday - something which Tamsin organises (and pays for out of her learning mentor salary at the local college).

This year, my pennyworth was to wait on hold listening to Club Med's choice of music for half an hour in the hope of discovering the exact (and exorbitant) cost of their flights. Then Lottie asked the family WhatsApp group how we were getting to the airport, now that the ancient Toyota people carrier had failed its MOT one time too many.

Tamsin had forgotten all about that - too much going on. Too many things to think about. Brain fog setting in, she told me via a series of messages while I attempted to put Samsara's cabin back together. Eventually, I had to explain that every time the phone pinged, I was obliged to put a screw in my mouth because I needed both hands to open the messenger app. When I had five in there and was beginning to worry about swallowing, she agreed that I didn't need all the updates.

It was the sort of thing we used to laugh about, and there was something comforting about finding that now, when I wondered whether I was being insensitive, it only took a moment to decide that, no, I wasn't.

But that's marriage for you, isn't it? You only discover how to do it towards the end, although it's at the beginning that you need the handbook.

I once talked this over with my sisters. The three of us had gathered in Alderney in the Channel Islands as our mother was eased through her final days at the little hospital. We noted that all three of us had been divorced. Was it that our parents had made marriage look too easy?

What is the secret? Is it, as all the Golden Wedding couples told me when I went to interview them for the Mitcham News and Mercury, "Give and Take"?

I think it's all down to that much undervalued human quality: Kindness.

Love and passion will send you storming through the early years. Shared interests and mutual respect will smooth the way and, of course, if you can manage to listen to what anybody else says, that helps a bunch.

But I believe that kindness will take you all the way. I wanted to add it to our marriage vows, but Tamsin vetoed the idea. Maybe she was right. Kindness doesn't spring from making a vow any more than you can expect love and honour - and certainly not "obedience".

But, in the end, kindness does count for more than all the others put together.

Chapter 30
Death

I'm supposed to be dead.

A defendant in a French courtroom had snatched a gun from the gendarme and took the judge hostage.

This happened early in the morning on a slow news day. The news editor was wrestling with his schedule and, quite frankly, didn't have a thing for the Splash – and that was not something you could admit to in Conference when all the heads of departments gathered in the editor's office to show how very clever they were (it was a competition).

On the other hand, saying: "The siege at the French courthouse: Passmore's on his way," merited instant Brownie points.

I can't even remember if it did make the splash. What I do remember is arriving in the square in front of the *Palais de Justice* and finding the world's press all lying on the ground (it was clearly a slow news day everywhere else as well).

"Why is everybody lying on the ground," I asked of nobody in particular.

The gunman – who had, apparently, abandoned the judge – was now standing alone on the steps, congratulating himself on subduing the world's press.

All except one. There was one who was still on his feet. The gunman raised his pistol. He fired. He missed.

Well, he missed me. Instead, the bullet smashed the lens of the BBC camera next to me. The cameraman, I remember, was ecstatic: "I got it, I got it…" he kept saying. I think he had the idea that he had captured on tape the bullet getting bigger and bigger until it went right through the lens and finally embedded itself in the closely-packed electronics an inch in front of his nose.

It was the same in Milltown Cemetery for the funeral of the IRA's Gibraltar bombers – I mentioned earlier that my Brother typewriter was a casualty of this story. I was supposed to be writing the lengthy "colour piece" which must have been why I had the typewriter with me instead of my usual school exercise book. Colin Adamson was there for the news story.

It's possible that this also explains why I was not paying attention to minute-by-minute developments around me, but instead had elevated myself to some higher plane full of adjectives and historical significance.

Maybe that was why, when the first explosion went off, I did not fling myself on the ground like everyone else. I now put this down to **lack of attention to detail** but I was told later that what I actually said was (again): "Why is everyone lying on the ground" (because there's a feller throwing hand grenades).

This story made it back to London before I did (just like my reaction at being introduced to one of Belfast's ubiquitous burning buses: "Good God. You mean to tell me this place is part of the United Kingdom?")

Fortunately, other people were more on the ball. The Standard's photographer Clive Howes chased the grenade-thrower all the way down the hill – despite him pulling out a gun and turning to fire directly at Clive who, famously, kept shooting back (at five frames a second). He won an award for that, I seem to remember.

I didn't.

Of course, journalists are supposed to be brave – it's just that they're just not supposed to write about how brave they are. Fortunately, nobody had told me this. As it says at the front of the book, Tamsin had observed early on, and most astutely: "The reason you can't write fiction is because you're not interested in other people. But you're good when you're writing about yourself."

The ADHD Foundation should include that in their list of symptoms – but it meant I got plenty of column inches out of a variety of close shaves.

Like the time in Iraq, covering Sadam Hussain's invasion of Iran in 1980. The Iraqi Ministry of Information invited the world's press to witness their glorious victory over the Persian hordes. Some 30 of us flew in from the USA and Japan and all points in between – there was even a solitary East German who couldn't speak a word of any other language. This meant he had no idea what was going on (and the West German wasn't going to tell him).

Unfortunately for the Minister of Information, by the time we had all gathered in Baghdad, the magnificent Iraqi advance had stalled somewhat.

Frustrated by an itinerary that was rapidly degenerating into a tour of cultural sites and the occasional artillery position well behind the lines, the Dutch correspondent and I slipped off in a taxi to go and find the real action. The best we could manage was an island in the Shatt-al-Arab waterway where a couple of Iraqi snipers were hiding in an abandoned fisherman's hut and taking pot shots at the Iranians a few hundred yards away on the opposite bank. One of the snipers lent me his rifle so I could look through the telescopic sight and see them – which, of course, I couldn't: If they'd shown themselves, the Iraqi's mate would have shot them.

But it did mean I could write: "Through the telescopic sight of a Russian-made sniper's rifle, I watched as the Iranian… etc… etc…

And that would have been fine if the sniper next to me hadn't decided to add a bit of colour by loosing off a round with an enormous *bang*. This set off what I believe is called in military circles "an exchange of fire". The Dutchman and I decided we had enough for our respective publications and it was time to get back to the hotel and the single ancient telex machine.

With 30 correspondents in residence, the telex machine was in use 24 hours a day – and heaven help you if you didn't beat the Japanese to it: Japanese reporters had to file their copy phonetically since the Telex keyboard could not accommodate Japanese characters.

So, we elected to run back across the pontoon bridge to the taxi on the mainland. Maybe this wasn't such a good idea – at any rate, it seemed to attract the attention of the Iranian snipers who shifted their aim from the abandoned fisherman's hut to the two running figures on the bridge.

In those days, I used to pride myself on my running – when I was at home, I ran around Chiswick House grounds every morning. I was well ahead of the cigar-smoking Dutchman when I heard a fizzing noise as if some particularly speedy insect had flown over my shoulder. That's how I know that you really can hear bullets. Apparently, if you're close to the gun, the bullet makes a crack – something to do with the sound barrier. But a long-range shot (such as from the other side of the Shatt-al-Arab) makes a definite fizzing sound.

I covered the remaining few yards faster than Seb Coe while the Dutchman dived over the side.

A footnote to this story is that when we got back and gleefully reported our scoop to our colleagues who had spent the day driving nowhere in particular for some purpose that was never explained, a bunch of them promptly jumped into another taxi to re-create the excitement.

Unfortunately, they elected to drive across the bridge – on which the Iranians had taken the time to zero their sights. The taxi took one bullet in the engine, one in the boot – and a third hit one of the reporters in the face. She survived, but I feel awful now that I can remember nothing more than that. I was too busy re-reading the hero-gram that had dropped during a moment's idleness in the Telex room.

* * *

I mentioned that I was in Tiananmen Square when the Chinese People's army came in shooting – that's really a bit of journalistic licence. They didn't actually do any shooting in the square itself – something to do with the communist party's PR department wanting to confine any bloodshed to less iconic locations – such as Chang-an Avenue, which runs alongside the square. The avenue was the venue for *that* photograph – the lone man standing in front of the column of tanks. Later, the tanks lined up across the road and opened up with the heavy machine guns.

Actually, it was just one short burst – maybe only three or four rounds – and it's different when they're just shooting into the crowd rather than at you personally. On the other hand, when the shooting starts, everybody still runs like hell – and the problem with running anywhere in Beijing is that pretty soon you run into a couple of thousand parked bicycles … you and the other couple of thousand people running from the same machine gun.

Anyway, it was carnage.

But you don't have to go to war to dice with death in the cause of journalism. You can do it just as effectively in Trafalgar Square and I had forgotten all about this until I was alerted to the unlikely fact that I am the star of the LOAD ZX Spectrum Museum in Portugal – a museum dedicated to the world's first personal computer.

Admittedly the world's first personal computer doesn't look very impressive today – I remember it as just a black box with a keyboard that you plugged into your TV. I gave one to Oliver for his tenth birthday in 1982. He programmed a clock on the screen which counted the seconds – we were all amazed.

Much more exciting than the little black box was Sir Clive's next invention, the C-5, his electric-powered vehicle of the future, unveiled in 1985.

Not many people will remember this since it sank without trace soon afterwards – largely due to the many derisory reviews.

Nonetheless, in pride of place on the museum's wall next to the historic little electric trike, is an enormous picture of me driving it through London's traffic. This was given to the museum by Sir Clive's nephew, Grant Sinclair – probably because the picture from the Daily Mail accompanied the C-5's only positive review.

The Mail's then editor, David English, loved everything about new technology – even if it didn't work. Without a moment's hesitation, he insisted the plastic dodgem was the future of urban travel.

Maybe that was why he was so blasé about it nearly killing the test pilot.

I remember it well: The whole episode was conducted with typical Daily Mail (in those days) extravagance.

The thing was delivered by lorry to my flat in Chiswick at about 7.30 in the morning. Fellow reporter Gareth Woodgates arrived too, in his battered yellow Citroen 2CV. Woodgates and I were known for somewhat foolish escapades.

The idea was that this was going to be a race to the office (the old one in Fleet Street). The Mail's photographer Neville Marriner with whom I was to survive many adventures over the years (but only just) undertook to record the event.

When I say I "just" survived adventures with Neville – this was a classic example. He insisted we must give the impression of speed - and since the C-5 had the top speed of a shopping trolley, the only way to achieve this was by flinging it downhill... like, for instance, down the east side of Trafalgar Square.

According to Neville, if I could take the bottom corner at

about 30mph just in front of a Number 12 bus, the photograph would show not only velocity but also comparative size.

I positioned myself at the top of the square for a Le Mans start as soon as a bus should appear. All went according to plan. I pedalled furiously (the pedals were merely to assist Sir Clive's revolutionary electronics).

The speed built up impressively – Trafalgar Square is a surprisingly steep hill if you are in something the size of a soap box cart, only closer to the ground.

Also, having only three wheels and therefore the handling characteristics of a wheelbarrow, the C-5 takes corners at speed by lifting the inside rear wheel.

This is not something that fills the driver with confidence – particularly when there is a 13-ton Routemaster following six feet behind.

The Mail didn't use that picture. Apparently, my face failed to display the required confident expression demanded in the editor's memo.

So, they used another one of me beaming at the camera as I nip through the traffic and Woodgates in his disreputable 2CV is stuck in the queue.

Apparently, it is just the thing for the museum, which the director informs me is not only a "celebration of technology and history but also a tribute to remarkable individuals who have left an indelible mark."

He says that my contribution to journalism and my adventurous spirit - as captured in the canvas - is the very essence of what the museum aims to showcase.

He doesn't know the half of it.

Actually, you don't even have to leave home to come face to face with eternity. I did it in my Edwardian mansion flat one Friday afternoon.

I had bought it in an attempt to "get back on my feet" after the divorce. The estate agent described it as having "potential for improvement". The long, dark hall was painted in chocolate brown gloss and heating was by ancient storage heaters in huge grey metal cabinets.

One day, on a whim, I decided to remove these heaters, disconnecting them by turning off every switch I could find in the airing cupboard, removing the dozens of bricks and carrying them two at a time down three flights of stairs to stack on the floor of my long-suffering VW beetle.

Then, all I had to do was disconnect the wiring to the cabinets. This was when I touched the screwdriver across two bare wires. This should have gone unnoticed because I had turned off all the switches I could find in the airing cupboard.

The relevant phrase here is "all the switches I could find". Apparently, there was one I hadn't found.

The result was the most enormous bang and I was dazzled by the biggest spark I had ever seen. It melted the silvering on the screwdriver.

I have since investigated storage heaters and it seems they need very large amounts of current and require special heavy-gauge wiring. Anyone getting an electric shock at that voltage is going to be killed stone dead instantly – or, at least, their chances are pretty poor if they are all alone in a third-floor flat and nobody is going to raise the alarm until they fail to turn up for work on Tuesday…

There were other scrapes which could have turned nasty, no doubt – riding a BSA Bantam up Streatham High Street and hitting one mirror against the bus I was overtaking and the other against a lorry coming the other way, wrestling the headsail on my parents' boat when an unannounced hurricane appeared off the coast of Brittany – and then looking down to see the clip for my safety harness lying uselessly on the deck.

Statistically speaking, sailing is surprisingly dangerous – more so than skiing - you only have to look at the RNLI Safety at Sea advice. Visit any marina on a Saturday morning and you can see all the sailing school students setting off with everyone trussed up in lifejackets and harnesses. Personal EPIRBs (Emergency Position Indication Rescue Beacons) are all the rage and there's even an app for your phone to sound an alarm when someone falls overboard – and then point the helmsman in the right direction to go and get them.

None of which applies to me. I am 75 years old and decided long ago that the Health and Safety regulations do not apply to me. Regulations are for other people. I'm supposed to be dead already.

So, in the seven years and thousands of ocean miles I have sailed with *Samsara*, I have never carried an EPIRB. Also, I have told Tamsin that I don't want her raising the alarm if I am late arriving. Instead, she should wait six months and then set about diverting the Amazon royalties to her bank account instead of mine. Without a body, it's going to take her seven years to apply for a death certificate so she can get at my will.

Think about it – when five of us sailed across the North Sea in a 25ft Folkboat in 1957, we didn't have an EPIRB. In fact we didn't have a transmitter of any kind. We didn't even have a liferaft. If we had sunk, we would have taken our chances in the 6ft plywood dinghy which didn't really accommodate five people getting from the yacht club to the mooring.

But we did have an enormous pump.

I have four pumps – two of them might be described as "enormous". I have a liferaft which is out of date (but the manufacturers tend to build in a bit of a safety margin).

Instead, I have a Plan of Action: First, I shall try to keep the ship afloat – there are any number of long-forgotten techniques for doing this which I learned from reading too much *Hornblower*. Mind you, I have never actually tried to fother a topsail.

Anyway, well-found ships do not sink as a rule – no matter how many shipping containers there are floating around. It could be argued that the containers are merely replacing the icebergs which are becoming more and more difficult to find thanks to global warming.

No, it is far more likely that I shall meet my end by falling overboard.

This is something that used to worry me greatly back in my 30s – and rightly so, since I had my whole life before me. I never left the cabin without clipping on to one of the two jackstays I had running the length of the decks.

And if I should have fallen over, I had a Plan of Action for that as well: As I was dragged along, half drowning at six knots, I would reach up to the deck and fumble for a 3mm line I had rigged all the way around the boat. This line was thought out in such a way that pulling it would disconnect the self-steering and cause the boat to stop. Then I would unclip my harness and manhandle myself round to the stern where I had stowed a collapsible boarding ladder. All I had to do was hook this over the rail and climb up.

It was only later that I discovered the boat was quite capable of keeping her course for hours at a time with the steering disconnected – which meant that I would continue to be dragged along at six knots until I drowned. Then the boat would carry on for a couple more weeks before eventually beaching herself somewhere in South America where I would be discovered hanging over the side, partially dissolved.

Also, I read the great singlehanders – Knox-Johnston, Moitessier, Slocum… none of them clipped on except in the most extreme conditions. In fact, the father of French singlehanding, Éric Tabarly never clipped on at all – even at the end of the bowsprit of his 100-year-old Fifer *Pen Duick*. Mind you, he was lost over the side one filthy black night in the Irish Sea – smacked in the chest by the gaff while reefing the main.

So I stopped wearing a harness. To begin with, this took some getting used to. Climbing out of the cockpit without a tether attached seemed as peculiar as settling into the driving seat and not buckling up the seatbelt. The first time I doused the spinnaker without being clipped on, I kept looking at the water going past and working out that I could never swim fast enough to catch up.

But on the other hand, there was something about moving around the decks without having to disconnect and reconnect every time I switched sides, or being brought up short when the tether got itself wedged under an obstruction which induced a wonderful sense of freedom. It was like walking barefoot on a beach.

Now I don't even think about it – but, on the other hand, holding on absolutely all the time, even in the calmest weather, has become second nature.

Just this year we lost a contestant in the Jester Challenge – a short hop for singlehanded small boats to Crosshaven in Ireland. Every day in the pub, people were asking if there was any news of Duncan Lougee – and then they found his boat with nobody aboard.

It was a slow crossing with light winds all the way – not at all the sort of conditions you associate with people going over the side. But that's just when it happens. Probably he tripped over something. With the boat gliding along at a couple of knots, he wouldn't have had a hope of catching her.

That's probably what's going to happen to me in the end. I must get old and doddery sometime. Much better to fall in the water and watch the boat sail away than fall and break a hip in Sainsburys and end up in a care home with a cheery girl in a plastic apron saying: "Never mind, let's get you cleaned up…"

I'm in no hurry. In fact, there's a video of me on the internet somewhere saying that I'm going to celebrate my 100th birthday by sailing around the world non-stop.

Well, either all the way around or just some of the way…

Afterword

Oh dear, I seem to have annoyed someone else. Today, I changed my mind (for the second time in two days). It was a small thing: I had asked the electronics engineer to come and look at my switch panel and then decided against it… and then thought I might as well get him around anyway…

He never called back.

Sometimes we should see ourselves as others see us.

I could have explained myself: **I'm sorry. I have ADHD. I change my mind a lot**…

Of course, I didn't. I have never found a way of explaining it without sounding like an idiot.

Reading through the first draft of this book all those years ago, all I could hear was the whining voice of someone going on and on about how *It's not my fault*…

But as time passed and I edited and rewrote and, in great bouts of self-obsession, slowly came to terms with this ridiculous condition, so I have tried to find the silver lining.

And this bit – which I truly believe is the end – I am writing as I sail somewhat slowly into the Cape Verde islands off the coast of West Africa. It is five o'clock in the morning and I am still up, trying to keep the boat moving – which she is doing most obligingly with that swooping motion that feels as if you're sailing through time and space rather than water. Also, because I haven't been able to put down *Tomorrow and Tomorrow and Tomorrow* by Gabrielle Zevin (and Nanci Griffith is singing *From a Distance* on Spotify), I do find myself getting a bit emotional.

So, maybe it's no surprise that at last, I have decided I don't want to shoot the people who got me to sign that very expensive contract, after all.

In two months, I shall be 75 years old – and three-quarters of a century entitles a person to look back on their life and be the judge of it.

In which case, not shooting people is one decision I feel I can be proud of – like Ranulph Fiennes in *Schindler's List:* "I forgive you."

Except that, unlike Amon Göth, the concentration camp commandant who couldn't see the point in it, I find that I rather revel in the concept of forgiveness. For me, it does feel good.

So, I hope that if you have this thing too, then I have been able to show you that there is a silver lining – that no matter how much you might annoy yourself and everybody else around you, it's still better than the alternative.

Because the alternative is to be like ordinary people.

And you wouldn't want that, would you?

Amazon Stars & Reviews

These are so important. Nobody buys a book on Amazon if it doesn't have enough stars.

If you are reading this on Kindle, you will be invited to leave between one star and five stars. Fill them in and your device will upload them next time you're connected.

If you have the paperback edition, the person who bought it can award stars by finding the book on their Amazon "My Orders" page.

Good books tend to have at least 4½ stars – and since there are always going to be some people who object violently to something or other and leave only one star, the only way to get to 4½ is for the people who really do like it to leave 5 stars.

So, if you feel that this one does deserve 5 stars, that would be an enormous help.

Then there are the reviews. Most readers will look through half a dozen. Finding that a diverse group of people have been moved to write thoughtfully and in detail about what they have read is reassuring for someone unfamiliar with the author's work.

It doesn't do the author's ego any harm, either.

Thank you.

JP

Books by the Same Author
Also Available on Amazon

Old Man Sailing: Some Dreams Take a Lifetime

When COVID-19 struck the UK, the government advised the over-70s to "shield" while the country went into Lockdown. One old man went sailing instead. Single-handed and self-isolated, retired journalist, John Passmore, used the pandemic to achieve an ambition which had eluded him for 60 years. For 3,629 miles, he disappeared into a world of perfect solitude, adventure and adversity – arriving back 42 days later, short of water and with shredded sails to find himself celebrated on national radio as the embodiment of everybody's Lockdown dream. This is his story. It is also a story for anyone who ever thought a dream was unattainable. "A word-of-mouth bestseller." - Yachting Monthly

> This title is also available in French as
> *Le vieil homme hisse la voile.*

The Voyage #1: BVIs to Falmouth

This is what it is like to sail an ocean alone. Not the world-girdling marathon of the Southern Ocean racers or the "cruise in company" as part of a trade-wind rally, but what it is really like to set off for 3,496 miles from the British Virgin Islands to Falmouth in the UK, totally alone.

That means no contact with the shore, no high-frequency radio or satphone. No weather forecasts, no texts from loved ones. No news….

Just complete and uninterrupted isolation for 44 days. In other words, this is singlehanded ocean sailing at its purest: One man in a world shrunk to its bare essentials. John Passmore is a lifelong sailor and professional writer. His book Old Man Sailing was described by *Yachting Monthly* as "a word-of-mouth bestseller."

In *The Voyage,* he takes it a step further. At times truly hilarious, at others, quite frankly weird; as Yachting World's Tom Cunliffe said of the author: "*A professional storyteller who always sees the funny side, even when laughs must have been hard to find.*"

Audiobook available from the oldmansailing website.

The Voyage #2: Falmouth to Grenada

These "Voyage" books began as an experiment: If a retired foreign correspondent sailing across an ocean alone in a small boat with no long-range communications were to sit down every day and write down what he was thinking, would anyone want to read it?

It turns out they did.

John Passmore's Voyage #1 became an implausible success. As one Amazon reviewer put it: "You wouldn't think John had the necessary ingredients for a compulsive page-turner, but he did and what's more the finished product was just that. It rather reminded me of the Monty Python sketch that included the wonderful line "...all of a sudden ... nothing happened..." The Voyage had me hooked from beginning to end. A great read."

That reviewer was right. Nothing did happen on The Voyage #1.

But plenty happened on The Voyage #2: A knockdown, 1,500 miles with a broken rudder – some local difficulty with the Cape Verdean Maritime Police…

As another reviewer said: "John is my kind of sailor. Down to earth, humorous, passionate about what he does – and full of adventures."

The Voyage #2 has got the lot…

The Good Stuff – Book One

John Passmore is the author of *Old Man Sailing: Some Dreams Take a Lifetime* – the story of his escape from Lockdown by sailing alone into the Atlantic for 42 days and 3,629 miles. Yachting Monthly called it "A word-of-mouth bestseller". Many of the five-star reviews claimed it worked so well because there was more to the story than the adventure: There were humorous anecdotes. There was a love story…

What the readers did not know was that all of this was chronicled in detail as it happened. Throughout the early 80s and into the noughties, Passmore was writing for yachting magazines and national newspapers.

Here, for the first time, is a complete and chronological account: Everything from levitating the dog and navigating by smell to meeting his wife, Tamsin, through the Lonely Hearts column of Time Out and attempting to run away to sea and raise a family on a 27ft boat.

It is a laugh-out-loud, real-life story of love and exasperation afloat – when it's not making you cry. It is, as the editor of Yachting World said at the time – "Good Stuff."

The Good Stuff – Book Two

In this second volume of The Good Stuff, John and Tamsin have a baby on the boat – and then another one. The idyllic lifestyle, sailing where the wind blows them, sitting over a glass of wine as the sun turns the estuary to liquid gold is suddenly more complicated. Where do you find a launderette in the middle of the French countryside? How do you keep to the maintenance schedule with help from a two-year-old?

At least it was good copy. There was Yachting World's *Dogwatch* column to feed every month and the Daily Telegraph's travel page. Apparently, the readers were captivated by the couple's determination to put a brave face on even in the most desperate situation – or maybe they just liked the dog.

Here you will discover how to win third prize in the Tayvallich Regatta one-oar race and what the home counties school nurse said to the Liverpool "Scally." And where else do you think you would find detailed instructions for casting *The Curse of the Stones* on troublesome neighbours? It is, as the editor of Yachting World said at the time – "Good Stuff."

Trident: The Future Is Out of Control – And It's Happening Now

A new Prime Minister committed to scrapping Britain's nuclear deterrent – a Russian president meddling in other countries' elections and an isolationist in the White House... Does any of this sound familiar?

John Passmore's prescient novel, written in the 1980s and set in what was then the future, suddenly becomes terrifyingly relevant today. As NATO collapses and Russia looks to the West, the future of the world rests in the hands of a submarine captain, his aged father, an old-fashioned reporter and a government secretary in love with a man who is not what he seems... "

Fast-moving and immensely prescient, there are echoes of the early works of Ken Follett and Frederick Forsyth." – Daily Mail

Printed in Great Britain
by Amazon